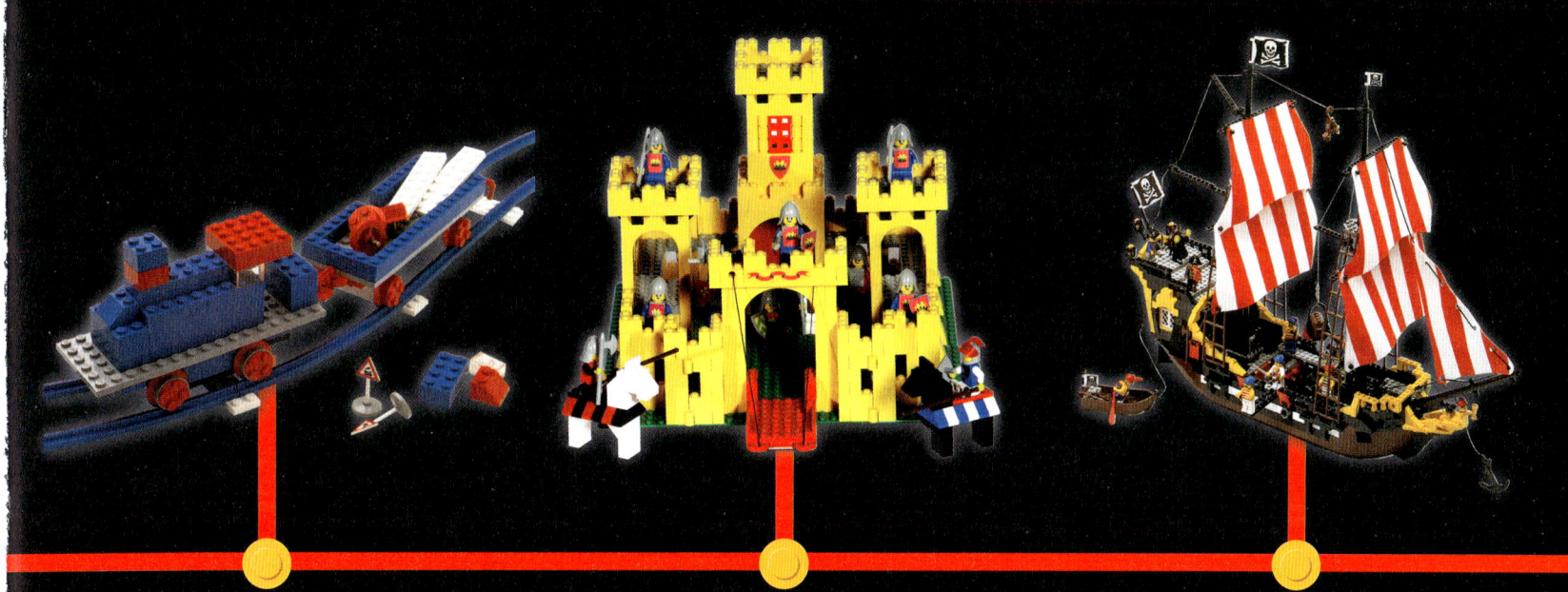

TIMELINES

A VISUAL JOURNEY THROUGH TEN DECADES OF LEGO® HISTORY

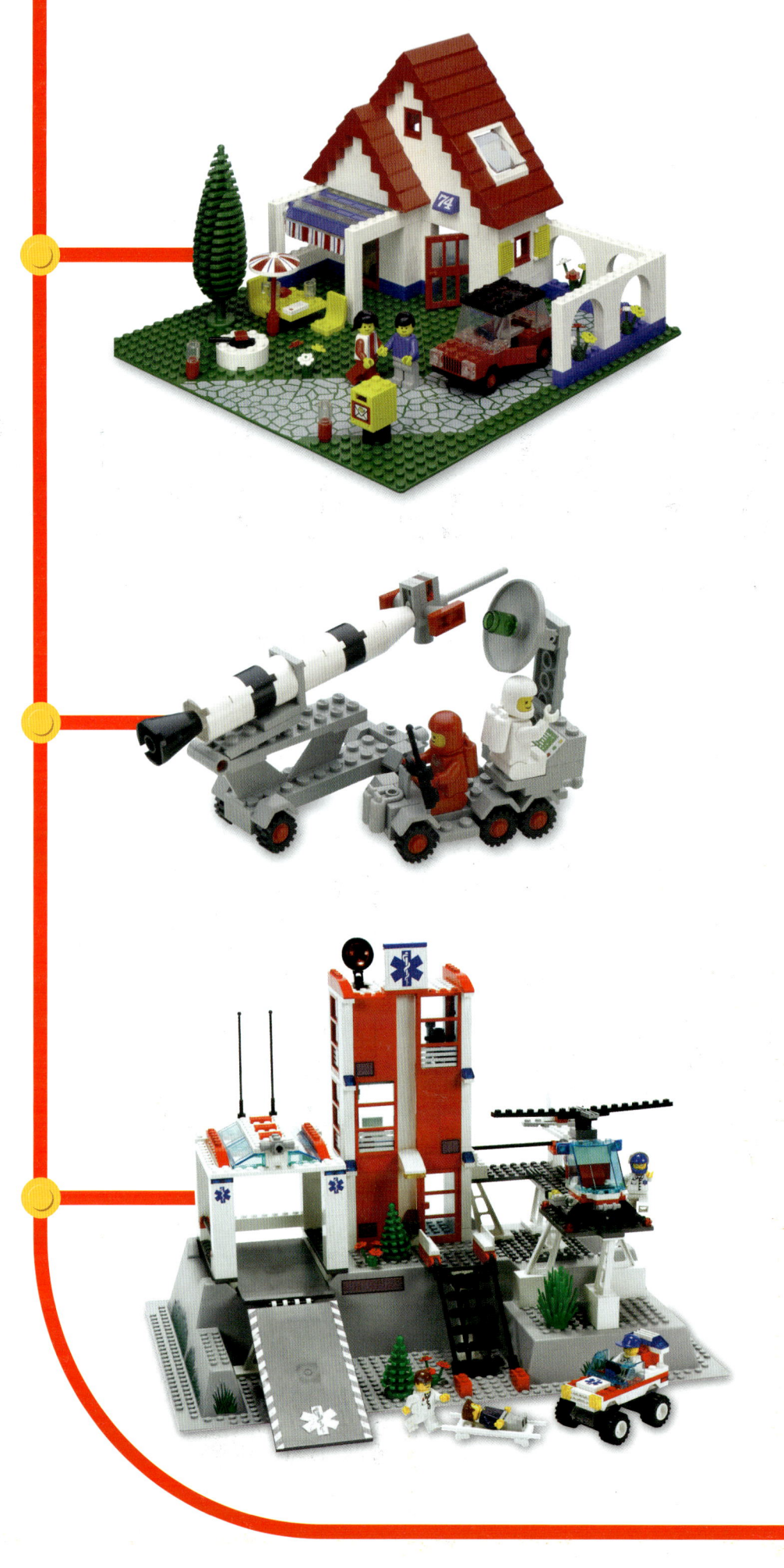

TIMELINES

A VISUAL JOURNEY THROUGH TEN DECADES OF LEGO® HISTORY

Written by Simon Hugo

DK

CONTENTS

Introduction	6
Early Years: the beginnings of the LEGO Group	8
Brick by Brick: innovative LEGO® elements	12
Mid-Century Marvels: the LEGO® Town Plan range	14

The 1960s: an overview — 16

Wheels of Progress: LEGO® wheels through time	18
Lights, Motors, Action!: electronic LEGO® sets	20
Full Steam Ahead: LEGO® trains	22
Set Focus: The Orient Express Train	26
Small Hands, Big Ideas: LEGO® DUPLO®	28

The 1970s: an overview — 32

Minifigure Milestones: a characterful evolution!	34
Gripping Gear: Minifigure tools and accessories	38
A Town Through Time: LEGO® Town	40
History in the Making: LEGO® Castle	44
Set Focus: Lion Knights' Castle	48
Through Space and Time!: LEGO® Space	50
Set Focus: Monorail Transport System	54
Gears and Years: LEGO® Technic	56
Set Focus: LIEBHERR Crawler Crane LR 13000	60
Fabulous Fabuland: LEGO® FABULAND™	62
Go Figure: LEGO® figures of all shapes and sizes!	64
Animal Evolution: LEGO® creature figures	66

The 1980s–1990s: an overview — 68

Treasure Trail: LEGO® Pirates	72
Set Focus: Eldorado Fortress (2023)	76
We Are the Robots: programmable LEGO® sets	78
Destination: Adventure: quest-led LEGO® themes	82
Galactic History: more than 3,000 years of LEGO® Star Wars™!	86
Size Matters Not!: special LEGO® Star Wars™ sets	90
Set Focus: Millennium Falcon	92

The 2000s: an overview — 94

Sports for All: sports-themed LEGO® sets	98
Mata Nui Matters: LEGO® BIONICLE®	100
Life in the Fast Lane: LEGO® Racers	104
Magic Moments: LEGO® Harry Potter™	106
Set Focus: Gringotts Wizarding Bank Collectors' Edition	110
The Creator Master Plan: LEGO® Creator sets	112
Teams and Schemes: faction-led LEGO® themes	116
Space Is the Place: sets inspired by space exploration	118
Streets Ahead: LEGO® City	122
Set Focus: Downtown	126
New Heights: the LEGO® Modular Buildings Collection	128
Set Focus: Natural History Museum	132
Landmark Achievements: LEGO® Architecture	134
Happy Holidays!: Christmas-themed LEGO® sets	136
Keeping up with the Joneses: LEGO® Indiana Jones™	138

The 2010s: an overview — 140

Meet the Minifigures: collectible LEGO® Minifigures	144
Disney Time: LEGO® Disney sets	150
Set Focus: Disney Castle	154
Ninja, Go!: LEGO® NINJAGO®	156
Set Focus: Ninjago City Markets	160

Ideas Welcome: fan-designed
LEGO® sets ... 162
Friends Forever:
LEGO® Friends ... 164
Set Focus: Andrea's
Modern Mansion ... 168
**Super Sets and Bat-tastic
Builds!:** LEGO® DC Comics™
Super Heroes ... 170
Set Focus: Batcave—Shadow Box ... 174
Make Mine Marvel!:
LEGO® Marvel Super Heroes ... 176
Set Focus: Hulkbuster ... 180
A Chronicle of Middle-earth:
LEGO® The Lord of the Rings
and LEGO® The Hobbit ... 182
Set Focus: The Lord of the
Rings: Rivendell ... 184
Can You Dig It?:
LEGO® Minecraft® ... 186
Set Focus:
The Mountain Cave ... 190
Massive Machines: display
sets inspired by vehicles ... 192
Mega Monuments: display
sets inspired by landmarks ... 196
Fair Play: the LEGO® Fairground
Collection ... 198
Brick Flicks: LEGO® adventure
on the big screen ... 200
Set Focus: Welcome to
Apocalypseburg! ... 204
Fast and Fabulous:
LEGO® Speed Champions ... 206
Jurassic World:
LEGO® Jurassic World ... 208
Build Me Up!: brick-built
LEGO® characters ... 210

**Bricks That Go Bump in the
Night:** ghostly LEGO® sets ... 212
Worlds of Wonder: LEGO® themes
set in fantasy lands ... 214
TV Times: LEGO® sets inspired
by TV shows ... 216
Big-Screen Builds: LEGO® sets
inspired by movies ... 218
Next-Level Sets: LEGO® sets
inspired by video games ... 220

The 2020s: an overview   **222**

Years of the Monkie:
LEGO® Monkie Kid™ ... 224
Statement Pieces: LEGO® sets
inspired by art and design ... 226
Time, Pieces: the biggest
LEGO® sets keep getting bigger! ... 228
Learning Curve:
LEGO® Education ... 230
Brickish Broadcasting:
LEGO® adventure on the
small screen ... 232
Designing a LEGO® Set: from
early ideas to play perfection! ... 234
Inside the Factory: how
LEGO® bricks are made ... 236
The Changing LEGO® Logo:
a mark of quality through the years ... 238
From Post to Posts: how
the LEGO Group stays in
touch with fans ... 240
Wonder Lands: LEGOLAND® Parks
around the world ... 242
What's in Store?: the evolution
of LEGO® Stores ... 244

Welcome To Our House:
the LEGO® House
visitor attraction ... 246
Set Focus: LEGO® House ... 248
Tomorrow's World: the sustainable
future of the LEGO Group ... 250

Index   **252**
Acknowledgments   **256**

INTRODUCTION

We all have our own LEGO® timelines. Mine begins as far back as I can remember, and is the thread that defines my 1980s childhood. It takes in the dozens of LEGO® Town, Space, and Castle sets I was lucky enough to own, and many more I coveted in well-thumbed LEGO catalogs. It includes a tenth-birthday trip to LEGOLAND® Park in Billund, Denmark (at the time, the only LEGOLAND Park in the world), and many attempts to re-create its wonders when I returned home to the UK.

The trail goes cold in the mid-1990s, as study and then the grown-up world of work got in the way of my LEGO fun. But I never strayed far from the brick-built path, and the launch of THE LEGO® MOVIE™ in 2014 was enough to reel me in all over again. Soon after, I started writing about LEGO sets, and the book that you now hold in your hands is the result of a personal timeline almost 45 years in the making.

In the pages that follow, you can see how your own LEGO timeline weaves into wider LEGO history. It doesn't matter if your journey is just beginning, or whether it stretches back much farther than mine. Every time you pick up a handful of bricks and make something new, you are connecting to a long tradition and shaping the future all at once. As long as we all keep doing that, the LEGO timelines need never end!

INTRODUCTION

The author on safari at LEGOLAND Park, Billund, in 1989.

My first set: the LEGO Space Surface Rover (set 6804).

EARLY YEARS

The LEGO® story may be built on bricks, but it doesn't begin with them! It starts with Ole Kirk Kristiansen, **a carpenter** carving out a niche in small-town Denmark, and then molding the future with new technology. When his son Godtfred Kirk Christiansen makes the first LEGO bricks, he invents a whole new "System" to make them click around the world!

Ole Kirk Kristiansen is born in the tiny village of Omvrå, near Billund, Denmark. He is number 10 out of 13 children.

1891

After ruling out the name "LEGIO," Ole Kirk decides to call his products "LEGO" toys. He is inspired by the Danish phrase *"leg godt,"* meaning "play well."

1934

The wooden duck toys were produced into the 1960s, and they are a LEGO Group mascot to this day!

The LEGO workshop produces its first construction toy—made up of wooden blocks for assembling a ball run in a sandbox—and its first pull-along wooden duck toy.

1935

Wooden construction set Kirk's Kuglebane ("Kirk's Ball Track" in English) is also known as Kirk's Sand Game.

The LEGO workshop hires its tenth staff member as demand grows for Ole Kirk's high-quality products, including cars designed by Godtfred Kirk.

Dagny designs several toys during her internship, including pull-along character Clumsy Hans.

1936

1937

1939

Ole Kirk's niece Dagny Holm joins the business for a three-month internship. She goes on to study sculpture before returning as chief model designer in the 1960s.

Ole Kirk coins the company motto, "Only the best is good enough," and his youngest son, 17-year-old Godtfred Kirk Christiansen, starts designing LEGO models for production.

Godtfred Kirk makes a carving of his father's motto (in Danish) and hangs it in the LEGO workshop.

8

EARLY YEARS

1905–1911: The 14-year-old Ole Kirk starts to train as a carpenter, working for his older brother Kresten Bonde Kristiansen. He completes his apprenticeship six years later.

1916–1920: Ole Kirk goes into business as a carpenter in Billund, making doors, furniture, and tools, and doing carpentry work on buildings. He marries Kristine Sørensen and they have four children together.

Workers pose with wooden toys displayed on ladders and ironing boards, all made in Ole Kirk's workshop.

1932: Ole Kirk Kristiansen starts a production of wooden toys to cope with the Great Depression that brings his normal carpentry business to a halt. His early designs include cars, planes, and yo-yos.

1924: Fire destroys Ole Kirk's workshop and the adjoining family home. He rebuilds both, bigger and better, complete with Billund's first concrete sidewalk!

The new house eventually becomes a LEGO museum!

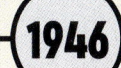

Yo-yos are Ole Kirk's first must-have toy! When the fad passes, he turns the leftover yo-yo casings into wheels for other toys.

1942: The workshop built after the 1924 fire is destroyed by another blaze. Once again Ole Kirk rebuilds, this time creating a factory dedicated to toy-making.

Ole Kirk working to re-create the design for the wooden duck after the original template was lost in the fire.

1946: This year's new toys include stackable wooden blocks called LEGO Klodser and a train adorned with a new LEGO logo on its wooden engine.

INTO THE ERA OF LEGO BRICKS!

9

Convinced that plastic toys are the future for his company, Ole Kirk imports a plastic injection-molding machine from the UK at great expense.

The LEGO Group now has more than 60 employees. The first LEGO toys made from plastic are created, including counters for the Monypoli road safety board game, baby rattles, and "Automatic Binding Bricks."

1947

1949

Godtfred Kirk visits the first British Toy Fair with a representative from a Danish department store. They agree that there is no "system" to link different toys together.

The Kubus range is made exclusively for the Norwegian market.

Automatic Binding Bricks are renamed LEGO Mursten (bricks), with the LEGO name molded into every stud. One of the first LEGO products to be sold abroad is called LEGO® Kubus.

 **1954**

1953

Godtfred Kirk perfects the design of the LEGO brick, adding inner tubes so bricks grip more firmly and in more ways. This becomes known as "clutch power."

The interlocking stud-and-tube principle is patented on January 28, 1958.

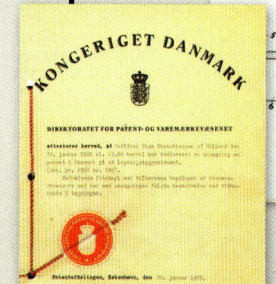

1955

1958

The LEGO Group launches its "System in Play," based on Godtfred Kirk's realization that brick-built toys can be endlessly combined, year after year.

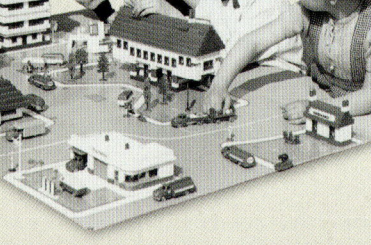

The first System sets form a Town Plan, with LEGO brick buildings and a range of vehicles at a consistent scale.

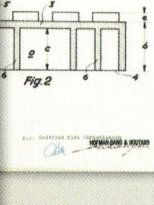

EARLY YEARS

A box of 128 "Automatic Binding Bricks" is launched—hollow plastic pieces with studs on top for building.

Godtfred Kirk's two-year-old son, Kjeld Kirk Kristiansen, makes his first appearance on a LEGO box! He is playing with a range of large, cube-shaped bricks for preschoolers.

Ole Kirk's son Godtfred Kirk becomes junior managing director of the thriving family company.

1950

A realistic tractor becomes the best-selling plastic LEGO toy so far. More than 75,000 are sold, and the model is rereleased as a buildable kit the following year.

Ole Kirk, Godtfred Kirk, and Kjeld Kirk pose for a family portrait in 1951.

1951

The LEGO Group stops making wooden toys when a fire guts the woodworking department. LEGO bricks, which are now sold across Europe, become the company's sole focus.

A new era begins in earnest when LEGO System sets go on sale in the US and Canada. The sets are made under license by the Samsonite luggage company into the 1970s.

1960   **1961**

Ole Kirk dies on March 11, 1958, at age 66. Godtfred Kirk becomes managing director of the LEGO Group, which now employs 140 people.

The burned-out woodworking department, with no roof or upstairs windows, in 1960.

Godtfred Kirk Christiansen stands on a LEGO display at the New York Toy Fair to demonstrate the bricks' strength!

11

BRICK BY BRICK

LEGO® building was never just about basic bricks! For more than 70 years, pioneering new parts have kept things fresh while still fitting into one interlocking System. These **brick breakthroughs** have earned their place in history and have never gone out of date, as each innovation clicks with the last!

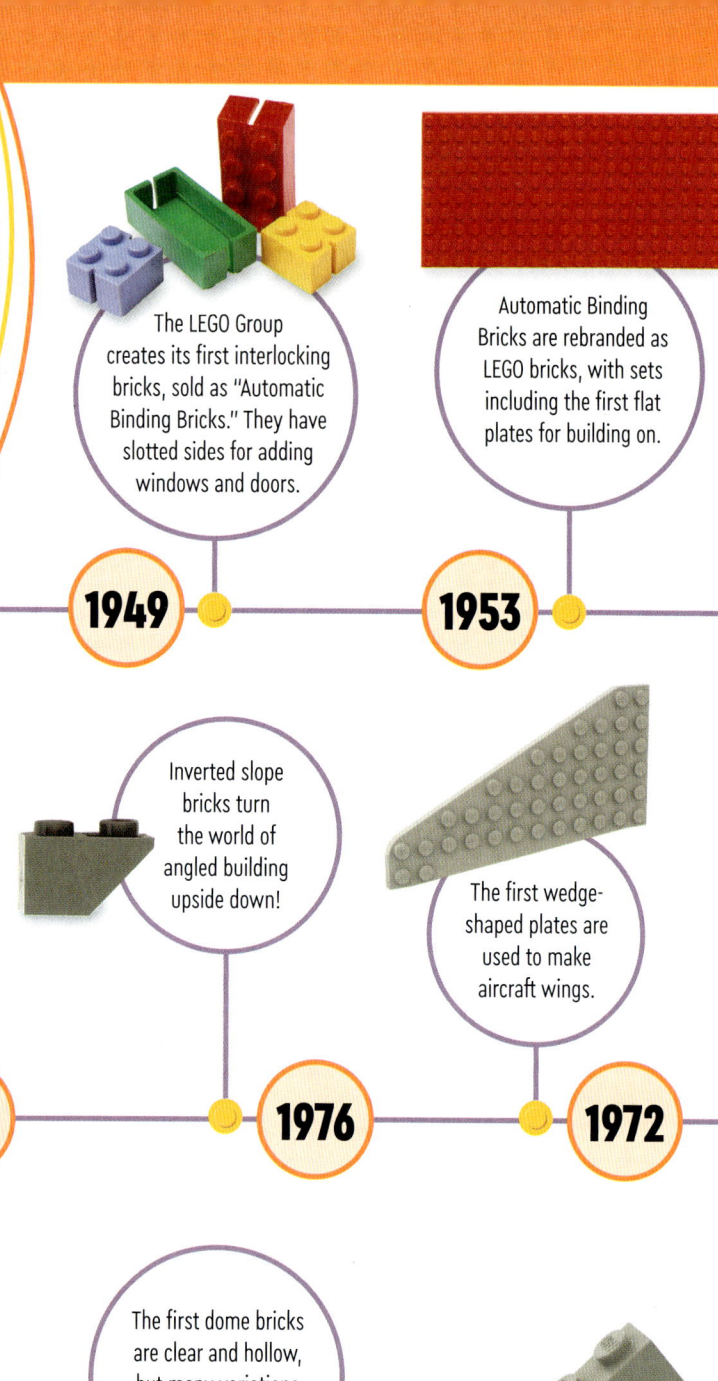

1949 — The LEGO Group creates its first interlocking bricks, sold as "Automatic Binding Bricks." They have slotted sides for adding windows and doors.

1953 — Automatic Binding Bricks are rebranded as LEGO bricks, with sets including the first flat plates for building on.

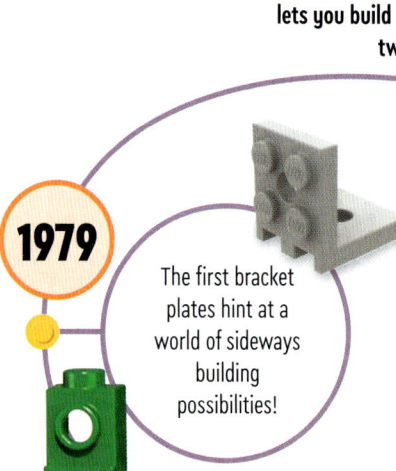

The first sideways hinge bricks are designed for folding out the walls of LEGO® Castles.

Jump for joy! The jumper plate lets you build halfway between two standard studs

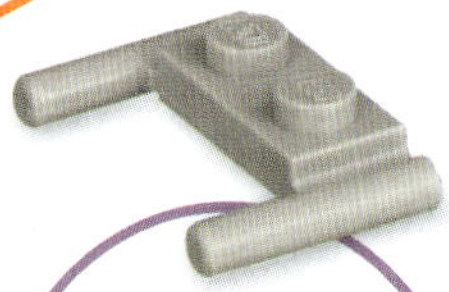

1978 — Plates with bars arrive at the same time as minifigures, who can grip onto them.

1976 — Inverted slope bricks turn the world of angled building upside down!

1972 — The first wedge-shaped plates are used to make aircraft wings.

1979 — The first bracket plates hint at a world of sideways building possibilities!

1984 — Castle wall pieces are the first of many panel pieces for building large, sturdy walls.

1998 — The first dome bricks are clear and hollow, but many variations follow, including R2-D2's head.

1980 — Headlight bricks are designed for minifigure cars, but go on to have many other uses.

1985 — Plates with clips hold minifigure accessories and can make hinge connections with bars.

Bricks with studs on all sides are first used to make robot heads.

1999 — Click-hinge bricks combine to make all kinds of angles, and lock in place once positioned.

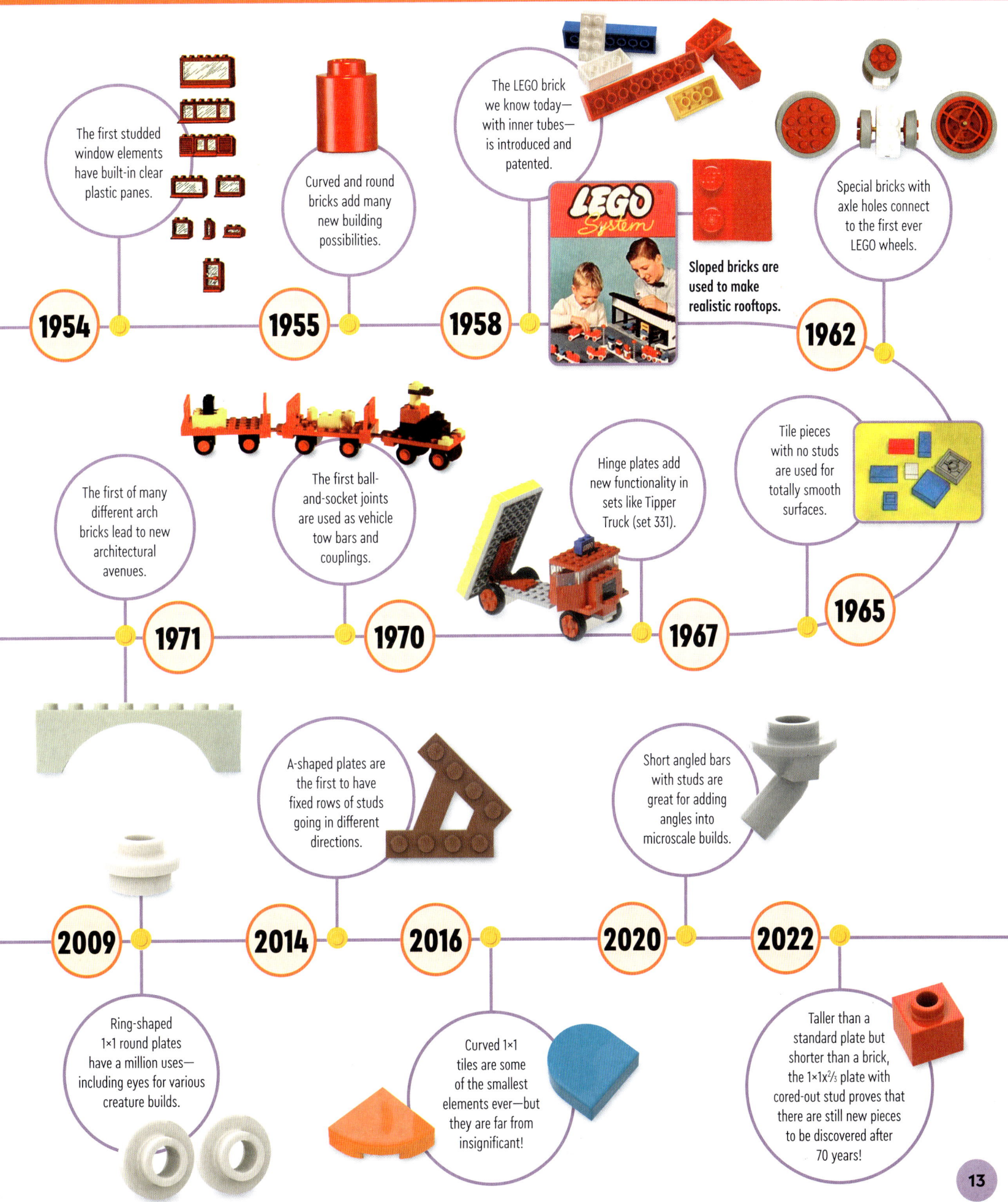

MID-CENTURY MARVELS

In the early days of LEGO® sets, one box of bricks was much like another. That all changed in 1955, with the launch of **LEGO® Town Plan**. For the first time, sets were designed to make specific buildings and to fit together as a structured system of products—"System in Play." They came with realistic vehicles and other urban essentials.

This year's sets include a car showroom with a Volkswagen Beetle model, a church, and a fire station with a fire engine. Signs for other shops and services can be made from new 1×1 bricks with printed letters on them.

Trucks aren't the only vehicles on this year's new, rigid Town Plan boards! Motorcycles, bicycles, and a camper all take to the roads, with traffic lights and police officer figures to keep everyone moving safely.

1957

1956

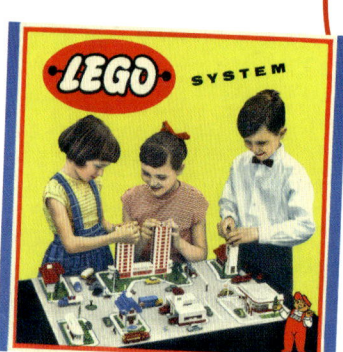

Several Town Plan sets feature future LEGO Group owner Kjeld Kirk Kristiansen and his siblings Hanne and Gunhild on the boxes!

Town Plan vehicles such as the Bedford Flatbed Truck (set 1253), Bedford Fire Truck (set 1255), and Bedford Tow Truck (set 1256) are made in 1:87 scale, to match popular model train ranges.

The first Town Plan (set 1200) is a roll-up sheet with a printed streetscape. A range of five brick buildings; eight single-piece trucks; and various trees, bushes, and street signs are available to customize the layout.

1955

14

MID-CENTURY MARVELS

1959 — A new, folding Town Plan board opens like a book to reveal its road layout. The outer covers show a bustling Town Plan scene, building ideas, and pictures of all the available parts, including battery-powered light bricks.

1961 — The first set to include a board and the parts to populate it is simply called Town Plan (set 810). It comes with five trucks, three cars, four cyclists, eight road signs, seven trees, and more than 700 bricks!

1962 — The first full range of Town Plan cars includes Ford Taunus, Karmann Ghia, Mercedes 220 S, and Opel Rekord models. Each one comes in a garage-style plastic box with a lift-up door and building studs on top.

1963 — As Town Plan sets gain fans in more and more countries, models of two British cars are made just for the UK and Australia. The Jaguar E-Type and Vauxhall Victor soon become sought-after around the world!

1964–1967 — The final additions to the Town Plan range include several Mercedes trucks, a new VW camper, a Morris Marina, a Citroën DS, and a Fiat 1800. All prove popular, but the future of LEGO vehicles is brick-built.

2008 — Celebrating 50 years since the LEGO brick was patented, Town Plan (set 10184) is a modern reimagining of the classic range. Lots has changed over the years, but Kjeld Kirk Kristiansen is still having fun on the front of the box!

THE 1960s

1960

The LEGO Group stops making wooden products and focuses on plastic toys.

By the end of 1960, there are LEGO® offices in Belgium, Finland, France, Germany, the Netherlands, Sweden, Switzerland, and the UK.

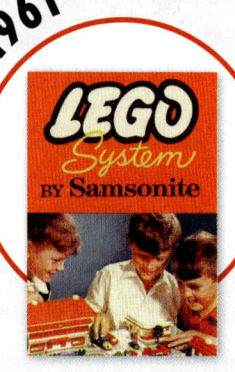

1961

LEGO sets are sold in the US and Canada for the first time, made under license by the Samsonite luggage company.

The quality of LEGO bricks improves as acrylonitrile butadiene styrene (ABS) replaces cellulose acetate as the main production material.

The LEGO Group launches Modulex— a range of bricks to help architects and planners visualize their ideas.

The LEGO Group sets up a new office in Austria.

LEGO products are sold in Spain for the first time.

1966

The first battery-powered LEGO® Train sets run on new, blue LEGO rails.

The first official LEGO Club is established in Canada.

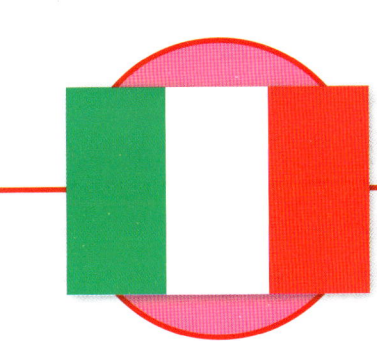

LEGO Italy is the ninth overseas outpost of the LEGO Group.

1962

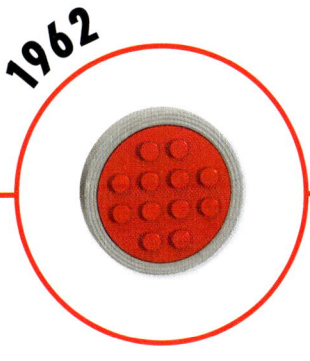

The first LEGO® System wheels combine plastic, metal, and rubber parts.

LEGO sets are sold in Oceania, Asia, and Africa for the first time (in Australia, Singapore, and South Africa).

1963

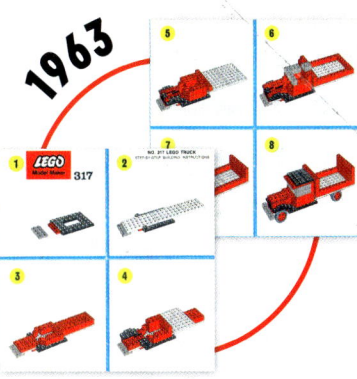

The first step-by-step building instructions come with sets such as Truck (set 317).

1964

The Ole Kirk Foundation is established to improve the lives of children and families through art, culture, and other means.

LEGO products are sold in the Middle East for the first time (in Lebanon).

1965

The first LEGO motor is used to power LEGO Samsonite sets in the US.

The Terapi range for schools and preschools is produced for three different age groups.

1967

The LEGO® DUPLO® system for preschool children is patented.

Europe's first official LEGO Club is founded in Sweden.

1968

The first LEGOLAND® Park opens in Billund, Denmark, welcoming more than half a million visitors during its first year.

1969

The LEGO® DUPLO® range is launched internationally, following a successful test run in Sweden.

17

WHEELS OF PROGRESS

They say you can't reinvent the wheel, but LEGO® designers think differently! There have been more than 100 different **LEGO wheel** and tire elements since the early 1960s, bringing movement to cars, trains, wheelchairs, and roller coasters—each one as revolutionary as the last!

The steering wheel in 1972's Tractor (set 378) features in just four sets.

Minifigure-scale cars run on new plate elements with built-in wheels. They also feature the first minifigure steering wheels and wheel-arch pieces.

1978

The special wheels and chunky tires that go on to drive many LEGO® Technic vehicles make their debut in other sets. Elsewhere, the first LEGO steering wheel really functions!

1972–1974

The 4.5V Motor Set with Rubber Tracks (set 103) comes with a choice of standard wheels or train wheels, plus the first LEGO caterpillar tracks.

1969

The first spoked wheels adorn this classy Antique Car (set 329).

Wheels with working steering are built into sets such as Breakdown Truck (set 332). Turning the LEGO sign on top of the cab moves the special front axle brick.

1967

New LEGO train wheels roll on the first LEGO train tracks! Just like the real thing, they have a flange around the inside edge that holds them on the rails.

1966

1962

Knud's design goes into production, with minor modifications. The first LEGO wheels come in two sizes, with rubber tires and metal axles that plug into new axle bricks.

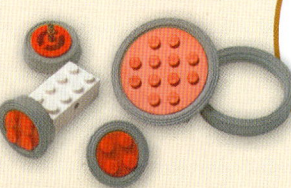

1958

LEGO designer Knud Møller Kristensen quietly invents the LEGO wheel before filing away his design to focus on other projects.

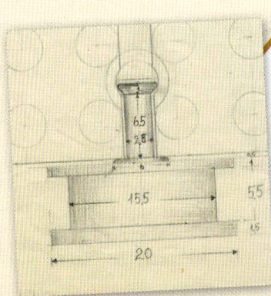

18

WHEELS OF PROGRESS

All I need now is a roof!

Knights turn somersaults when LEGO® Castle gets its own cartwheel piece! A supply wagon, a siege tower, and a blacksmith shop all use the piece in its first year.

1984

1985

Brand-new bicycle wheels fit onto the first LEGO bicycles in this year's LEGO® Town and LEGO® Dacta (LEGO® Education) sets.

A tiny new wheel element clips onto a luggage trolley (dolly) in three LEGO® Train sets. It goes on to serve as baby carriage, wheelbarrow, and skateboard wheels in more than 400 sets!

1991

2003

This year's LEGO *Star Wars* Hailfire Droid boasts the biggest LEGO wheels of all time! The unique elements measure 8 in (210 mm) across and have no axles or tires.

2005

The first decorative wheel trims (hubcaps) add style to the LEGO® Racers Enzo Ferrari 1:10 (set 8653). Trims later become standard in the LEGO® Speed Champions theme.

2016

The largest LEGO tires of all time add off-road heft to the LEGO Technic CLAAS XERION 5000 TRAC VC tractor (set 42054). They stand 4.2 in (107 mm) high!

2022

The smallest ever LEGO wheels are part of a minifigure-scale duck toy, which is only available at the LEGO® House in Denmark. The 3D-printed pull-along is based on a LEGO wooden duck from the 1930s.

The duck's bill opens and closes as its tiny wheels turn.

A new wheelchair element gets brand-new rear wheels in this year's LEGO® City range.

19

LIGHTS, MOTORS, ACTION!

These days, it's not unusual to find LEGO® **sets with light bricks, motors, and remote controls**. It wasn't that unusual in the old days, either! It's more than 65 years since the first battery-operated LEGO product, and every decade since has introduced its fair share of building power-ups!

The first powered LEGO parts are light-up bricks that connect directly to 4.5-volt batteries with no battery box!

1957

The first powered LEGO car with wireless control is Radio Control Racer (set 5600). A radio receiver and a battery-powered motor are built into the base.

The first LEGO pull-back motor works on the same principle as 1981's wind-up design, but without the need for a key.

The 9-volt system comes to LEGO Technic, with a new motor, battery box, and—in the case of Control Center (set 8094)—a programmable command panel.

1998   **1996**   **1990**

Listen up! LEGO® DUPLO® Zooters boast a battery-powered memory chip for recording and playing back what you say to them.

A new 9-volt fiber-optics element adds a different kind of lighting to LEGO Technic sets, bouncing light along thin, transparent cables.

New light bricks and sound bricks with built-in batteries add authenticity to LEGO Creator sets such as Mythical Creatures (set 4894) and Revvin' Riders (set 4893).

2001   **2002**   **2003**   **2006**

The smallest LEGO pull-back motors yet power LEGO® Racers cars. Each motor is the size of a 2×8 brick, and the cars are not much bigger.

A battery-powered memory module in LEGO® Creator Record and Play (set 4095) remembers how you moved a model and then repeats those movements!

20

LIGHTS, MOTORS, ACTION!

North American LEGO builders are the first to add powered movement to their builds, with a 4.5-volt motor and battery-box set.

1965

Electric motors arrive in Europe! Some come in 4.5-volt battery-powered train sets, while others are sold with swappable train and car wheels.

1966

LEGO® Trains get a power-up with the first 12-volt motors, which connect to grid power using a big, blue transformer with forward/reverse and speed controls!

1969

The first LEGO® Technic motor is a 4.5-volt battery-powered device. Far smaller than its 1960s predecessors, it connects to a wide range of gears.

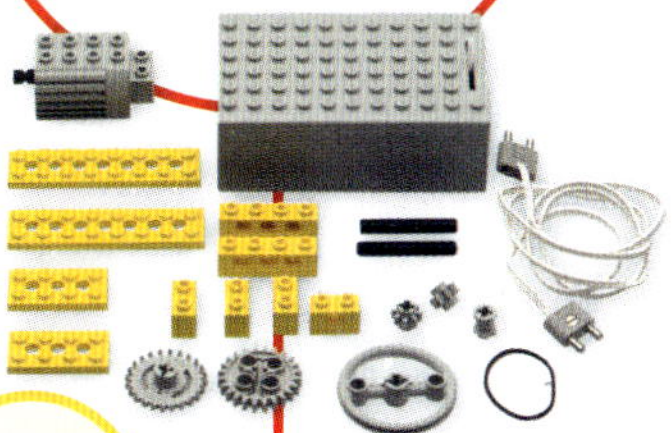

1977

The 9-volt battery box pairs with a new motor to power the first LEGO monorail. It goes on to power every other working LEGO monorail too!

1987

A new 9-volt battery box is used to power the latest light bricks and the first sound bricks, which play a choice of sirens.

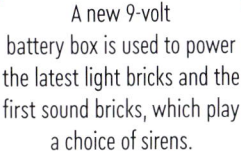

1985

Not every motor needs electricity to run! The first LEGO wind-up motor uses a special key to generate kinetic energy from a coiled spring.

1981

LEGO Creator, LEGO Technic, and LEGO® Star Wars™ sets introduce LEGO Power Functions, with its new range of 9-volt motors and infrared remote-controllers.

2007

The Powered UP system replaces Power Functions, adding smart components and app control to sets such as the LEGO® City Cargo Train (set 60198).

2018

The latest LEGO motors to not need batteries are the tiny, flywheel-powered friction ones in LEGO City Stuntz sets. Give them a push and watch them go!

2021

21

FULL STEAM AHEAD

LEGO® train sets have been on a roll for almost as long as there have been LEGO wheels! Some trains are powered and some are push-along. Some carry minifigure passengers, while others haul realistic cargo. All put LEGO builders in the driver's seat, racing down the LEGO track to stops marked fun, excitement, and adventure!

1964
The simply-named Train (set 323) is the first rail-themed LEGO building set—even though it doesn't include any actual rails for the push-along vehicle to run on!

1966
LEGO® Trains launches as a dedicated range of 12 sets, including push-along and 4.5-volt battery-powered engines, running on blue tracks.

Motorized Train Set (set 113) is one of the first battery-powered LEGO sets.

1968
Electronic train (set 118) can be remote-controlled... with a whistle! One blast starts the engine and a second makes it stop.

Train with 12V Electric Motor (set 720) draws its power from a wall socket.

1969
The first grid-powered LEGO trains run on tracks with metal center rails. These channel 12 volts of power into the engines from underneath.

1975
After a decade on the rails, LEGO Trains finally get somewhere to stop with Central Station (set 148), the first Trains set to include figures.

22

FULL STEAM AHEAD

TO 21ST CENTURY TRAINS →

Gotta love these flesh-colored trousers!

1998
Train fans can build their biggest-ever track layouts with the LEGO® Loco PC game, which comes with an exclusive stationmaster minifigure.

1991
Sets such as Metroliner (set 4558) run on a new 9-volt grid-powered system, replacing both the 4.5-volt battery and 12-volt grid systems.

1976
Western Train (set 726) is the first LEGO train designed to carry passengers, with room for three cowboy figures and their brick-built horse.

1978
Fully-fledged minifigures take to the rails in sets compatible with LEGOLAND® Town, such as Passenger Coach (set 164) and Car Transport Wagon (set 167).

1980
It's all change as LEGO Trains is relaunched with realistic gray rails, a revamped 12-volt control system, and 28 new sets—all now at minifigure scale.

Inter-City Passenger Train Set (set 7740) is the largest LEGO Trains set of the 1980s.

23

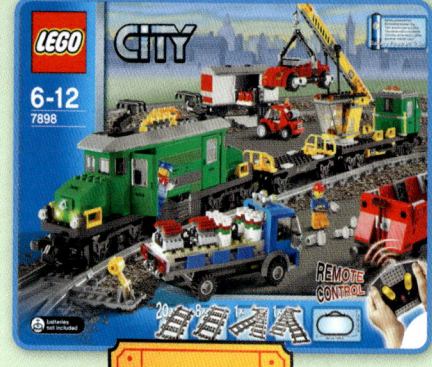

Toot toot! Cargo Train Deluxe (7898) includes a remote-controlled horn.

2002
Based on a famous US engine, Santa Fe Super Chief (set 10020) is the most realistic LEGO train so far, with equally accurate train cars available separately.

2001
From 2001 to 2003, the My Own Train website lets builders create and customize engines and train cars and then order the parts to build them.

2006
The LEGO Trains range becomes part of LEGO® City, and returns to battery-powered operation. Remote-control units now operate train speed, lights, and more.

2007
Part of the LEGO® Factory line of fan-designed sets, the 1,060-piece Hobby Trains (set 10183) is launched with instructions for building 30 different ways.

2009
Emerald Night (set 10194) is the result of consultation with 10 LEGO Trains fans who were flown to the LEGO headquarters in Billund and asked to describe their dream LEGO train!

2010
LEGO City trains start to run on the Power Functions system, bringing them into line with all other battery-powered sets in the LEGO range at this time.

Passenger Train (set 7938) comes with flexible tracks that can be used straight or curved.

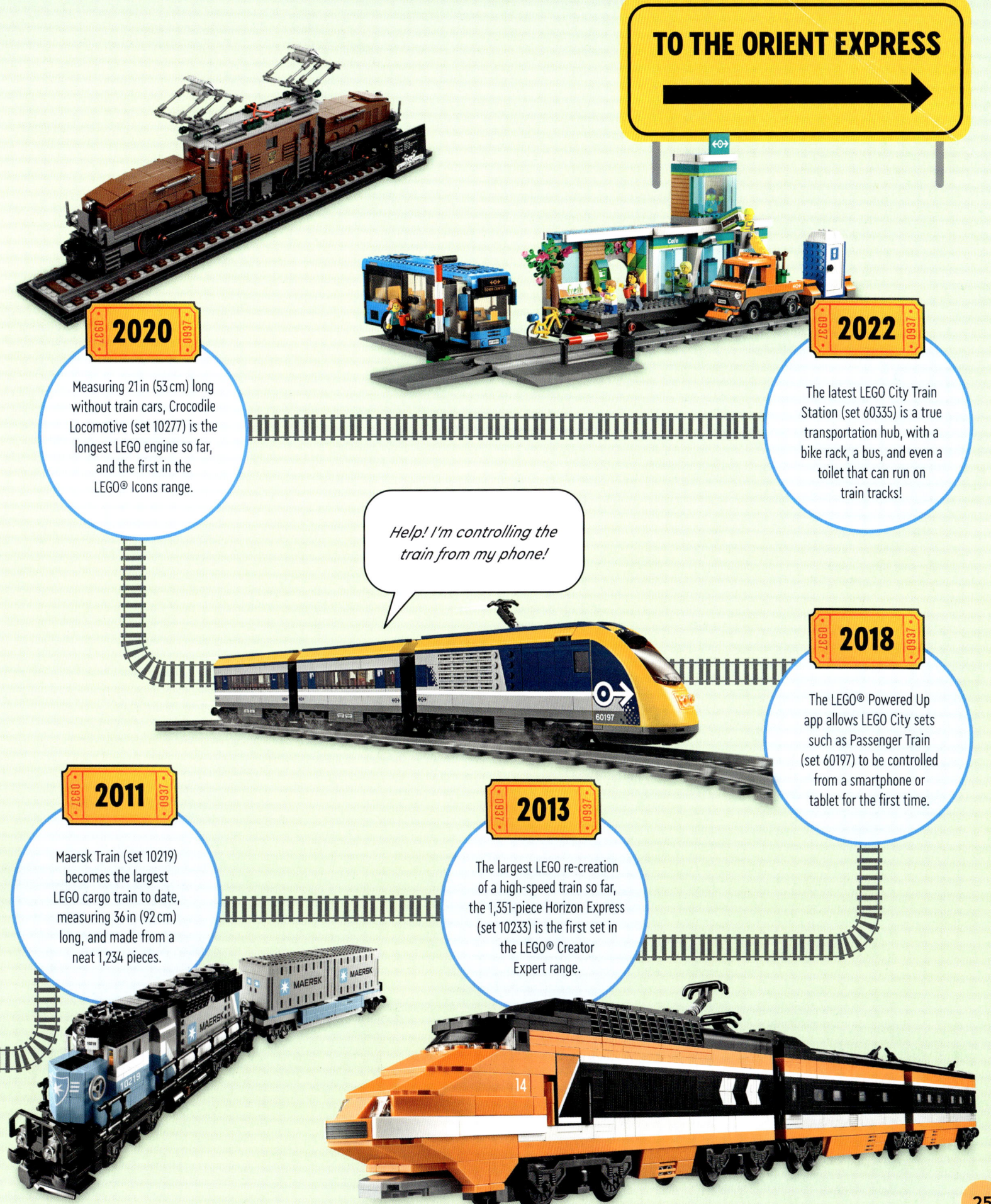

2023

THE ORIENT EXPRESS TRAIN

The most lifelike LEGO train so far is a fan-designed tribute to a legend of luxury travel. The LEGO® Ideas take on the Orient Express has a glamorous 1930s vibe, with passengers including a mustachioed movie director, an Art Deco duchess, and even one of the world-famous LEGO® Adventurers!

SET NUMBER	21344
PIECES	2,540
MINIFIGURES	8
SIZE	46 in (116 cm) long, 4.5 in (12 cm) high

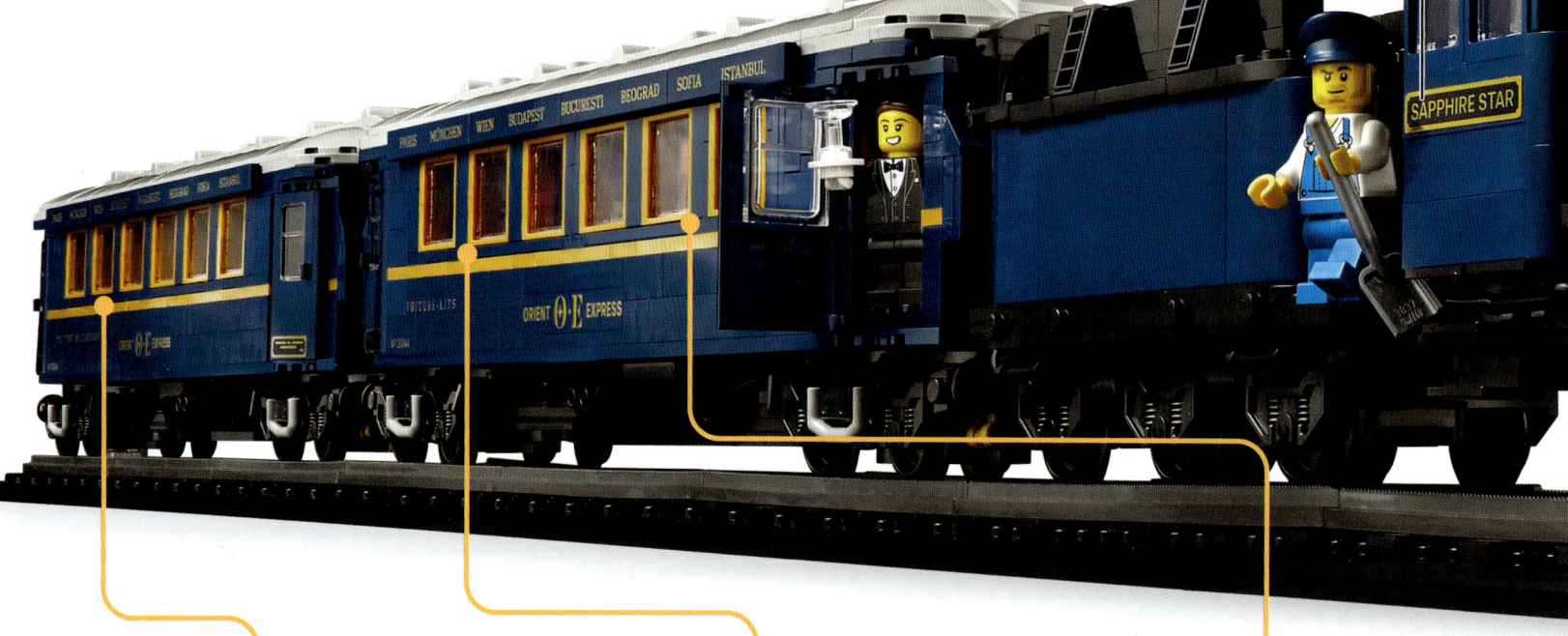

Engine name echoes 2009's Emerald Night train set

In the restaurant car, movie directors rub shoulders with duchesses while a white-gloved waiter tends to their every need.

At the back of the sleeper car, the first-class cabin has bedroom and lounge areas, and even an en suite bathroom.

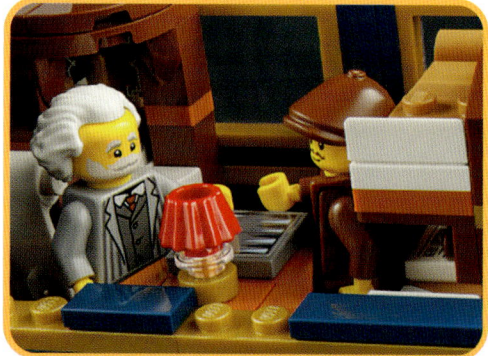

Closest to the engine is a smaller cabin with bunk beds and room for two bunkmates to enjoy a game of backgammon.

FULL STEAM AHEAD

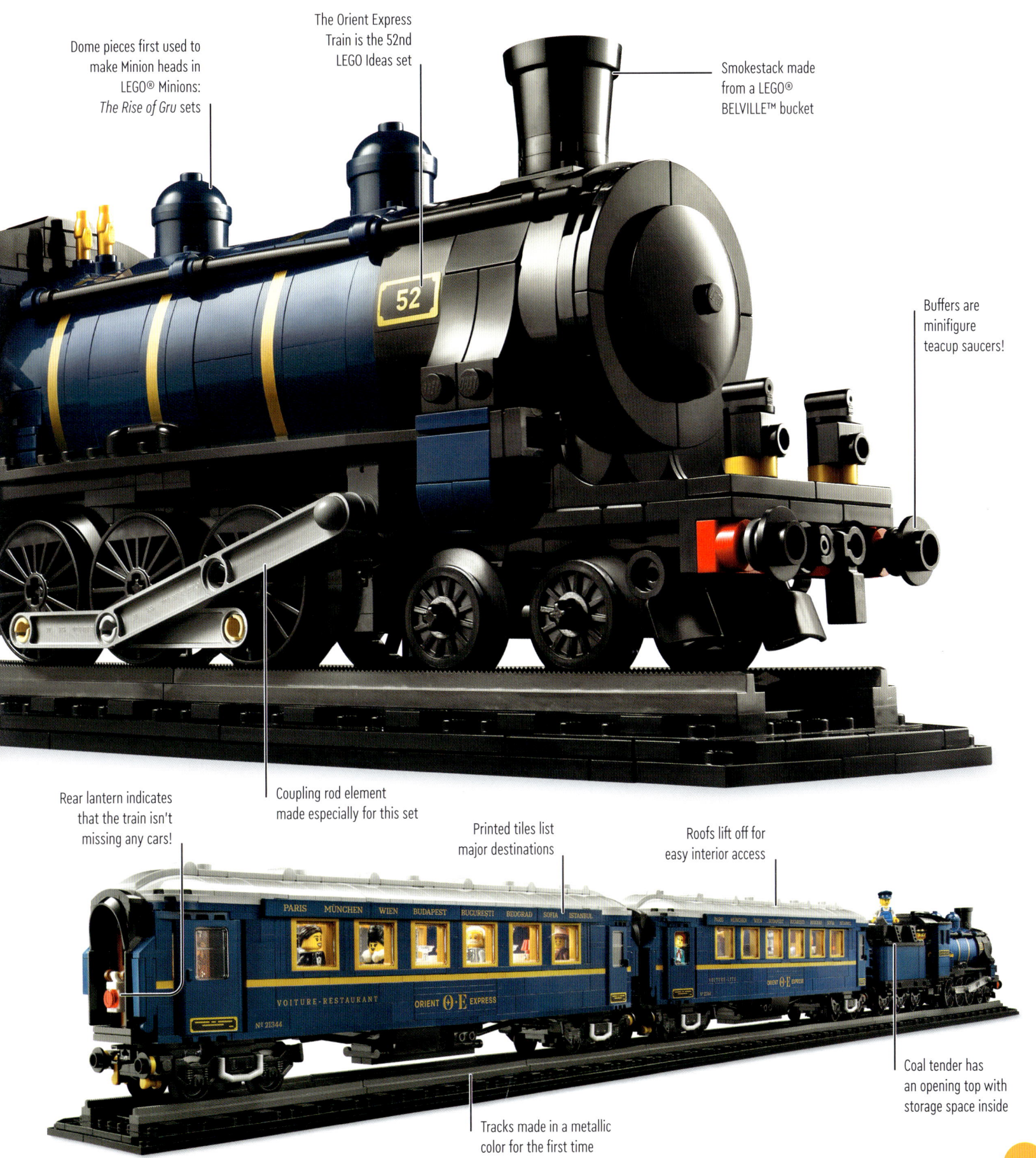

- Dome pieces first used to make Minion heads in LEGO® Minions: *The Rise of Gru* sets
- The Orient Express Train is the 52nd LEGO Ideas set
- Smokestack made from a LEGO® BELVILLE™ bucket
- Buffers are minifigure teacup saucers!
- Rear lantern indicates that the train isn't missing any cars!
- Coupling rod element made especially for this set
- Printed tiles list major destinations
- Roofs lift off for easy interior access
- Coal tender has an opening top with storage space inside
- Tracks made in a metallic color for the first time

SMALL HANDS, BIG IDEAS

It may have been going for more than 50 years, but **LEGO® DUPLO®** still looks decidedly youthful! Designed for budding builders in their earliest years, the preschool range went worldwide in 1969 and launched its distinctive red rabbit logo in 1978. Today the range is still going strong, with sets designed to nurture preschoolers' confidence and inspire creativity.

1949

Long before LEGO DUPLO, the LEGO Group launches its first bricks for very young builders. The 2-in (5-cm) square bricks come in a colorful box featuring future company owner Kjeld Kirk Kristiansen as a toddler!

The iconic LEGO DUPLO rabbit logo first made an appearance one year earlier, in 1978.

1979

The first of many realistic animal figures join the LEGO DUPLO lineup, with sets such as Farm (set 045) including a cow, a horse, a sheep, a pig, two hens, and a rooster!

1983

New, articulated figures and the first LEGO DUPLO trains offer more play potential for older preschoolers, while children as young as four months can enjoy the first in a range of LEGO DUPLO rattles!

Figures with moving arms and legs travel on the Play Train (set 2705).

Duck Rattle (set 2024) has moving eyes and a spinning ball for a belly!

1992

Built for budding engineers, each LEGO DUPLO TOOLO set comes with a child-safe screwdriver for attaching and detaching wheels and jointed parts, such as the cherry picker on the back of Fire Truck (set 2940).

I can see the 1980s from up here!

SMALL HANDS, BIG IDEAS

Preschool LEGO sets featuring "jumbo bricks" go on sale in the US. Measuring about 4 in x 2 in (10 cm x 5 cm), the bricks initially come in just red and white and are not compatible with standard LEGO bricks.

1964

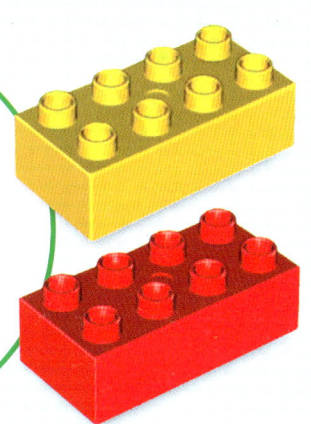

Sweden is the first country to get LEGO DUPLO bricks. At twice the height, depth, and width of standard LEGO bricks ("Duplo" means "I double" in Latin), the new pieces can be combined with other elements in the LEGO System.

1968

Mary's House (set 537) comes with three LEGO DUPLO figures—but which one is Mary?

All seven sets released this year include new LEGO DUPLO play figures. Their blocky bodies have no arms or legs, but their unique head pieces identify them as police officers, chefs, cats, and dogs!

1977

Following a successful trial in Sweden, LEGO DUPLO is launched around the world. In the US the range is initially called LEGO® Pre-school, while in Australia it is known as LEGO® Nursery Bricks until 1979.

1969

The LEGO® DUPLO® PRIMO™ range launches, with bigger, rounder bricks for children aged from 6 to 24 months. Sets include new-look figures, mirrored bricks, and rattling bricks for a range of sensory play.

1995

1999

A new era begins as LEGO DUPLO teams up with the Walt Disney Company to make sets based on the world of Winnie the Pooh. The sets boast all new figures for Pooh and his many friends.

Pooh, Piglet, Eeyore, and Tigger all appear in Welcome to the Hundred Acre Wood (set 2987).

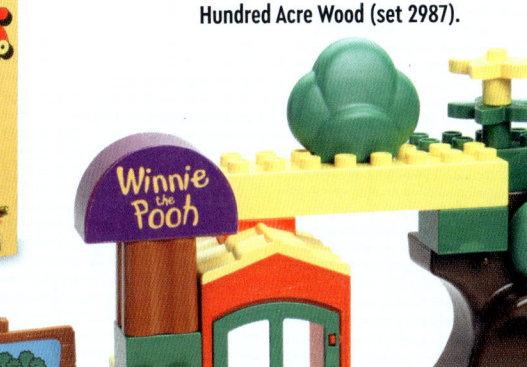

LEGO DUPLO KEEPS ON GROWING!

29

The LEGO DUPLO Dolls range features the biggest LEGO figures ever made, with four lifelike dolls each standing around 7 in (18 cm) tall. Meanwhile, TV favorite Bob the Builder™ gets his own range of sets.

Like all LEGO DUPLO Dolls, Marie (set 2952) comes with a smaller doll of her own!

Little Robot Tiny appears with his dog, Messy, in Tiny and Friends (set 7441).

This curvy croc is part of LEGO Explore's African Adventures (set 3515).

Now called LEGO® Explore, this year's range includes unique figures based on the BBC children's series *Little Robots*, and accordion-like flexi bricks for extra bendy builds.

 **2001**

2003

Super Heroes make their LEGO DUPLO debut, with sets featuring Superman and Batman. Meanwhile, sets such as Creative Ice Cream (set 10574) let kids build real-world objects at real-life size!

Sets such as Snow White's Cottage (set 6152) feature new fabric skirt pieces.

The long-running LEGO® DUPLO® *Disney Princess*™ range launches, with four sets featuring Cinderella, Sleeping Beauty, and Snow White. Later sets add Disney princesses Ariel, Belle, and Rapunzel to the lineup.

2014

2012

LEGO DUPLO goes digital, with Cargo Train (set 10875) working both as a traditional push-and-go toy and an app-controlled engine. This year's sets also include the first to be based on the *Jurassic World* film series.

LEGO DUPLO celebrates its 50th birthday in style, with a prominent role in THE LEGO® MOVIE 2™, and DUPLO figure versions of the film's heroes in Emmet and Lucy's Visitors from the DUPLO® Planet (set 10895).

This is a great look for me!

2018

2019

30

SMALL HANDS, BIG IDEAS

The new-look LEGO DUPLO figures were first seen in LEGO® Education sets.

LEGO DUPLO figures get a new, more realistic look, complete with button noses. New range LEGO® QUATRO™ launches with bricks that are twice the height, width, and depth of LEGO DUPLO ones, for even younger builders.

My First QUATRO Figure (set 5470) is one of just 10 LEGO QUATRO sets.

With 380 pieces and guidance for rebuilding it as a 67-in (170-cm) tower, Black Castle (set 4785) becomes the biggest ever LEGO DUPLO play set! Elsewhere, steam engines Thomas & Friends™ make their LEGO DUPLO debut.

2004

2005

LEGO DUPLO teams up with Disney Pixar for sets based on the *Cars* and *Toy Story* movies. Unique parts are used to re-create much-loved characters such as Lightning McQueen and Buzz Lightyear in DUPLO form.

2010

Learn About Chinese Culture (set 10411) takes LEGO DUPLO in yet another new direction, celebrating traditional Chinese family life. Details include traditional dress, calligraphy, and dumplings.

2022

2023

Wild Animals of Asia (set 10974) includes a sound brick that plays animal calls!

The Wild Animals of… range introduces children to the creatures of Africa, Asia, Europe, South America, and the world's oceans. Also, the LEGO DUPLO logo gets the latest of several updates.

THE 1970s

1970
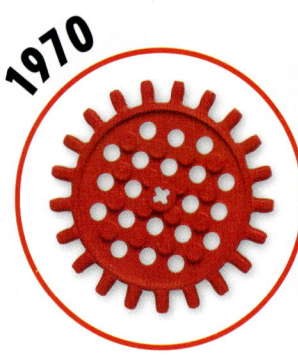
Gears sets are the forerunners of LEGO® Technic.

The LEGO® Minitalia and OLO ranges are made exclusively for Italy and Japan, respectively.

1971

LEGO® Homemaker sets feature doll-size furniture—but no dolls!

1974

Buildable LEGO figures populate the LEGO Homemaker range and other sets.

The LEGOLAND® Park in Billund, Denmark, welcomes its five-millionth visitor.

The first LEGO operated brick factory outside Denmark opens in Switzerland.

1977

All-new LEGO Technic elements add a range of mechanical movement to brick-built vehicles.

LEGO® DUPLO® gets its own range of simple, smiling figures.

1978

Everything changes with the launch of LEGO minifigures and the first LEGO play themes—Castle, Town, and Space!

1973

Kjeld Kirk Kristiansen joins the LEGO Group management in Switzerland after completing his second business degree.

A bold new LEGO logo makes its debut.

LEGO boats really float with new watertight hull pieces.

The LEGO Group sets up an office in the US.

LEGO Spain is the latest overseas outpost for the LEGO Group.

1975

Simple figures with no moving parts or faces are the forerunners of LEGO minifigures.

Hobby Sets for older builders re-create classic cars. The LEGO Group also sets up an office in Portugal.

1976

Thatcher Perkins Locomotive (set 396) is one of the most ambitious LEGO sets yet.

LEGO Japan is the first LEGO Group office in Asia. LEGO Singapore opens the following year.

1979

Adorable new animal figures star in LEGO® FABULAND™ sets.

The LEGO® SCALA™ range is the first to feature wearable LEGO accessories.

Kjeld Kirk Kristiansen becomes President and CEO of the LEGO Group.

MINIFIGURE MILESTONES

It's hard to imagine a world without **minifigures**, but until 1978 the LEGO® world was exactly that! The iconic design was worked up over several years and remains essentially unchanged to this day. But there is always room for innovation, and modern minifigures are more representative of the real world than ever!

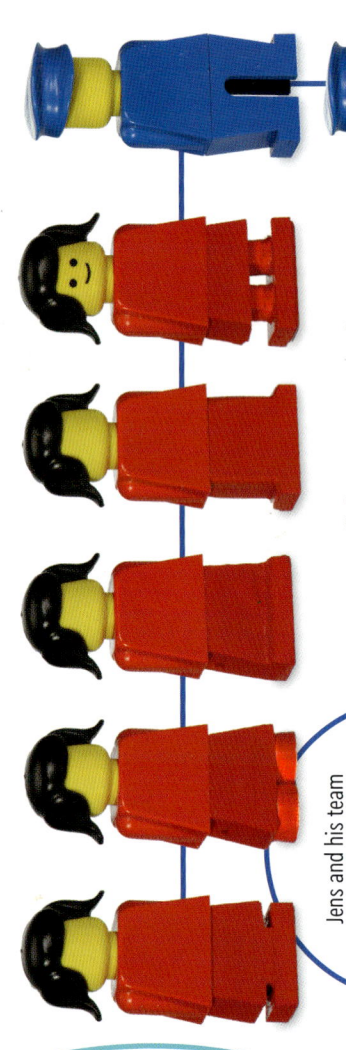

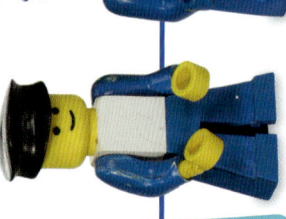

All these concepts use the same head piece, perfected in 1975.

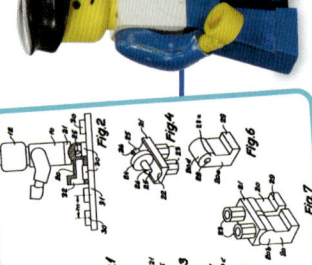

The finished design is registered at the Danish patent office in August 1977.

LEGO sets enter a whole new era with the launch of three play themes designed around the first minifigures: LEGO® Castle, LEGO® Town, and LEGO® Space.

Jens and his team continue to work on figure concepts, creating more than 50 variants before arriving at the now-famous minifigure design.

1976–1977

A minifigure also serves as a doll in this year's Homemaker Nursery (set 297).

1978

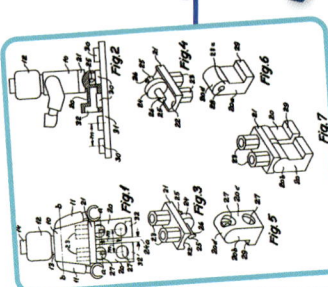

The figures in Hospital have no printed faces or jointed parts. These two stretcher-bearers are built into their stretcher!

1975

LEGO designer Jens Nygaard Knudsen leads a team to develop smaller figures. The first results of their efforts appear in sets such as Hospital (set 363).

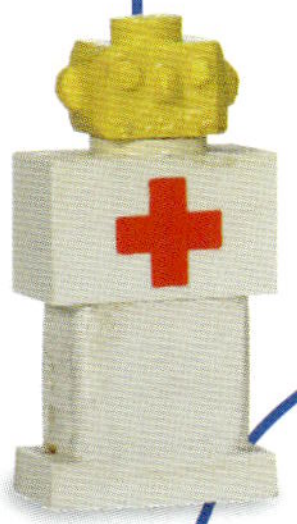

This concept model for a hospital figure has sculpted facial features.

We're the future!

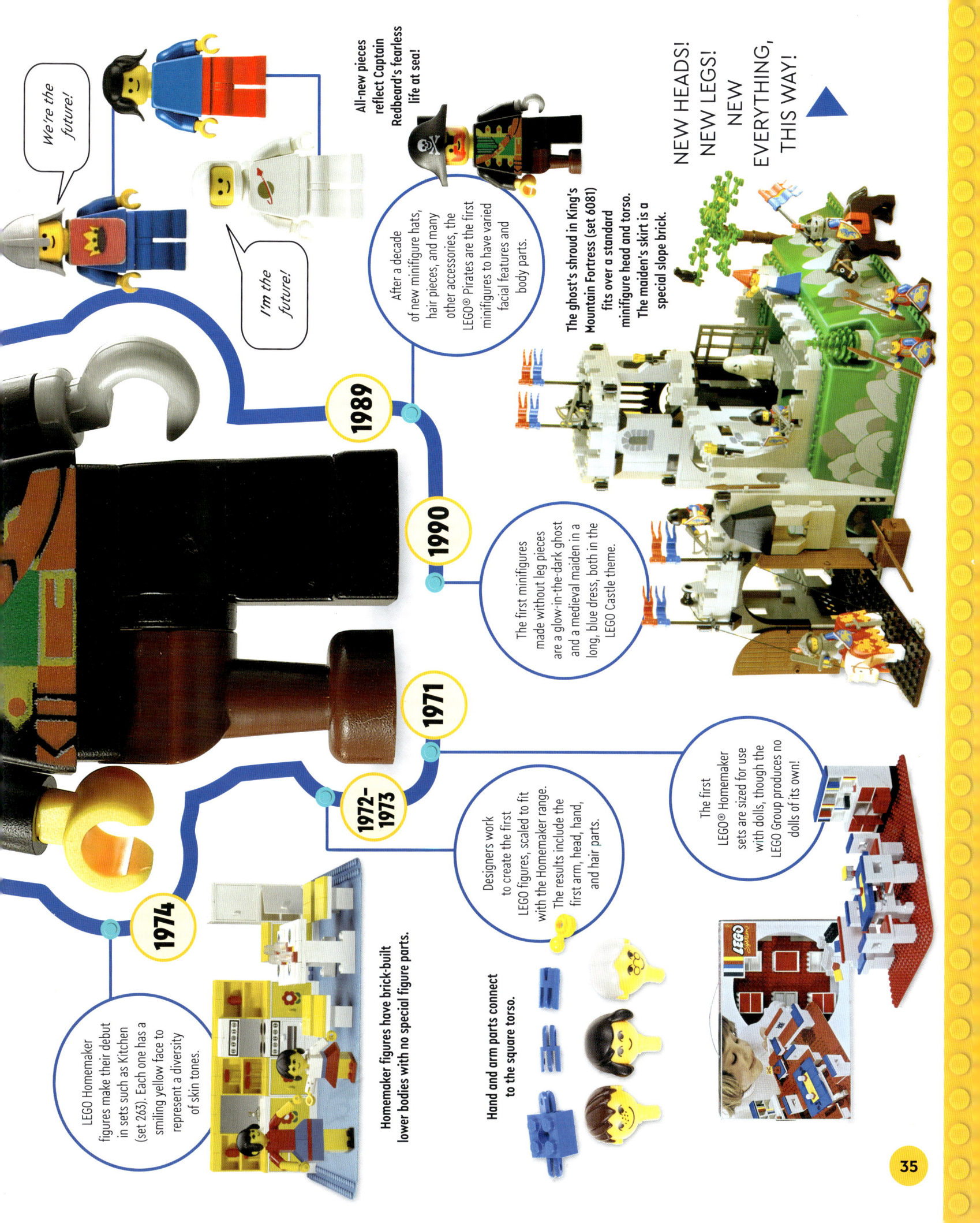

I'm the future!

All-new pieces reflect Captain Redbeard's fearless life at sea!

After a decade of new minifigure hats, hair pieces, and many other accessories, the LEGO® Pirates are the first minifigures to have varied facial features and body parts.

The ghost's shroud in King's Mountain Fortress (set 6081) fits over a standard minifigure head and torso. The maiden's skirt is a special slope brick.

NEW HEADS! NEW LEGS! NEW EVERYTHING, THIS WAY!

1989

1990

The first minifigures made without leg pieces are a glow-in-the-dark ghost and a medieval maiden in a long, blue dress, both in the LEGO Castle theme.

1971

1972–1973

Designers work to create the first LEGO figures, scaled to fit with the Homemaker range. The results include the first arm, head, hand, and hair parts.

The first LEGO® Homemaker sets are sized for use with dolls, though the LEGO Group produces no dolls of its own!

1974

LEGO Homemaker figures make their debut in sets such as Kitchen (set 263). Each one has a smiling yellow face to represent a diversity of skin tones.

Homemaker figures have brick-built lower bodies with no special figure parts.

Hand and arm parts connect to the square torso.

35

1993
LEGO Castle is at the cutting edge once again, with the first fabric minifigure garments—and at the no-hair-cutting edge with the first beard piece!

1999
The launch of LEGO® Star Wars™ calls for the first all-new head mold—used for Gungan hero Jar Jar Binks. Many more special head designs will follow.

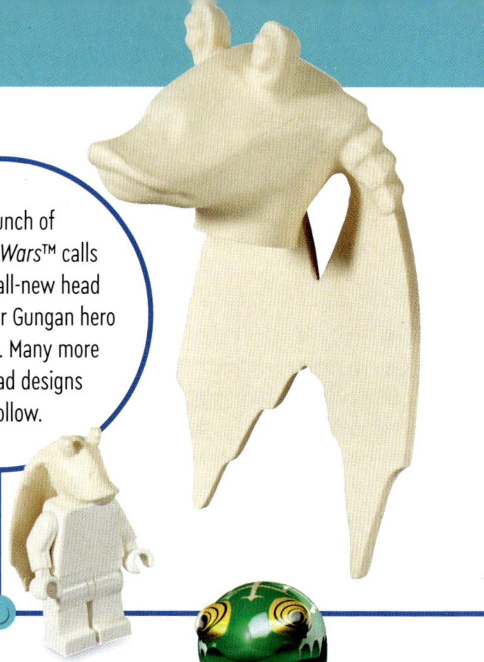

2010
The debut series of collectible LEGO® Minifigures introduces the first all-new arm piece—a robot arm with a slot for a chunky claw hand!

2009
LEGO Space alien Frenzy is the first four-armed minifigure, while hair pieces with slots for accessories let minifigures wear headgear on top of hair!

2014
Rocket from LEGO® Marvel Super Heroes is one of the first minifigures to have a tail! It fits between his legs and torso.

2018
New, posable, medium-length legs let young minifigure characters stand taller (and sit down) in the first collectible LEGO® Minifigures Harry Potter™ series.

It's okay, I'll stand!

2020
A minifigure with a hearing aid in LEGO® City Main Square (set 60271) is the first to be printed wearing realistic adaptive equipment.

MINIFIGURE MILESTONES

2001 — The LEGO® Harry Potter™ theme is the first to feature a minifigure with two faces, as Professor Quirrell hides Voldemort's visage on the back of his head!

2002 — Short leg pieces are first used to depict Ewoks in LEGO Star Wars and goblins in LEGO Harry Potter. They are later used by many minifigure children.

2003 — The first minifigures to approximate real-life skin tones are Lando Calrissian in LEGO Star Wars and NBA basketball players in LEGO® Sports sets.

2004 — Varied skin tones become the norm for minifigures based on existing fictional characters and real people such as racing driver Rubens Barrichello.

2022 — Two new minifigure skin tones bring the total up to six. All feature in Table Football (set 21337), which also includes a face print with vitiligo.

GRIPPING GEAR

For as long as LEGO® minifigures have been around, they have had LEGO tools to hold in their little yellow hands! Over the years, these **accessories** have become ever more diverse — expanding role-play options beyond the world of traditional work to include high-tech gadgets, fun food items, musical instruments, and more!

The very first minifigures are devoted to hard work, with tools including a broom, an ax, and a shovel.

Medieval sword and shield

1978

Just like the real thing, LEGO laptops fold shut when not in use. They are first used by super spies the LEGO® Agents.

LEGO® Adventurers sets introduce minifigure magnifying glasses. They may be small, but they really work!

2008 **2001** **1998** **1997**

2009

Telescope

Gold-colored keys unlock a world of adventure in LEGO® Harry Potter™ sets. They have since taken turns in many other themes.

Croissant

Camera

Tennis racket

Scissors

2010 **2011** **2014** **2015**

The LEGO® World Racers' daring minifigure drivers, bikers, and pilots are the first to compete for shiny trophy pieces.

New guitar and saxophone pieces mean minifigures can form bands that aren't entirely bugle-based!

38

GRI

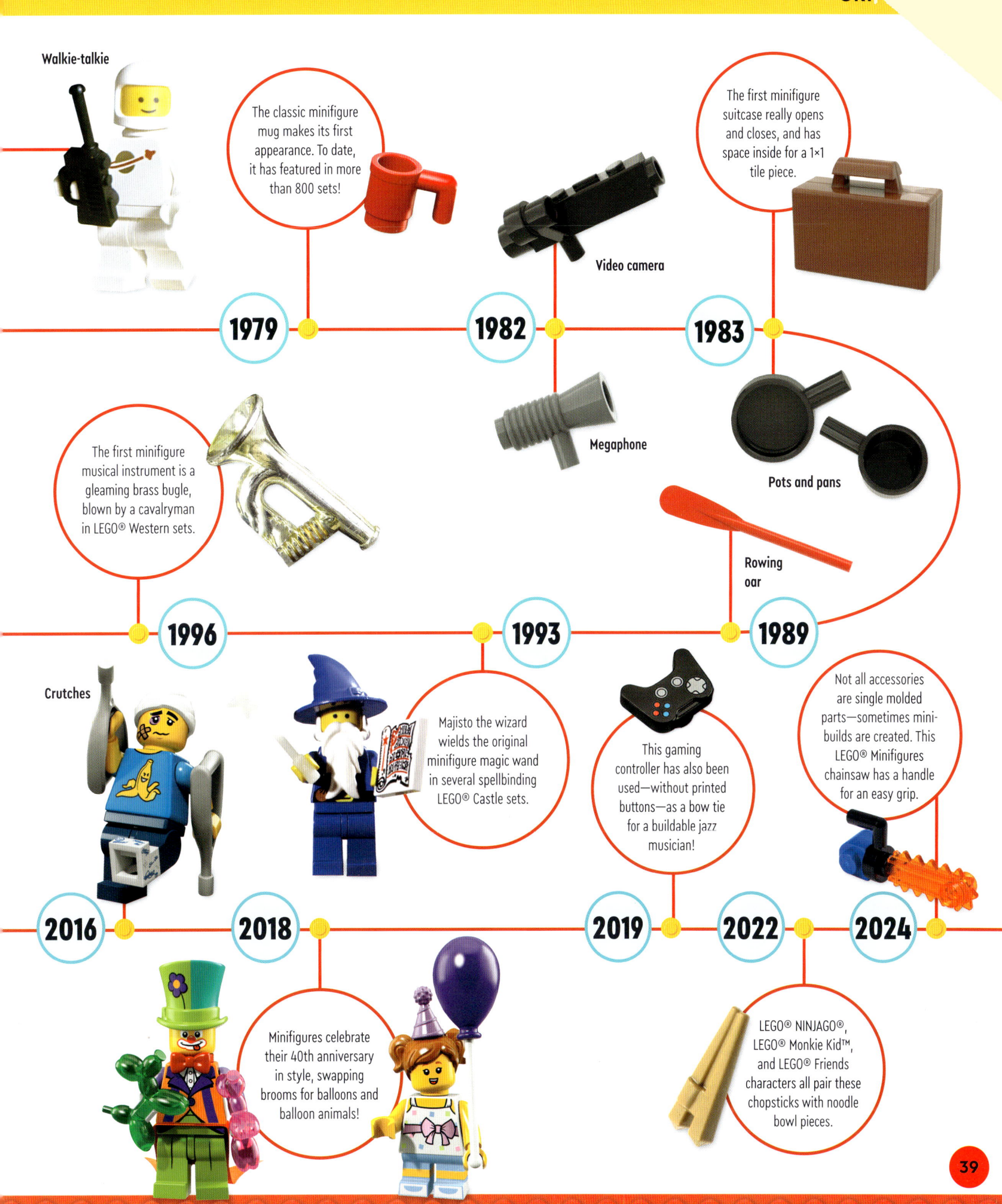

Walkie-talkie

1979
The classic minifigure mug makes its first appearance. To date, it has featured in more than 800 sets!

1982
Video camera

Megaphone

1983
The first minifigure suitcase really opens and closes, and has space inside for a 1×1 tile piece.

Pots and pans

Rowing oar

1996
The first minifigure musical instrument is a gleaming brass bugle, blown by a cavalryman in LEGO® Western sets.

1993
Majisto the wizard wields the original minifigure magic wand in several spellbinding LEGO® Castle sets.

1989
Not all accessories are single molded parts—sometimes mini-builds are created. This LEGO® Minifigures chainsaw has a handle for an easy grip.

2016
Crutches

2018
Minifigures celebrate their 40th anniversary in style, swapping brooms for balloons and balloon animals!

2019
This gaming controller has also been used—without printed buttons—as a bow tie for a buildable jazz musician!

2022
LEGO® NINJAGO®, LEGO® Monkie Kid™, and LEGO® Friends characters all pair these chopsticks with noodle bowl pieces.

2024

39

TOWN THROUGH TIME

Of the first three LEGO® play themes to feature minifigures, **LEGO® Town** most closely followed from earlier LEGOLAND® and LEGO® Town Plan sets. Proving that there's nothing dull about everyday life, the theme delighted in the details of work, leisure, home life, and travel, and laid the foundations for its blockbuster follow-up, LEGO® City.

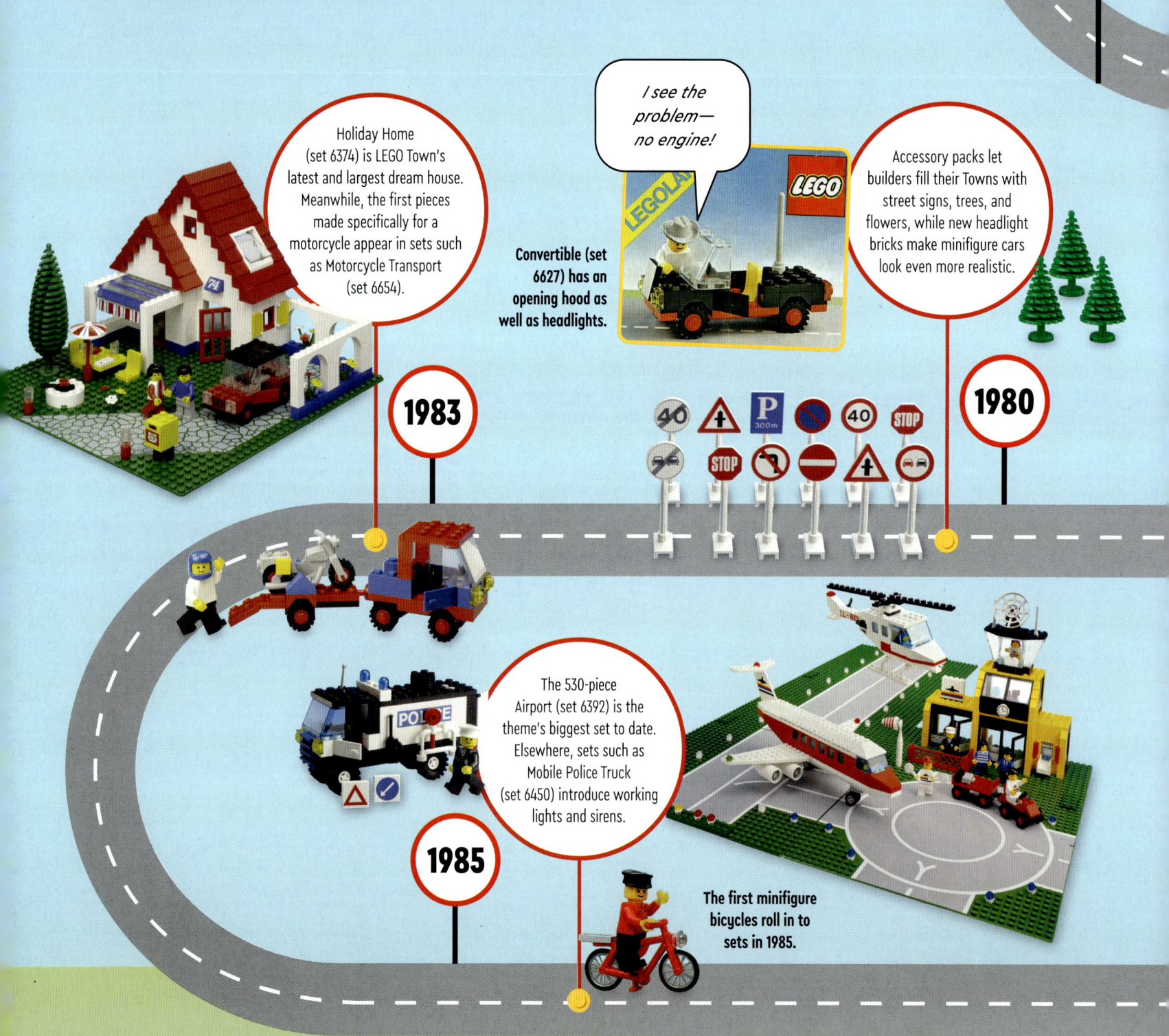

Holiday Home (set 6374) is LEGO Town's latest and largest dream house. Meanwhile, the first pieces made specifically for a motorcycle appear in sets such as Motorcycle Transport (set 6654).

I see the problem—no engine!

Convertible (set 6627) has an opening hood as well as headlights.

Accessory packs let builders fill their Towns with street signs, trees, and flowers, while new headlight bricks make minifigure cars look even more realistic.

1983

1980

The 530-piece Airport (set 6392) is the theme's biggest set to date. Elsewhere, sets such as Mobile Police Truck (set 6450) introduce working lights and sirens.

1985

The first minifigure bicycles roll in to sets in 1985.

A TOWN THROUGH TIME

1976 — Sets such as Coast Guard Station (set 369) are forerunners of the LEGO Town theme, featuring static, faceless figures in real-world vehicles and settings.

This coastguard set is updated in 1978 to include actual minifigures (set 575).

1978 — LEGO Town launches with an array of vehicles and all-new road plates. Most sets now come with minifigures, and destinations include a fire station, a gas station and—in Europe, as part of a co-promotion—even a chocolate factory!

Town Square (set 1589) includes two of the new road plate pieces.

1979 — LEGO Town gets the first of many Police Headquarters (set 381), and a public transportation system courtesy of Bus Station (set 379) and its three-seater bus.

While most Town sets have minifigures, some—like Police Car (set 600) and Ambulance (set 606)—are not quite minifigure scale!

1987 — LEGO Town gets its first and only hospital, Emergency Treatment Center (set 6380), while Refuse Collection Truck (set 6693) deals with the first LEGO bins.

1988 — It's a big year in Town, as the 606-piece Victory Lap Raceway (set 6395) offers epic motor-racing thrills. The 620-piece Parking & Service Tower (set 6394) gives spectators a place to park.

NOW APPROACHING PARADISA, TOWN SPACE PORT, AND THE ARCTIC!

41

1990

The incredible Airport Shuttle (set 6399) is LEGO Town's largest motorized set, whizzing air passengers high above the streets before they even board a plane.

The 767-piece Airport Shuttle measures 54 in (138 cm) from one end to the other!

1991

This year's flagship set is Launch and Load Seaport (set 6542). The detailed dock scene is the only LEGO Town set to have more than 1,000 pieces.

Rough-seas recovery action is the focus of sets such as RES-Q Hovercraft (set 6473).

Beach Action (set 6572) showcases the Extreme Team logo on a dune buggy and a land yacht.

New subthemes Extreme Team and RES-Q keep the focus on out-of-town action and unusual vehicles, but are designed to feel like part of the LEGO Town family.

1998

Sets such as Deep Reef Refuge (set 6441) introduce new manta ray and dolphin pieces.

1999

With an eye on the stars and one foot on the ground, LEGO Town Space Port sets are inspired by real-life moon missions, rather than the fantasy worlds of LEGO® Space.

The space shuttle in Space Port Shuttle Launch (set 6456) has light-up engines and sound effects.

2000

Back from space, this year's LEGO Town minifigures are on top of the world in a range of Arctic sets. The largest, Polar Base (set 6575), includes the first LEGO polar bear!

2002

With the recent introduction of LEGO City, LEGO Town looks back with pride. Two sets are reissued under the LEGO® Legends banner, confirming them as all-time classics.

A TOWN THROUGH TIME

1992

Gas 'N' Wash Express (set 6397) introduces the fictional Octan fuel brand to LEGO sets. Elsewhere, LEGO® Paradisa whisks LEGO Townsfolk to a tropical vacation destination.

Octan branding is still used in LEGO City sets to this day.

LEGO Paradisa sets such as Poolside Paradise (set 6416) introduce new colors, pieces, and face prints.

1993

23768 is my lucky number!

With 615 pieces, LEGO Town's fifth police station is its largest, and is the first set to feature a minifigure crook—Jailbreak Joe—dressed in striped prison gear!

The Outback Airstrip (set 6444) is too isolated to boast its own airport monorail!

With a newfound thirst for adventure, LEGO Townsfolk venture into the desert in five Outback-themed sets and underwater in 11 diving-themed sets.

1997

Central Precinct HQ (set 6398) is LEGO Town's only four-story building.

Breezeway Café (set 6376) first opened to diners as set 6332 back in 1990.

The final LEGO Town set is another Legends rerelease. Main Street (set 10041) was first issued in 1980, and includes a car showroom and an under-construction hotel.

Unlike the 1980 version (set 6390), the 2003 Main Street has added cycle lanes.

2003

Pizza-To-Go (set 10036) was fresh from the oven as set 6350 in 1994.

43

HISTORY IN THE MAKING

Launching with one huge set in 1978, the **LEGO® Castle** theme built on firm foundations to become a historic favorite. As one of the first three minifigure play themes, its brave knights crossed swords with outlaws, Bat-Lords, trolls, and more over 35 action-packed years.

1970s
Plans for the first historical LEGO play theme focus on Vikings—until set designer Daniel August Krentz presents his vision for a medieval theme based around jousting knights.

1978
LEGO Castle debuts with just one set—but what a set! With 767 pieces and eight knights, Castle (set 375) remains the largest minifigure-scale set until the 1990s.

1990
King's Mountain Fortress (set 6081) is the first castle to be built on a raised baseplate. It is also one of the first LEGO sets to be haunted by a glow-in-the-dark ghost!

1993
The Dragon Knights take LEGO Castle in a new direction, introducing actual dragons to the medieval mix! Majisto, the first ever minifigure wizard, adds to the fantasy fun.

This dragon design makes use of existing crocodile head and tail elements.

Majisto is one of the first minifigures to have a name, and the first with a detachable beard.

"Be amazed as I make my beard DISAPPEAR!"

1995
As aptly named as the Dragon Knights, new faction the Royal Knights are sworn to protect the first king minifigure. He is unmistakable in his gleaming gold crown.

44

HISTORY IN THE MAKING

Hinge bricks are designed especially for the Castle so its walls can unfold.

Siege Tower (set 6061) includes many new elements, such as wall panels in black and gray.

Armor Shop (set 6041) and **Guarded Inn (set 6067)** expand the LEGO Castle story—and can expand actual castles by plugging into their walls with LEGO® Technic pins.

The much-loved Guarded Inn is later reissued as a LEGO® Legends set.

1984

LEGO Castle takes a more realistic turn, with gray castles built with new wall panel pieces, molded horse figures, and two factions: Lion Knights and Black Falcons.

1986

A merry band of outlaws emerge from the forest in Camouflaged Outpost (set 6066). They are the first minifigures to wear green, and get stag's head shields in 1988.

1987

This dress really goes with your horseshoes!

1988

The 702-piece Black Monarch's Castle (set 6085) adds a new faction to the LEGO Castle landscape. New barding elements set their horses apart in the fashion stakes!

The Fright Knights' Night Lord's Castle (set 6097) stands more than 18 in (46 cm) tall.

1997

Yikes! It's the Fright Knights! Led by Willa the Witch and Basil the Bat-Lord, these creepy characters command a black dragon and the tallest LEGO Castle set of all!

The creepy bat insignia appears on Fright Knights' shields and flags.

MORE KINGDOMS TO COME!

45

1998

Years before LEGO® NINJAGO®, 1998's Ninja sets explore the characters and castles of 16th-century Japan. Flying Ninja Fortress (set 6093) is the largest set in the range.

2000

The Knights' Kingdom theme pits bad guy Cedric the Bull against LEGO Castle's first royal family—King Leo, Queen Leonora, and their daring daughter, Princess Storm.

Every knight has her day!

Princess Storm is the first knight minifigure to be depicted as female.

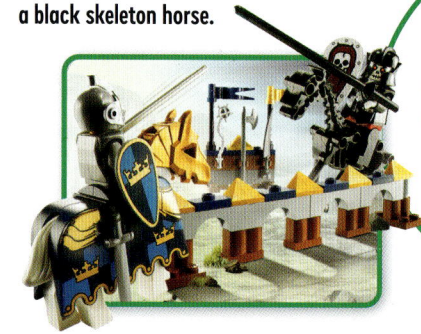

2008

The first jester minifigure appears in the first LEGO Castle Advent Calendar (set 7979), while the Castle Giant Chess Set (set 852293) pits wizards against giant trolls.

The Final Joust (set 7009) is the only Castle set to include a black skeleton horse.

2007

This year's sets are the stuff of legend! As LEGO Castle enters its Fantasy Era, brave knights must battle dwarves, trolls, and skeleton warriors riding on skeleton horses.

Why doesn't the sun ever shine on a LEGO castle? Because it's full of knights!

New-look Lion Knights defend this castle against Dragon Knights (without the dragons).

2009

With 1,601 pieces, Medieval Market Village (set 10193), is the biggest set in the original LEGO Castle theme. Instead of knights, it focuses on everyday village folk.

LEGO cow figures are new this year, also appearing in LEGO® City Farm.

2010

Briefly renamed LEGO® Kingdoms, the Castle theme goes back to basics, with few fantasy elements and a 933-piece fold-out fortress called King's Castle (set 7946).

HISTORY IN THE MAKING

2004

The color-coded young heroes of LEGO KNIGHTS' KINGDOM have a hint of LEGO NINJAGO about them.

A reboot of the LEGO® KNIGHTS' KINGDOM™ range takes its cue from BIONICLE®, offering large-scale buildable models of the main characters alongside minifigure versions.

The buildable version of villainous Vladek (set 8774) has 11 posable joints.

Viking Fortress against the Fanfir Dragon (set 7019) comes with three working catapults.

Separate from LEGO Castle, but with a shared heritage dating back to the 1970s, the LEGO Vikings finally make it off the drawing board and into their own fortress in 2005.

I'm the mean queen of... chess!

A Knights' Kingdom Chess Set (set 851499) from 2005 features this terrifying playing piece.

2005

2013

A second King's Castle (set 70404) gives the Lion Knights their biggest base to date. Not to be outdone, their rival Dragon Knights finally get their dragon back!

The massive LEGO Ideas Medieval Blacksmith (set 21325) towers over some castles!

The LEGO Creator 3in1 Medieval Castle (set 31120) can be rebuilt to include a windmill.

2021

Dragon Mountain (set 70403) and other 2013 sets mark the end of the LEGO Castle theme.

The spirit of LEGO Castle lives on, as LEGO® Ideas forges a second fan-designed blacksmith's shop and the Black Falcons find a new home in the LEGO® Creator range.

47

LION KNIGHTS' CASTLE

2022

The biggest and most realistic LEGO® castle celebrates 90 years of LEGO play. Ruled over by a smiling queen, it is home to nine Lion Knights, a wizard, a young prince, two servants, and three sneaky outlaws! A farmer brings the grain to keep the castle fed, while three Black Falcon knights drop in for friendly jousts!

What makes us Lion Knights?

Thatched and half-timbered living quarters

A cozy royal bedchamber includes the Queen's bed, her writing desk, and a miniature yellow castle for the young prince to play with.

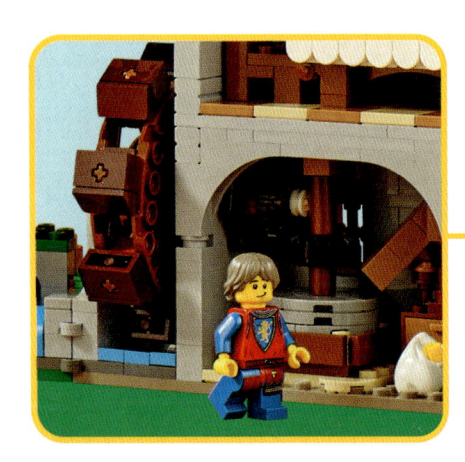

Black Falcon squire laden with supplies

Spinning the water wheel turns the millstone in the kitchen, just like in a real water mill. Grain milled here makes bread for the Queen's table.

48

HISTORY IN THE MAKING

"It must be the ... um... big... pause?"

Hinged balcony unfolds to become a bridge

This tower folds out to the front

Just like classic LEGO castles, this folding fortress can be displayed with its walls wide open or wrapped into a tight defensive ring.

Portcullis drops at the touch of a button

Archways lead to secret passages

Ox cart can fit through the castle gate

Hidden caves and tunnels make it easy for outlaws to sneak in and out of the castle—or simply to make a home in it!

SET NUMBER	10305
PIECES	4,514
MINIFIGURES	21 + 1 skeleton figure
SIZE	14 in (38 cm) tall, up to 27 in (69 cm) wide

49

THROUGH SPACE AND TIME!

In 1978, one small step for minifigures was a giant leap for LEGO® play! The first **LEGO® Space** sets established an iconic look (with a logo that is still in use today) and proved that yellow, posable figures really were the future! The LEGO Space universe went on expanding until 2013, and related sets still occasionally visit Earth.

LEGO Space becomes the first fantasy LEGO play theme, launching alongside lifelike LEGO® Town and historical LEGO® Castle. All three themes are the first to feature minifigures.

1978

The first astronaut minifigures, seen here in Launcher (set 462), all wear red or white.

Mission Commander (set 6986) is the Space Police's flying HQ.

I'll make my getaway while no one's looking.

1989

The latest LEGO Space faction is M:Tron, who defy gravity with their magnetic machines! Real magnets are used to carry cargo in all but the smallest M:Tron sets.

The first six Space Police sets bring order to a chaotic universe, locking Blacktron bad guys in the high-tech holding cells that attach to the backs of the police patrol vehicles.

The Space Police Solar Snooper (set 6957) runs on 12 wheels of justice!

1990

1992

Mega Core Magnetizer (set 6989) boasts seven real magnet pieces.

A second wave of Space Police vessels face off against a rebranded Blacktron. First seen in 1991, the new Blacktron minifigures don't look like such a bad bunch after all.

THROUGH SPACE AND TIME!

Galaxy Explorer is set 928 in Europe, in keeping with its printed registry number, "LL 928."

Blue- and black-suited astronauts complete the lineup of classic LEGO Space minifigures. Black-suited astronauts are the rarest, appearing in just eight sets between 1984 and 1986.

I'm from the dark side of the moon!

1979

1984

Red and white astronauts are joined by yellow-clad ones. Meanwhile, the 338-piece Galaxy Explorer (set 497) takes off in a big way, becoming one of the best-loved sets of the 1970s.

I look more sinister with my visor down.

Identical Blacktron minifigures feature in three 1987 sets.

The new 9-volt Light & Sound system adds a choice of sirens and steady or flashing lights in sets such as Sonar Transmitting Cruiser (set 6783) and Sonic Robot (set 6750).

1987

1985

Futuron minifigures command the Cosmic Laser Launcher (set 6953).

The galaxy gets a whole lot bigger, with the arrival of two new LEGO Space factions! Futuron revamps the classic Space colors, while Blacktron favors a more sinister look.

1993

There are thrills and chills to be had on Ice Planet 2002, where minifigure explorers use futuristic chainsaws and ships with skis to tackle the harsh environment.

Ice Station Odyssey (set 6983) is a classic LEGO Space moon base.

SET COURSE FOR MORE SPACE SETS!

1994

Two more factions stake their claim to an increasingly packed cosmos. Spyrius boasts an array of robots, while Unitron rides LEGO Space's second and final monorail.

Hands up if you like space robots.

The Spyrius Robo-Guardian (set 6949) stands 10 in (26 cm) tall.

This Unitron astronaut appears in Monorail Transport Base (set 6991).

1996

Engaged in an outer space treasure hunt, the Exploriens star in nine sets, featuring printed pieces that reveal different details when viewed through variously colored filters.

2009

The third outing for the LEGO Space Police is really all about the baddies! An intergalactic rogues' gallery includes "Four-Arms" Frenzy, Squidman, and the Skull Twins!

The mighty MT-61 Crystal Reaper (set 7645) holds a new-look alien in its high-tech hand.

2007

After six years in stasis, LEGO Space returns with the Mars Mission range. This time the local aliens are *not* friendly, and clash with a team of minifigure crystal miners.

Aero Tube Hanger (set 7317) uses an air pump to whiz Martians through flexible tubes!

2011

Squidman Escape (set 5969) offers cops-and-crooks action in just 42 pieces.

LEGO Space comes down to Earth with Alien Conquest sets. With gruesome green invaders attacking our home world, only the heroic Alien Defense Unit (ADU) can save us!

The ADU saves a flyaway farmer in UFO Abduction (set 7052).

2013

Galaxy Squad boasts the biggest LEGO Space sets yet, as astronaut heroes and their robot sidekicks battle alien Buggoids in their creepy-crawly craft!

Galactic Titan (set 70709) is the first LEGO Space set with more than 1,000 pieces.

52

THROUGH SPACE AND TIME!

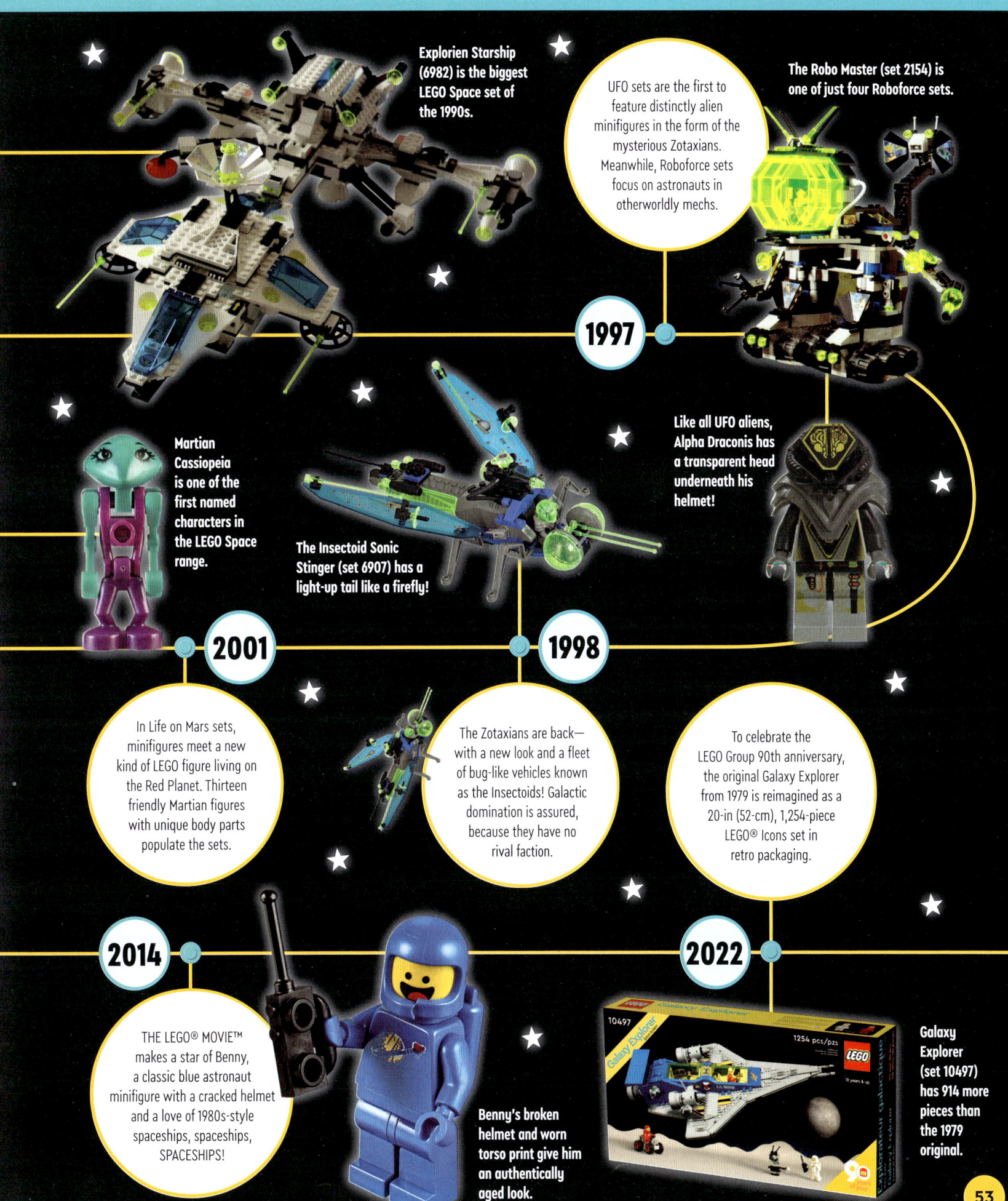

Explorien Starship (6982) is the biggest LEGO Space set of the 1990s.

UFO sets are the first to feature distinctly alien minifigures in the form of the mysterious Zotaxians. Meanwhile, Roboforce sets focus on astronauts in otherworldly mechs.

The Robo Master (set 2154) is one of just four Roboforce sets.

1997

Martian Cassiopeia is one of the first named characters in the LEGO Space range.

The Insectoid Sonic Stinger (set 6907) has a light-up tail like a firefly!

Like all UFO aliens, **Alpha Draconis** has a transparent head underneath his helmet!

2001

In **Life on Mars** sets, minifigures meet a new kind of LEGO figure living on the Red Planet. Thirteen friendly Martian figures with unique body parts populate the sets.

1998

The **Zotaxians** are back—with a new look and a fleet of bug-like vehicles known as the Insectoids! Galactic domination is assured, because they have no rival faction.

To celebrate the LEGO Group 90th anniversary, the original Galaxy Explorer from 1979 is reimagined as a 20-in (52-cm), 1,254-piece LEGO® Icons set in retro packaging.

2014

THE LEGO® MOVIE™ makes a star of Benny, a classic blue astronaut minifigure with a cracked helmet and a love of 1980s-style spaceships, spaceships, SPACESHIPS!

Benny's broken helmet and worn torso print give him an authentically aged look.

2022

Galaxy Explorer (set 10497) has 914 more pieces than the 1979 original.

53

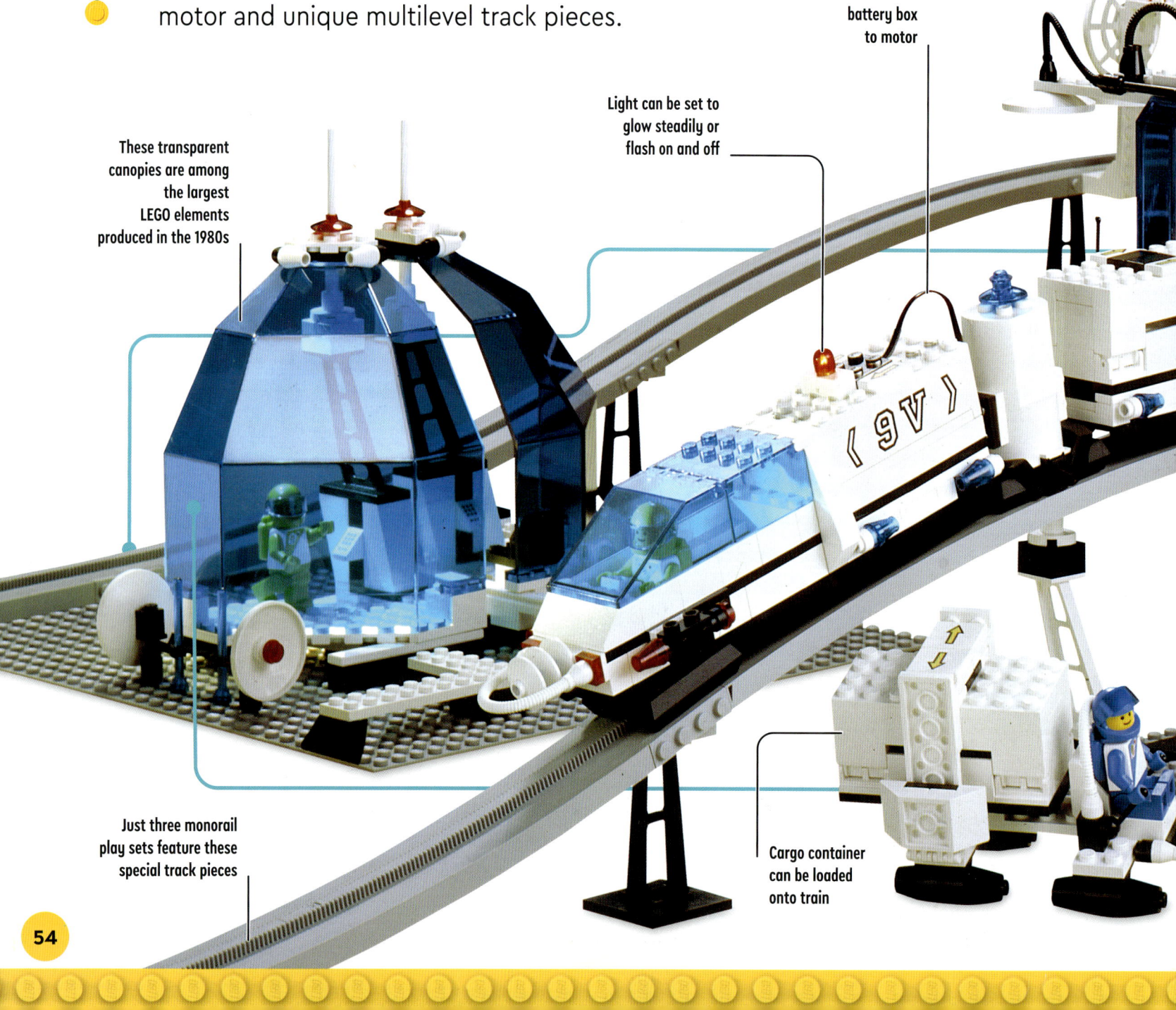

1987 MONORAIL TRANSPORT SYSTEM

SET NUMBER	6990
PIECES	731
MINIFIGURES	5
SIZE	55 in (140 cm) long, 19 in (48 cm) wide

LEGO® Space never looked so futuristic as when the aptly named Futuron faction touched down in 1987! The centerpiece of the range was the first powered LEGO monorail—driven by a new 9-volt motor and unique multilevel track pieces.

Cable links 9-volt battery box to motor

Light can be set to glow steadily or flash on and off

These transparent canopies are among the largest LEGO elements produced in the 1980s

Just three monorail play sets feature these special track pieces

Cargo container can be loaded onto train

THROUGH SPACE AND TIME!

MONO, MONO, MONO! The LEGO Space monorail was designed alongside a LEGO Town version called Airport Shuttle (set 6399, released in 1990), which also used the all-new track pieces. The third and final 9-volt monorail followed in 1994, and was one of just four sets in the LEGO Space Unitron range.

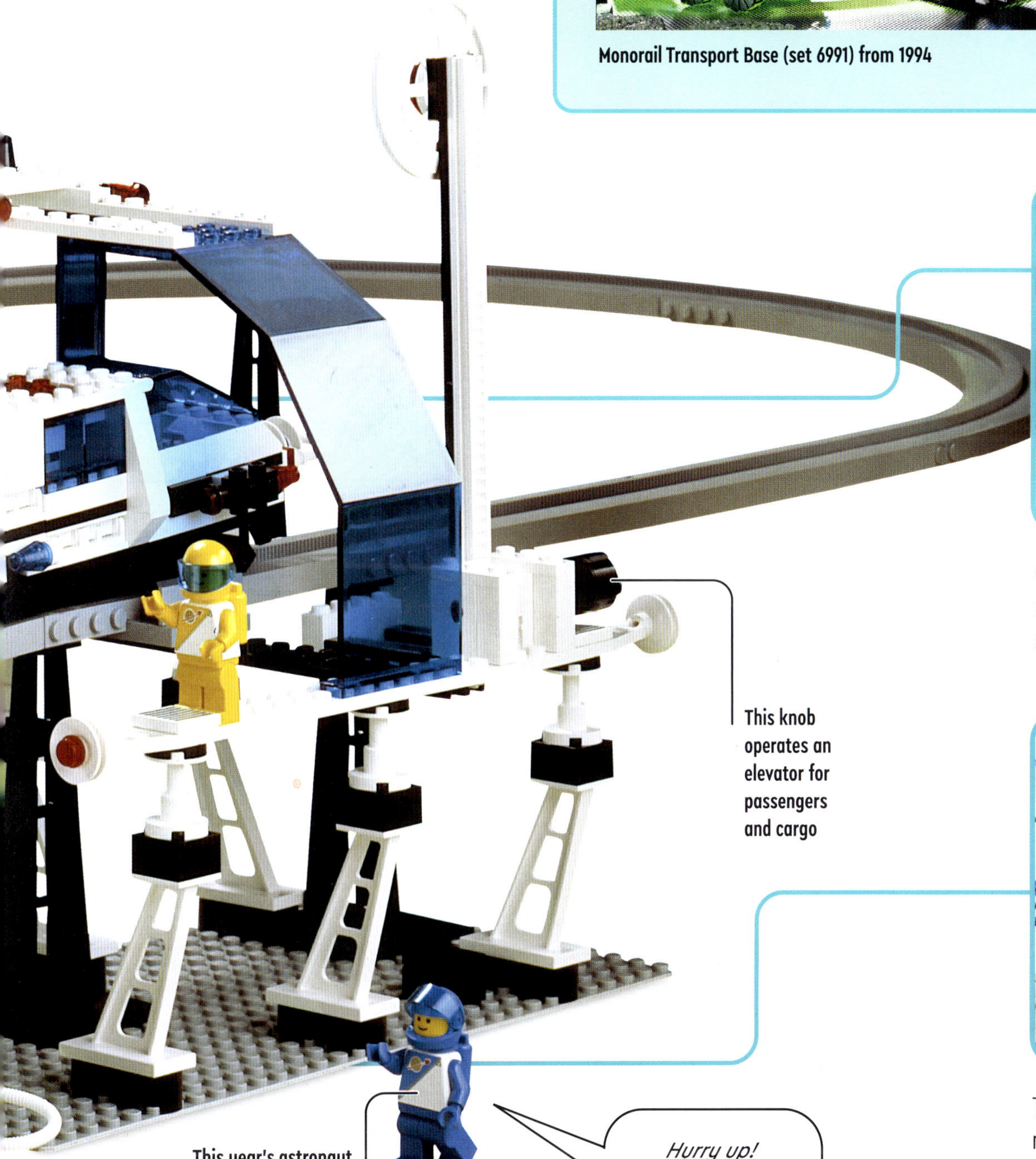

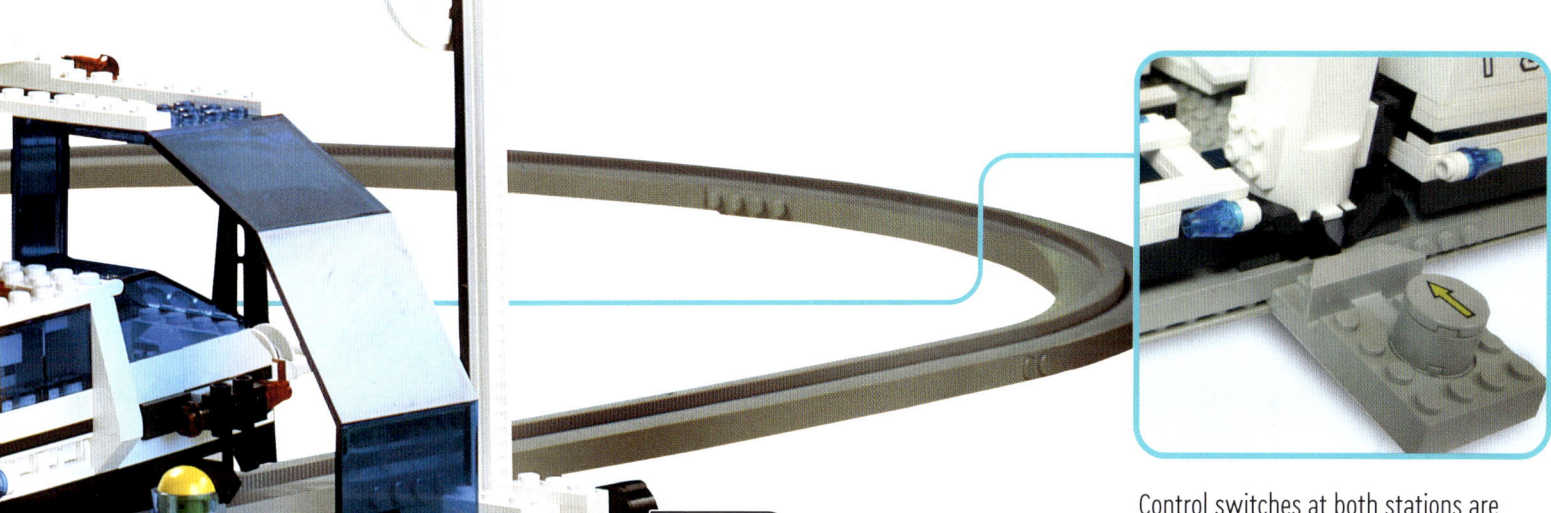

Monorail Transport Base (set 6991) from 1994

Control switches at both stations are used to stop and start the train and set its direction of travel.

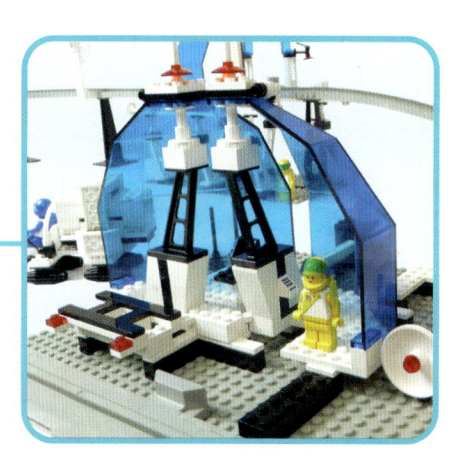

This knob operates an elevator for passengers and cargo

The canopies over the low-level station move back and forth along a sliding cargo platform.

This year's astronaut minifigures are the first to have helmets with opening visors

Hurry up! We've still got to buy tickets!

55

GEARS AND YEARS

Since the 1970s, **LEGO® Technic** sets have been turning builders into engineers. Today's stylish models may look very different from the purely functional builds of yesteryear, but lift the lid on any LEGO Technic set and you'll see that amazing machinery is still the driving force.

The first LEGO gearwheels look quite unlike their later LEGO Technic counterparts! These colorful cogs were only available in North America and are not compatible with today's LEGO Technic parts.

Gears (set 001)

1965

Other figures look tiny from up here!

Polar Copter (set 8640) has room for a pilot figure and storage space for his skis.

A range of Arctic-themed sets puts the emphasis on play with the first LEGO Technic action figures. Twice the height of minifigures, the Arctic explorers have jointed limbs.

The 347-piece Excavator (set 8851) is the largest of this year's Pneumatic sets.

1986

1984

Three LEGO Technic Pneumatic sets use compressed air pumps and rubber tubes to power realistic functions such as flatbed truck tippers, crane arms, handlike grabbers, and excavator scoops.

New 9-volt motors power innovative sets such as Control Center (set 8094). The first set to include a programmable computer, Control Center can be built as a working robot arm, a drawing machine, and more.

1989

1990

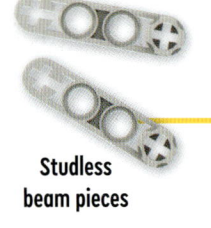

Studless beam pieces

Power Crane (set 8854) and Backhoe Grader (set 8862) are the first sets to use studless beam pieces. No one suspects that these slender, rounded elements will soon become the basis of a whole new building system!

The robotic arm can be programed to sort elements into two baskets.

56

GEARS AND YEARS

Gears, Motor, and Bricks (set 800) includes a 4.5-volt motor designed for LEGO Trains.

LEGO designers Jan Ryaa and Eric Bach dream of making a large LEGO car. The existing range of parts is not strong enough for their intended scale, and so they invent the "snap" to lock bricks with holes together!

These pins, known as "snaps" are not released to the public until 1977.

The first "Expert Builder" or "Technical" sets are released. Each one features working mechanisms, made possible using the new "snap" pieces, updated axles and bricks with holes, and new, smaller gears.

1970

Three sets pave the way for LEGO Technic, introducing long, thin axles that slot securely into new gear pieces and through bricks with holes to create hand-driven and battery-powered mechanisms.

1974

The growing range is officially named LEGO Technic. The chunky battery box used to power the first motors is replaced by a slimline version, available separately, or in Universal Motor Set (set 8050).

1976

Car Chassis (set 853) is the result of Ryaa and Bach's dream from 1974.

A new, compact motor (set 870) lets builders automate their Technical sets.

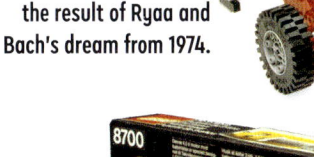

1982

Universal Set with Flex System (set 8074) comes with instructions for making four different machines.

1991

The Flex System adds curves to LEGO Technic builds, with cables that can control movement around corners. Later sets also use the system's outer tubes for purely decorative effect.

1994

Super Car (set 8880) is the first LEGO Technic model to have more than 1,000 pieces. It boasts a working gear box, four-wheel steering and suspension, and an eight-cylinder engine with moving pistons.

BEAM INTO THE NEXT ERA OF LEGO TECHNIC!

57

1995

Control Center II (set 8485) builds on the promise of its 1990 predecessor, using basic coding to create a helicopter, a hovercraft, and even a dinosaur that can all be programed to repeat a series of movements.

1996

Space Shuttle (set 8480) features 10 of these new beams along its "back."

It's a giant leap for LEGO Technic, as Space Shuttle (set 8480) marks the move toward building with studless beams for sleeker, more realistic structures. The set also boasts new fiber-optic lighting.

1997

Barcode Multi-Set (set 8479) offers pocket programming, with a handheld controller for scanning barcoded commands into a memory unit. Four builds can then be made to perform functions and play sounds.

2016

Measuring 28 in (72 cm) long, the motorized Bucket Wheel Excavator (set 42055) is the first LEGO Technic set with more than 3,000 pieces. In fact, with 3,929 elements altogether, its total is closer to 4,000!

The first LEGO Technic supercar is 2016's Porsche 911 GT3 RS (set 42056).

2017

To celebrate the range's 40th anniversary, every new LEGO Technic set in 2017 comes with a specially printed beam. Three of the sets can be combined to make an updated version of a car chassis set from 1980.

This anniversary build (set 8860) is made from parts of set 42057, set 42061, and set 42063.

2018

Rough Terrain Crane (set 42082) is—you've guessed it—the first LEGO Technic set to have more than 4,000 pieces! It reaches higher than 2005's Mobile Crane too—extending to more than 40 in (1 m).

GEARS AND YEARS

1999
Known as Throwbots in the US, LEGO Technic Slizers are disk-throwing alien robot figures. The range introduces many figure-building parts that make BIONICLE® a smash hit two years later.

The Millennium Slizer (set 8520) can be rebuilt as a motorcycle.

2003
Where earlier sets showed off their inner workings, Rescue Truck (set 8454) uses smooth panel pieces to suggest the vehicle's bodywork. This look will soon become the norm for LEGO Technic sets.

2005
With 1,884 pieces, Mobile Crane (set 8421) becomes the biggest LEGO Technic set to date. The motorized crane arm can rotate 360 degrees and, when fully extended, reaches 25 in (64 cm) into the air!

2007
Motorized Bulldozer (set 8275) is the first LEGO Technic set to use the Power Functions range of new and improved LEGO motors. A remote control operates its caterpillar tracks, steering, and more.

2011
The first LEGO Technic model to have more than 2,000 pieces, Mercedes-Benz Unimog U 400 (set 8110) is also the first of many sets to be designed in partnership with a real-world vehicle manufacturer.

2019
They just keep on getting bigger! The 4,108-piece Liebherr R 9800 (set 42100) is not only the largest ever LEGO Technic set, it is also the first to be controlled using new Powered UP motors and a smartphone app!

59

2023
LIEBHERR CRAWLER CRANE LR 13000

It takes six motors, two smart hubs, and a state-of-the-art app to power the tallest LEGO® Technic set of all! Together, they let master builders move the machine around on caterpillar tracks, rotate the superstructure through 360 degrees, raise and lower the boom and jib, and deploy the lifting block—all without touching the model itself!

Slim but sturdy axle pieces make stabilizing pendant cables

Warning beacons tell low-flying aircraft to steer clear at night

New rectangular frame elements are used to make the luffing jib and boom

In its tallest configuration, the top of the jib rises more than 39 in (100 cm) into the air

More than 32 feet (10 meters) of LEGO twine are used to operate the crane

A gear inside the lifting block allows the hooks to rotate

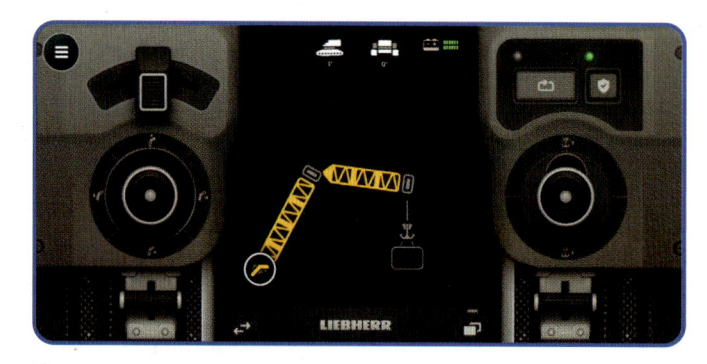

A LIEBHERR dashboard in the LEGO Technic CONTROL+ smartphone app features realistic virtual joysticks and levers for operating the crane remotely.

GEARS AND YEARS

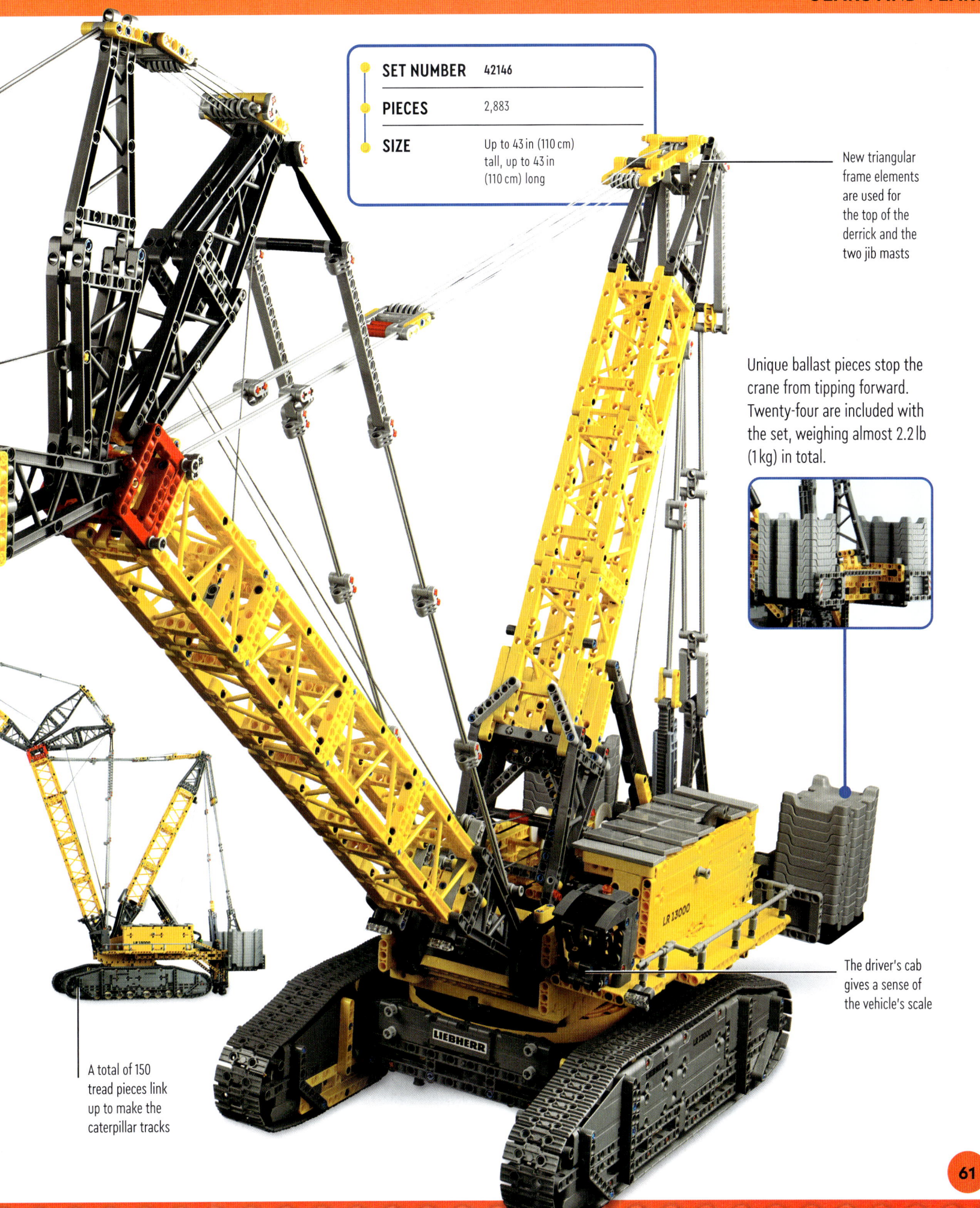

- **SET NUMBER** 42146
- **PIECES** 2,883
- **SIZE** Up to 43 in (110 cm) tall, up to 43 in (110 cm) long

New triangular frame elements are used for the top of the derrick and the two jib masts

Unique ballast pieces stop the crane from tipping forward. Twenty-four are included with the set, weighing almost 2.2 lb (1 kg) in total.

The driver's cab gives a sense of the vehicle's scale

A total of 150 tread pieces link up to make the caterpillar tracks

61

FABULOUS FABULAND

Designed to ease the move for young builders from LEGO® DUPLO® to System bricks, **LEGO® FABULAND™** introduced a range of adorable animal figures and special new parts for quick and easy building. The first LEGO theme to have named characters, it was also the first multimedia theme—with storybooks and a TV series.

1979 — The first LEGO FABULAND sets go on sale in mainland Europe, the US, and Canada. New parts include special doors, windows, vehicle parts, and trees, plus 11 unique animal figures—ranging from bears and bulldogs to lions and lambs!

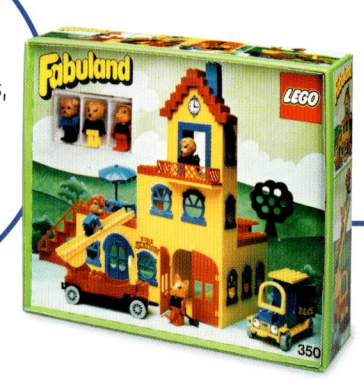

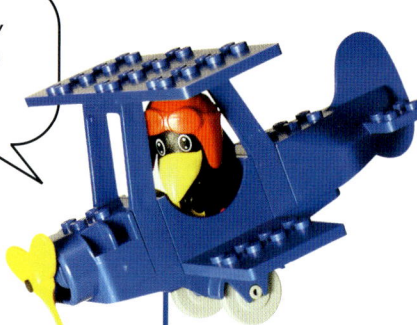

1986 — This year's FABULAND figures look a little different, with whites around their expressive eyes and printed torso designs. FABULAND storybooks also get a new look, and include *Max and Edward All at Sea* and *Edward's Butterfly*.

1985 — The first of several fair sets, Amusement Park (set 3681) has a rotating Ferris wheel with room for four FABULAND figure riders. Paddle Steamer (set 3673), meanwhile, is a huge blue boat that really floats!

How do you FABU-LAND this thing?

Like other FABULAND aircraft, the plane in Airport is flown by a bird!

1984 — Fast-growing FABULAND gets an Airport (set 3671), a Police Station (set 3664), and a Police Van (set 3639) with a crocodile crook. New resident Wally Walrus (set 3791) is the last new animal in the range.

1987 — The first ever LEGO TV series is stop-motion animation *Edward and Friends*, starring clay re-creations of Edward the Elephant and other FABULAND favorites. A new range of books follows, based on the series.

This year's sets include the first FABULAND Double-Decker Bus (set 3662), driven by Mike Monkey.

FABULOUS FABULAND

Larger sets such as Town Hall (set 350) come with storybook-style instructions showing figures building the sets.

The first FABULAND tie-in merchandise is a series of audio stories released on vinyl in Germany.

This year's new figures include Harry Horse, Clara Cow, and Charlie (also known as Joe) Crow. Small sets featuring a single figure and one or two accessories are forerunners of the collectible LEGO® Minifigures theme.

Ricky Raccoon and his Scooter (set 3605) is a rare example of a set with just two pieces!

Elton Elephant (set 3601) is known as Edward Elephant's Garden Table in some countries.

1980

1981

The first FABULAND storybooks are published in English, French, German, Swedish, and Dutch. The page-turning tales include *Edward's Skyscraper*, *Catherine Cat's Birthday*, *Morty's New Job*, and *Henry's Night Out*.

As LEGO FABULAND arrives in Asia, Australia, and the UK, sets such as Pat and Freddy's Shop (set 3667) introduce new large roof pieces and the first ever LEGO food element—a tasty looking baguette that still appears in sets today.

Bonnie Bunny and Edward (or Elton) Elephant join the FABULAND family, while Boris Bulldog sports a stylish new hat. There will be no doubt about Edward's name when he later becomes the most famous FABULAND figure of all!

1983

1982

Taking the total number of FABULAND sets to more than 90, the theme's final releases include a pair of fairground sets and Lionel Lion's Classroom (set 3647), starring the medallioned mayor of FABULAND himself!

1989

2022

Edward the Elephant returns after a 30-year break! Now rocking a brick-built look, the classic character is one of 15 mini-builds in 90 Years of Play (set 11021), celebrating FABULAND and other fan-favorite themes.

63

GO FIGURE!

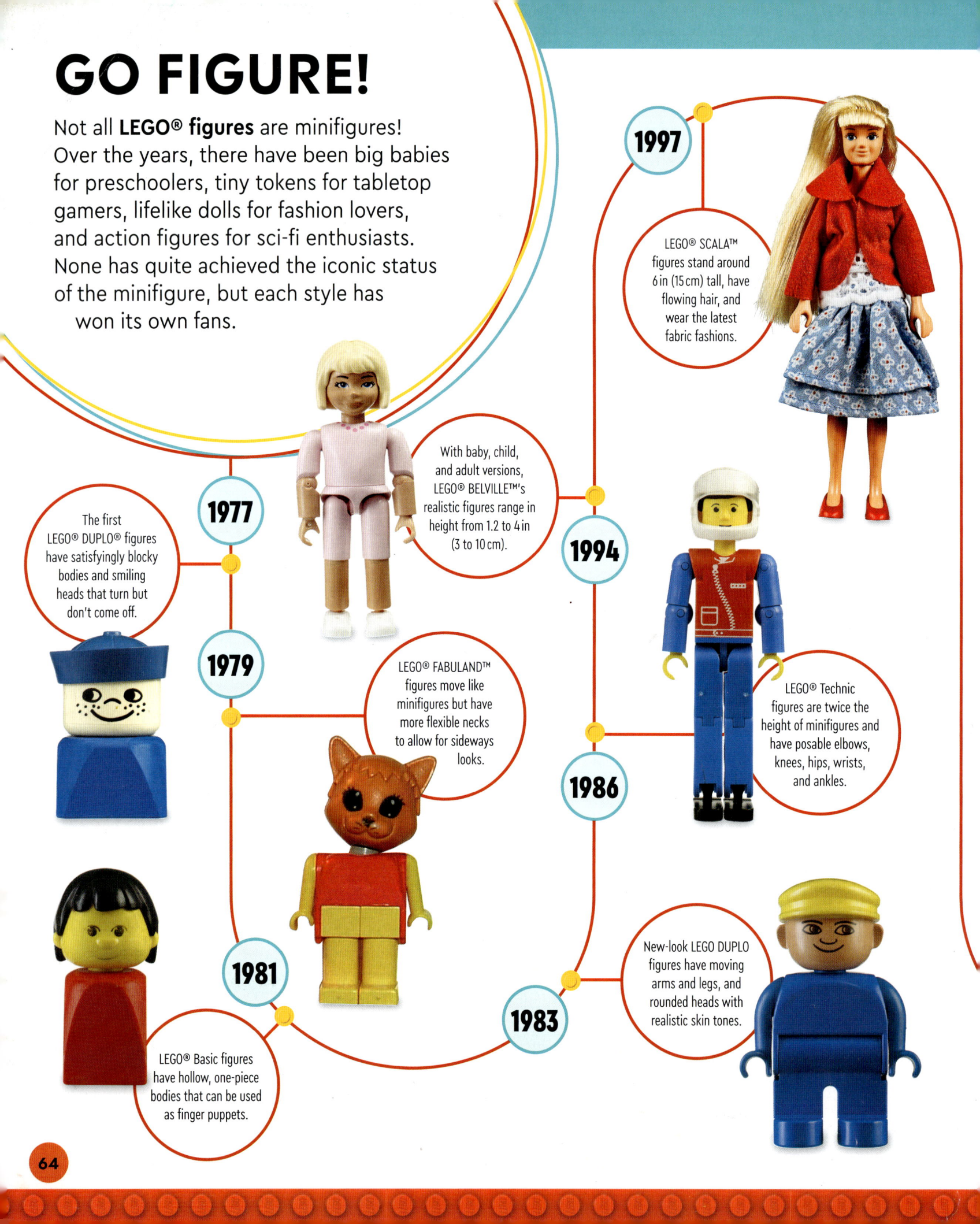

Not all **LEGO® figures** are minifigures! Over the years, there have been big babies for preschoolers, tiny tokens for tabletop gamers, lifelike dolls for fashion lovers, and action figures for sci-fi enthusiasts. None has quite achieved the iconic status of the minifigure, but each style has won its own fans.

1997 — LEGO® SCALA™ figures stand around 6 in (15 cm) tall, have flowing hair, and wear the latest fabric fashions.

1977 — With baby, child, and adult versions, LEGO® BELVILLE™'s realistic figures range in height from 1.2 to 4 in (3 to 10 cm).

1979 — The first LEGO® DUPLO® figures have satisfyingly blocky bodies and smiling heads that turn but don't come off.

1981 — LEGO® FABULAND™ figures move like minifigures but have more flexible necks to allow for sideways looks.

1994 — LEGO® Technic figures are twice the height of minifigures and have posable elbows, knees, hips, wrists, and ankles.

1986 — LEGO® Basic figures have hollow, one-piece bodies that can be used as finger puppets.

1983 — New-look LEGO DUPLO figures have moving arms and legs, and rounded heads with realistic skin tones.

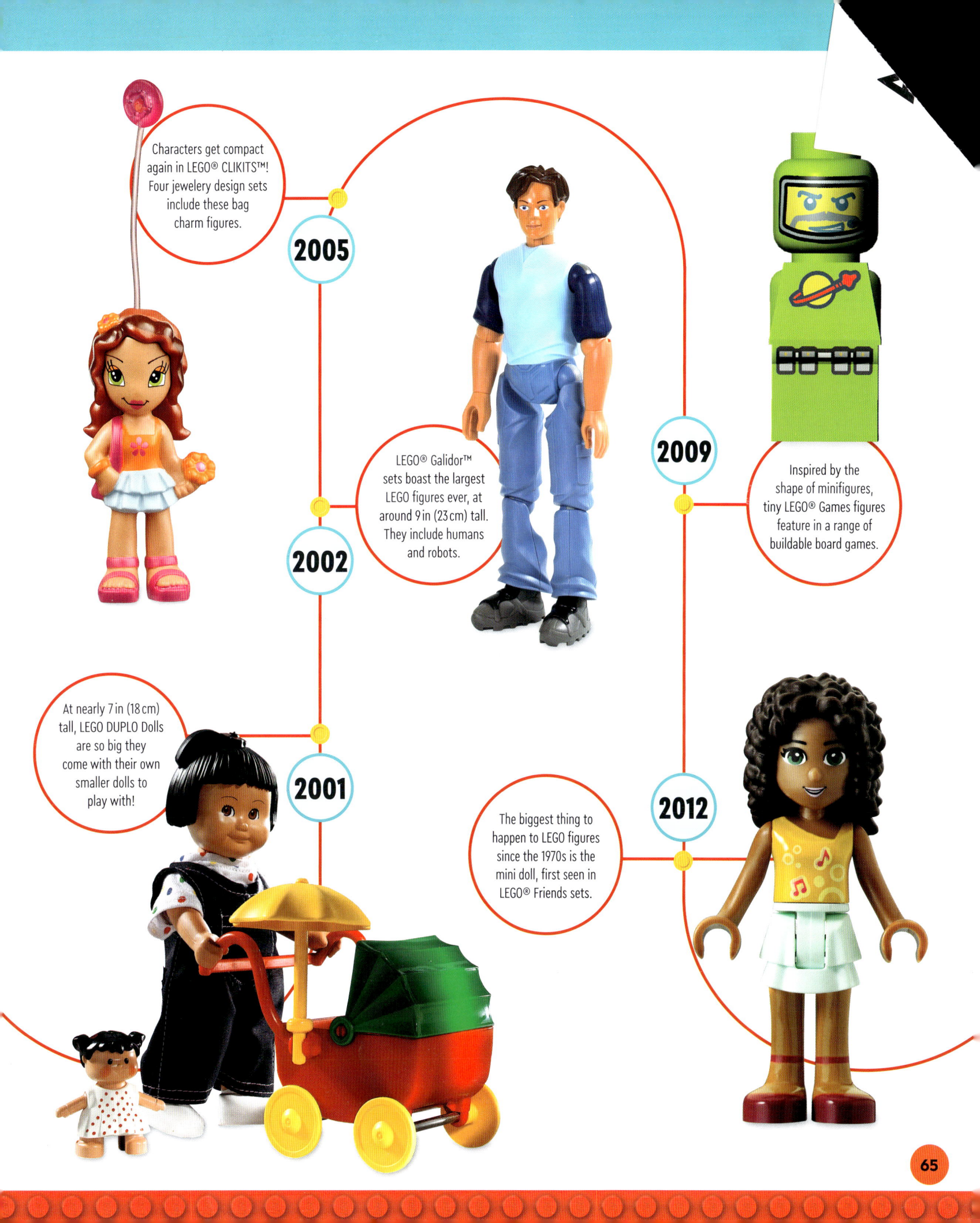

2005 — Characters get compact again in LEGO® CLIKITS™! Four jewelery design sets include these bag charm figures.

2002 — LEGO® Galidor™ sets boast the largest LEGO figures ever, at around 9 in (23 cm) tall. They include humans and robots.

2009 — Inspired by the shape of minifigures, tiny LEGO® Games figures feature in a range of buildable board games.

2001 — At nearly 7 in (18 cm) tall, LEGO DUPLO Dolls are so big they come with their own smaller dolls to play with!

2012 — The biggest thing to happen to LEGO figures since the 1970s is the mini doll, first seen in LEGO® Friends sets.

ANIMAL EVOLUTION

You can build any animal from LEGO® bricks, but some sets are that little bit more special when they come with their own **animal figures**! These are just some of the creatures to feature in minifigure themes throughout the years—becoming more realistic over time, but always holding on to their true LEGO nature!

Knights ride the first LEGO horse figures using new saddle pieces in LEGOLAND® Castle sets.

1984

Cow figures and fish pieces first feature in the LEGO Castle Medieval Market Village (set 10193).

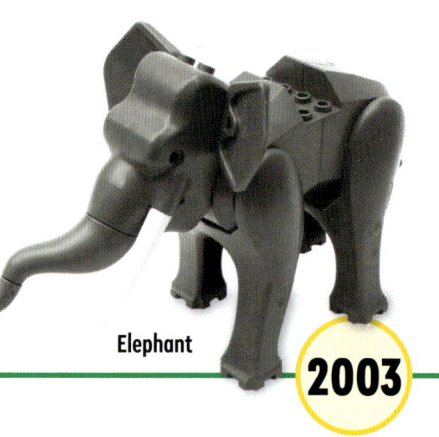

2009

The first of many dog figures appear in two LEGO Harry Potter sets and pull a sleigh in an advent calendar.

2004

Elephant

2003

Goats

2010

2011

Chicken

2012

Domestic cat

2013

Ostrich and camel pieces are made especially for the LEGO® *Prince of Persia*™ theme, and appear in no other sets.

Pig

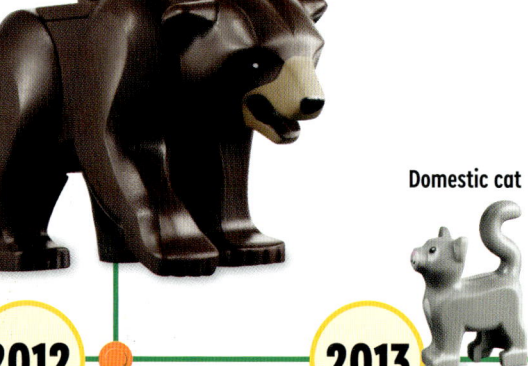

Unlike earlier bear figures, this brown bear can rear up on its hind legs to find food—or just to look extra scary!

66

ANIMAL EVOLUTION

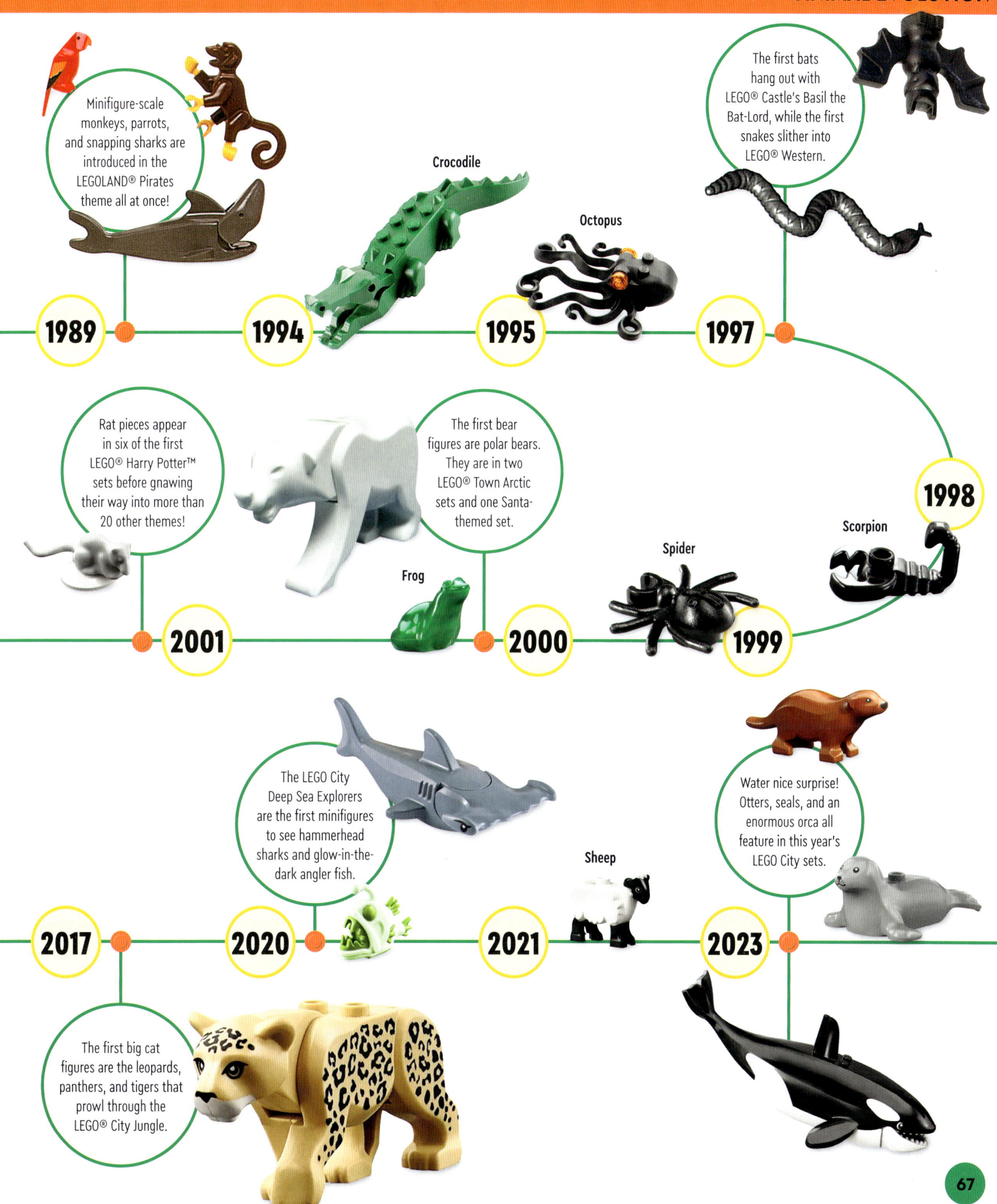

1989 — Minifigure-scale monkeys, parrots, and snapping sharks are introduced in the LEGOLAND® Pirates theme all at once!

1994 — Crocodile

1995 — Octopus

1997 — The first bats hang out with LEGO® Castle's Basil the Bat-Lord, while the first snakes slither into LEGO® Western.

1998 — Scorpion

1999 — Spider

2000 — Frog. The first bear figures are polar bears. They are in two LEGO® Town Arctic sets and one Santa-themed set.

2001 — Rat pieces appear in six of the first LEGO® Harry Potter™ sets before gnawing their way into more than 20 other themes!

2017 — The first big cat figures are the leopards, panthers, and tigers that prowl through the LEGO® City Jungle.

2020 — The LEGO City Deep Sea Explorers are the first minifigures to see hammerhead sharks and glow-in-the-dark angler fish.

2021 — Sheep

2023 — Water nice surprise! Otters, seals, and an enormous orca all feature in this year's LEGO City sets.

THE 1980s–1990s

1980

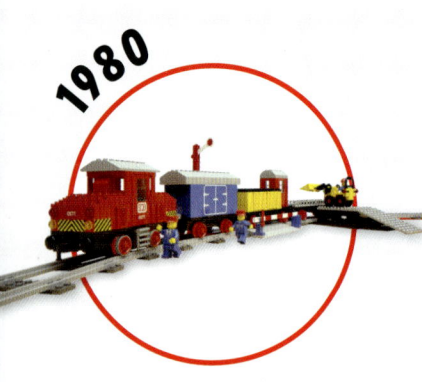

LEGO® Trains get a major overhaul for the minifigure era.

The LEGO Group sets up a department to make sets especially for schools.

A new LEGO brick factory opens in Connecticut.

1984

LEGO South Africa is the first office for the LEGO Group in Africa.

The LEGO Group opens new offices in Brazil and South Korea.

1985

The LEGO Prize is launched to reward people and groups who change children's lives for the better.

The first LEGO Technic figures go on an Arctic expedition!

A new LEGO brick factory opens in Manaus, Brazil.

1987

Official LEGO Clubs launch in Austria, France, Germany, Norway, Switzerland, and the United States.

1981
The first LEGO® World Show touring exhibition opens in Billund, Denmark.

The UK gets its own official LEGO® Club.

1982
The LEGO Group celebrates its 50th birthday with a book and a special song!

The LEGO® Technic name appears on sets for the first time.

A new LEGO brick factory opens in Kunpo, South Korea.

1986
The LEGO® Foundation is set up to help parents and schools harness the power of play in learning and development.

LEGO Technic Control I brings brick-based computer programming to schools.

LEGO® Model Team sets are the most detailed and lifelike builds to date.

1988
LEGO Canada is the latest LEGO office in North America.

Children from 14 countries take part in a LEGO World Cup building competition in Billund, Denmark.

1989
LEGO® Pirates is the first new minifigure play theme since 1978!

The LEGO Group founder, Ole Kirk Kristiansen is inducted into the Toy Industry Hall of Fame in the US.

69

New 9-volt motors power sets such as the programmable LEGO® Technic Control Center (set 8094).

LEGO Malaysia is the latest office for the LEGO Group in Asia.

1991

The LEGO Group now has more than 7,500 staff members and 1,000 element-molding machines across the world!

LEGO Mexico is the second office for the LEGO Group in South America.

1995

LEGO® Aquazone is the first theme based around undersea minifigure teams.

LEGO® DUPLO® PRIMO™ sets boast bigger, rounder parts for the very youngest builders.

1997

LEGO® SCALA™ is relaunched as a doll's house theme.

1998

LEGO® MINDSTORMS® makes smart bricks and programmable LEGO robots a reality.

The first LEGO® Adventurers sets tell tales of heroism in the Egyptian desert!

1992
LEGO® Paradisa launches with sets featuring pastel tones and a summertime vibe.

1993
The LEGO® Imagination Center opens in Minnesota.

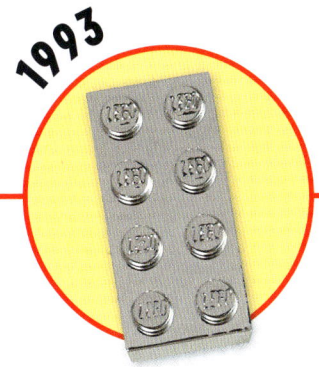

The LEGO Group celebrates the 35th anniversary of the LEGO® Brick patent.

1994
The first LEGO® BELVILLE™ sets feature large, lifelike figures in doll's house settings.

LEGO® *Fun to Build* is the first ever LEGO video game.

1996
New Western and Time Cruisers sets promise era-spanning adventure!

The second LEGOLAND® Park, LEGOLAND® Windsor, welcomes its first guests in the UK.

LEGO.com goes live on the World Wide Web!

The LEGO logo gets a subtle and long-lasting update.

1999
LEGO® *Star Wars*™ and LEGO® DUPLO® Winnie the Pooh sets launch a new era of sets based on preexisting characters.

Rock Raiders is the first LEGO theme to explore a fantasy underground setting.

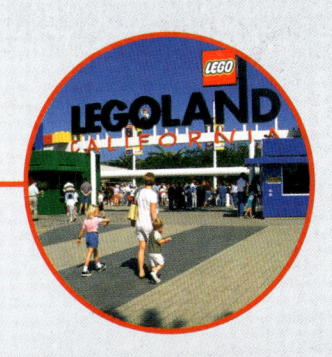

LEGOLAND® California opens its gates as the first LEGOLAND attraction in the US.

TREASURE TRAIL

With its named characters, rivalries, and facially distinct minifigures, the fourth LEGOLAND® play theme was very different from those that had come before it. Tales of the **LEGO® Pirates** were told in comics and books to inspire more exciting role play. This was the start of a storytelling trend that has defined almost every LEGO play theme since.

1984
Planning begins for a new historical play theme, with LEGO® Pirates, LEGO® Western (eventually released in 1996), and LEGO® Europa (an unmade 19th-century theme) all being considered.

1989
LEGO Pirates launches with 10 sets and a special comic book. The theme is the first to feature monkey and shark figures, working cannons, and minifigures with varied facial features.

Redbeard by name, red beard by nature!

Ship ahoy! Black Seas Barracuda (set 6285) is the first ever LEGO Pirates galleon.

1990
Four storybooks, two activity books, and six German audiobook adventures expand the exciting world of the LEGO Pirates. Titles include *The Royal Visit* and *Will and the Gold Chase*.

The pirates' first adversaries are the bluecoats of Eldorado Fortress (set 6276).

TREASURE TRAIL

1994

Five of this year's sets feature the first LEGO crocodile figure, complete with snapping head piece!

1995

From a brand-new base on scary Skull Island (set 6279), the pirates are up against returning redcoats—and one of the first ever LEGO skeleton figures.

1993

The Skull's Eye Schooner (set 6286) becomes the biggest ship in the Pirates theme—a record it still holds today! The 912-piece galleon measures 26 in (66 cm) from bowsprit to stern and stands 19 in (50 cm) tall.

1996

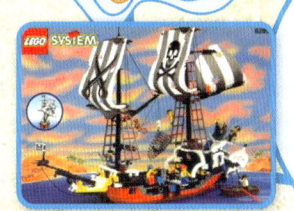

New pirate ship the Red Beard Runner (set 6289) is built with battle-damaged sails and collapsible sections for authentic clashes between the pirates and their latest enemies, the Imperial Armada.

1999

A LEGO Pirates-themed area at LEGOLAND® California opens. Today, there are Pirate-themed rides and water parks at LEGOLAND resorts around the world.

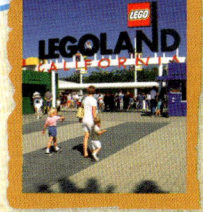

2002

After 13 years of pillage and plunder, the Black Seas Barracuda is rereleased as part of the LEGO® Legends range of undisputed classics (set 10040). Captain Redbeard and his crew don't look a day older!

1992

The pirates set sail for new waters, where redcoat soldiers rule the waves! Their Imperial Trading Post (set 6277) is the theme's largest land base and the only Pirates set to feature a merchant ship.

HERE BE MORE PIRATES!

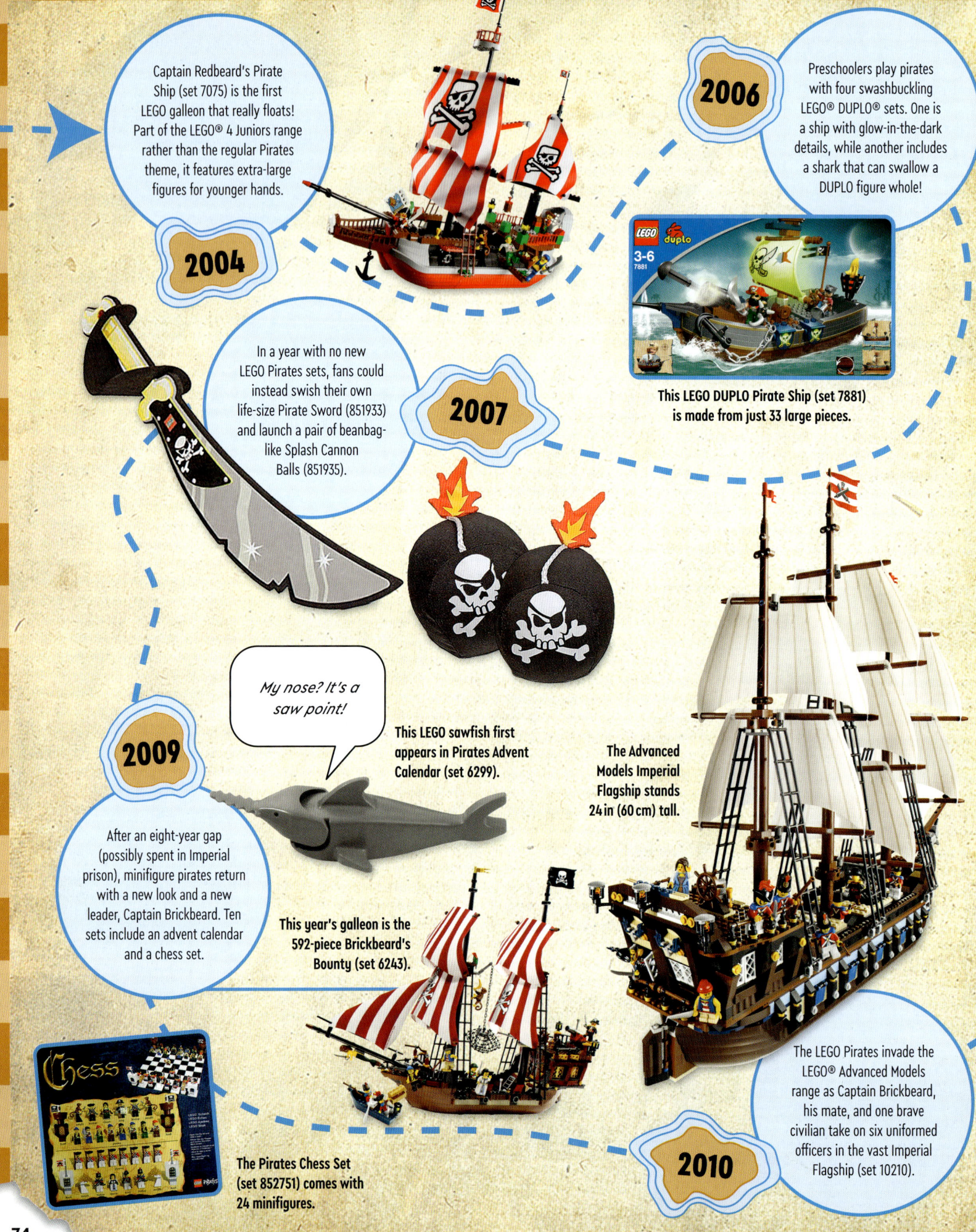

2004

Captain Redbeard's Pirate Ship (set 7075) is the first LEGO galleon that really floats! Part of the LEGO® 4 Juniors range rather than the regular Pirates theme, it features extra-large figures for younger hands.

2006

Preschoolers play pirates with four swashbuckling LEGO® DUPLO® sets. One is a ship with glow-in-the-dark details, while another includes a shark that can swallow a DUPLO figure whole!

This LEGO DUPLO Pirate Ship (set 7881) is made from just 33 large pieces.

2007

In a year with no new LEGO Pirates sets, fans could instead swish their own life-size Pirate Sword (851933) and launch a pair of beanbag-like Splash Cannon Balls (851935).

My nose? It's a saw point!

This LEGO sawfish first appears in Pirates Advent Calendar (set 6299).

The Advanced Models Imperial Flagship stands 24 in (60 cm) tall.

2009

After an eight-year gap (possibly spent in Imperial prison), minifigure pirates return with a new look and a new leader, Captain Brickbeard. Ten sets include an advent calendar and a chess set.

This year's galleon is the 592-piece Brickbeard's Bounty (set 6243).

The Pirates Chess Set (set 852751) comes with 24 minifigures.

2010

The LEGO Pirates invade the LEGO® Advanced Models range as Captain Brickbeard, his mate, and one brave civilian take on six uniformed officers in the vast Imperial Flagship (set 10210).

TREASURE TRAIL

2015
Now sailing aboard the 745-piece Brick Bounty (set 70413), the LEGO Pirates return in force, with new friends and foes including a scurvy ship's Cook and the swashbuckling Imperial Governor's Daughter.

2018
The celebratory 60 Years of the LEGO® Brick (set 40290) features microscale builds of four famous LEGO sets, including 1989's Black Seas Barracuda. The LEGO Pirates' place in history is assured!

The 2,545-piece Pirates of Barracuda Bay set is a shipwreck that can be rebuilt as an unwrecked galleon.

The LEGO Creator Pirate Ship has brick-built sails rather than fabric ones.

2020
The pirates continue to plunder other LEGO play themes—stealing their way into LEGO® Ideas with Pirates of Barracuda Bay (set 21322) and then into the LEGO® Creator range on board Pirate Ship (set 31109).

2013
Just when it seems safe to go back into the water, Classic Pirate Set (set 850839) comes out of nowhere! The 39-piece set comes with four pirate minifigures preassembled for an extra quick getaway.

2023
Standing 13 in (32 cm) tall and made from 1,041 pieces, a giant, limited edition version of pirate captain Redbeard goes on sale at the LEGO® House visitor attraction in Billund, Denmark.

Arr! 'Tis enough to make me big-headed!

Called A Minifigure Tribute (set 40504), this set is as tall as eight Redbeard minifigures!

2023
ELDORADO FORTRESS

This LEGO® Icons tribute to 1989's Eldorado Fortress (set 6276) shows some love to the non-pirate stars of LEGO® Pirates! The classic theme's Imperial Soldiers have a long and storied history of resisting Captain Redbeard and his crew. Now they have a base for the ages, befitting their swashbuckling status!

A gray-bearded governor controls the fortress from a room above the main gate. He's happiest studying maps by candlelight.

Large flag element was brand new in 1989

Cannons defend against far-off threats...

...while muskets warn off pirates who get too close!

The set splits into five sections that can be rearranged to make a wider fortress with a large jetty. The jetty serves as the central courtyard in the main version of the build.

Cobbled entry ramp made from round tiles and jumper plates

Two pirates prepare for a bold daylight raid!

SET NUMBER	10320
PIECES	2,509
MINIFIGURES	8 + 1 skeleton figure
SIZE	11 in (27 cm) tall, up to 28 in (70 cm) wide

76

TREASURE TRAIL

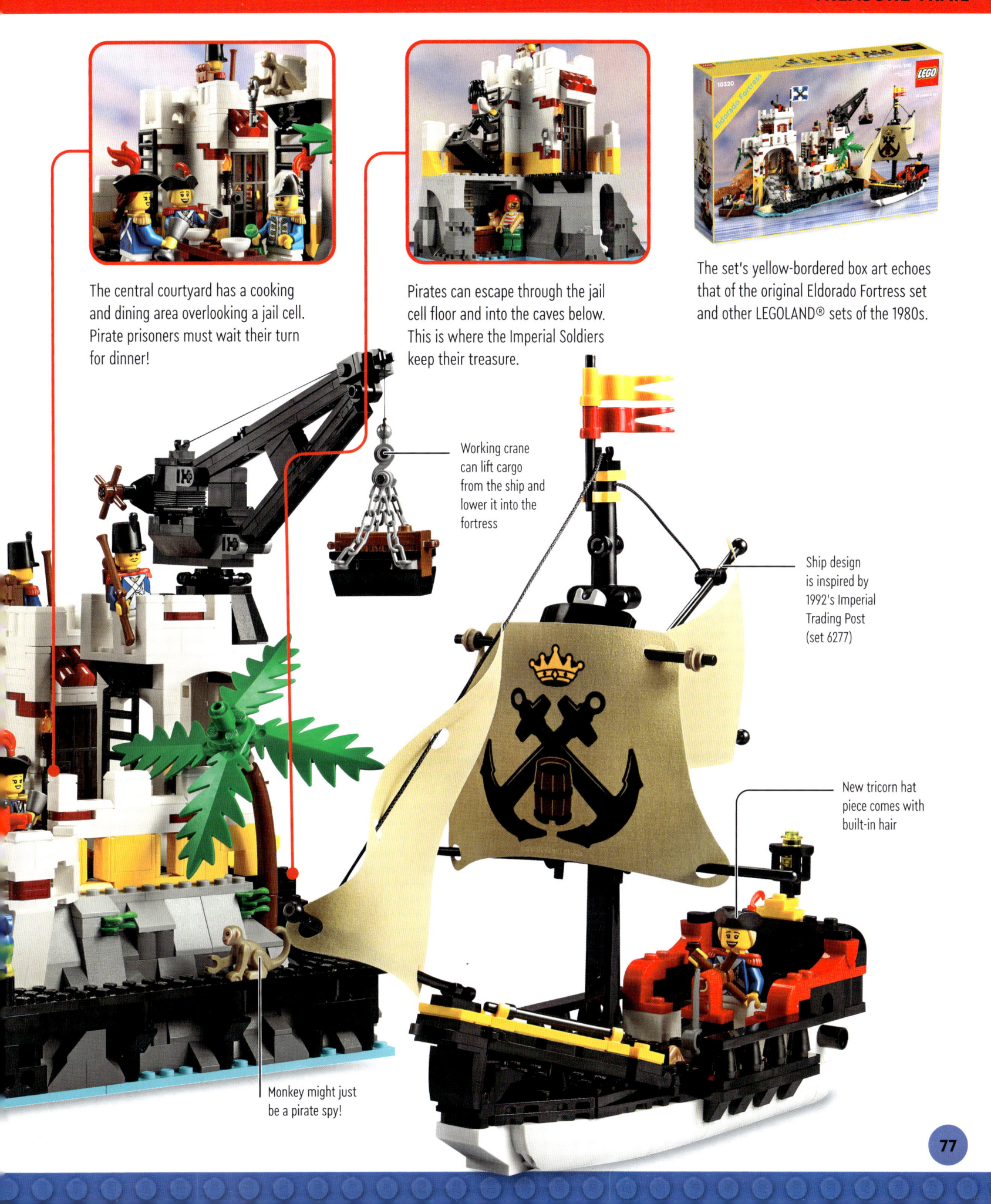

The central courtyard has a cooking and dining area overlooking a jail cell. Pirate prisoners must wait their turn for dinner!

Pirates can escape through the jail cell floor and into the caves below. This is where the Imperial Soldiers keep their treasure.

The set's yellow-bordered box art echoes that of the original Eldorado Fortress set and other LEGOLAND® sets of the 1980s.

Working crane can lift cargo from the ship and lower it into the fortress

Ship design is inspired by 1992's Imperial Trading Post (set 6277)

New tricorn hat piece comes with built-in hair

Monkey might just be a pirate spy!

77

WE ARE THE ROBOTS!

Back when LEGO® bricks were new, using them to make real robots was total science fiction! But, in just a few decades, innovations such as **LEGO® MINDSTORMS®** have made hands-on robotics a reality. Today, generations have come to grips with computer coding thanks to this LEGO robo-revolution.

1980

Massachusetts Institute of Technology (MIT) professor Seymour Papert writes *Mindstorms: Children, Computers, and Powerful Ideas*. The book sets out the case for teaching children about technology at a time when most schools do not have any computers.

1990–1996

LEGO robots come home—with the first programmable sets not exclusively for schools. Both the LEGO Technic Control Center (set 8094) and its follow-up, Control Center II (set 9753) connect to a battery-powered LEGO command console, rather than a computer.

1997

The Control Center sets can be used to build robotic arms, drawing machines, and even dinosaurs.

The LEGO Technic Barcode Multi-Set (set 8479) is the first free-roaming robotics set, controlled using an onboard "Code Pilot" with no external connections. It accepts commands in the form of 44 included barcodes, which can be combined for many different results.

The Barcode Multi-Set can be built as a dump truck, a moon rover, a dune buggy, or a robotic walker.

1998

Known as the RCX (Robotic Command eXplorer), the first smart brick is the large, yellow unit at the heart of this working robot.

After a decade of research, the smart brick makes its public debut in Robotics Invention System 1.0 (set 9719). It is the centerpiece of the new LEGO MINDSTORMS range, and has an infrared sensor for receiving programs written on a home computer.

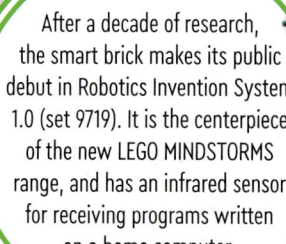

WE ARE THE ROBOTS!

1984 — The LEGO Group teams up with Professor Papert and MIT to find ways to combine LEGO building and computer programming in the classroom.

1986 — Combining work done with MIT and the UK's Microelectronics Education Programme, LEGO® Technic Control I (set 1090) is the first programmable LEGO set. Made for UK schools by the LEGO Group education division, it includes the first LEGO sensor bricks.

Like LEGO Technic Control builds, LEGO TC logo creations only work when wired up to a computer using a special interface.

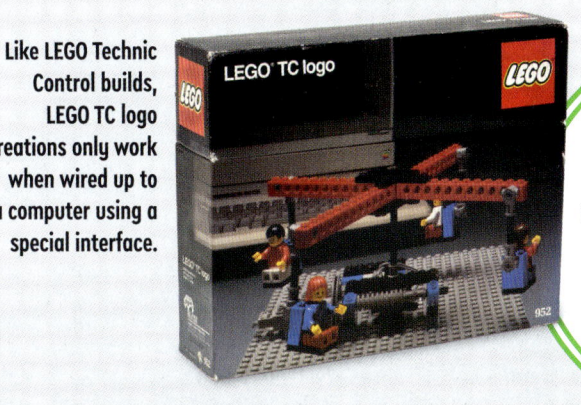

1987 — The ongoing partnership with MIT leads to LEGO TC logo (set 952). Named after the logo programming language used to control its builds, the LEGO® Education set introduces LEGO programming to many US schools.

1988 — MIT and the LEGO Group begin work on the first smart brick—a programmable LEGO element that can communicate with motors and sensors without being connected to a larger computer.

The initial MINDSTORMS range also includes expansion packs such as RoboSports (set 9730), with instructions and parts for making themed machines.

At the end of 1998, educational charity FIRST (For Inspiration and Recognition of Science and Technology) launches *FIRST* LEGO® League, a robotics competition for students that is still going strong today.

You wait 10 years for a LEGO smart brick, and then two come along at once! The second kind features in LEGO Technic CyberMaster (set 8482) and talks to a home computer using radio waves, but is not developed in any further sets.

MORE MINDSTORMS... AND BEYOND! ▶

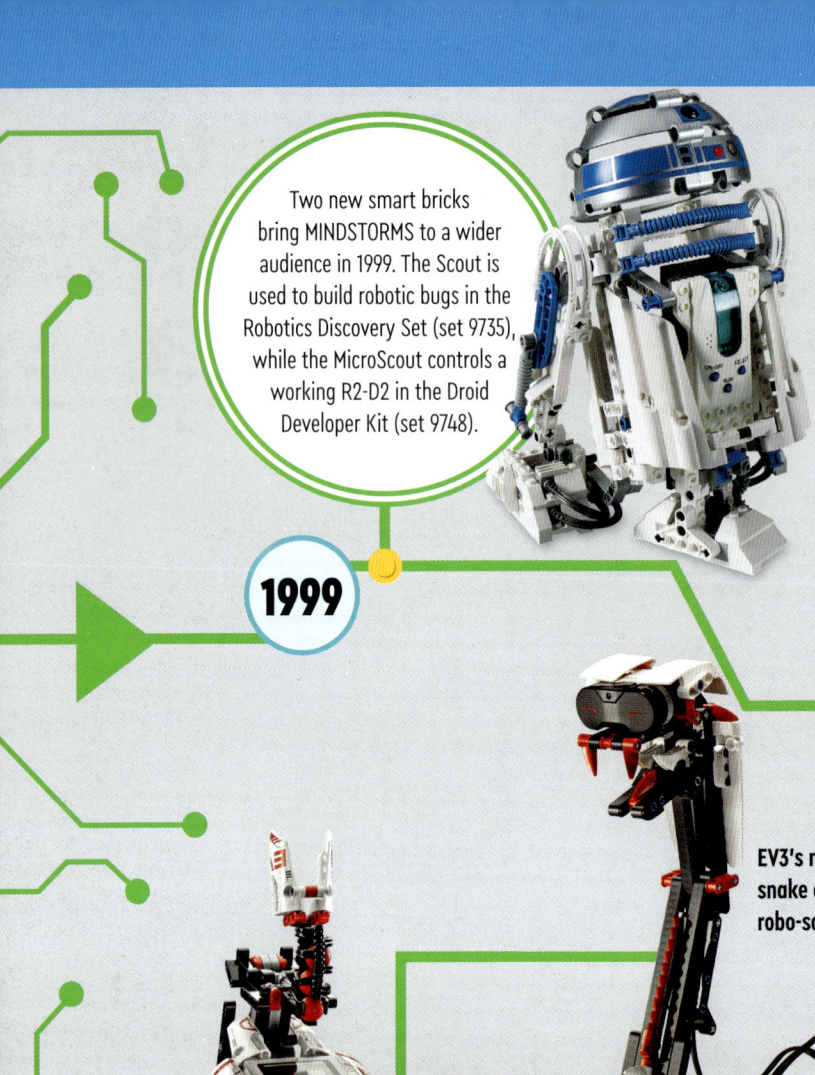

Two new smart bricks bring MINDSTORMS to a wider audience in 1999. The Scout is used to build robotic bugs in the Robotics Discovery Set (set 9735), while the MicroScout controls a working R2-D2 in the Droid Developer Kit (set 9748).

This year's MINDSTORMS expansion packs include Vision Command (set 9731), for making robots with built-in cameras, and Exploration Mars (set 9736), with missions for putting Martian rovers through their paces.

1999

2000

EV3's main builds include a snake called R3PTAR and robo-scorpion SPIK3R.

Celebrating 15 years of LEGO MINDSTORMS inventions, the new LEGO MINDSTORMS EV3 (set 31313) keeps things on the cutting edge with updated sensors, an EV3 smart brick with expandable memory, and complete control from your smartphone or tablet.

2013

R2-D2 returns in LEGO BOOST *Star Wars* Droid Commander (set 75253). This time he's joined by buildable, programmable Mouse and Gonk Droids and a new Droid Commander app packed full of missions set in that galaxy far, far away!

2017

BOOST robot Vernie can be programed to talk, dance, and fire a soft-tipped missile.

2019

There's a new name in LEGO robotics with the launch of LEGO® BOOST! Designed to get kids coding from a younger age, the LEGO BOOST Creative Toolbox (set 17101) is based around new smart brick (the Move Hub) and a colorful, intuitive app.

80

WE ARE THE ROBOTS!

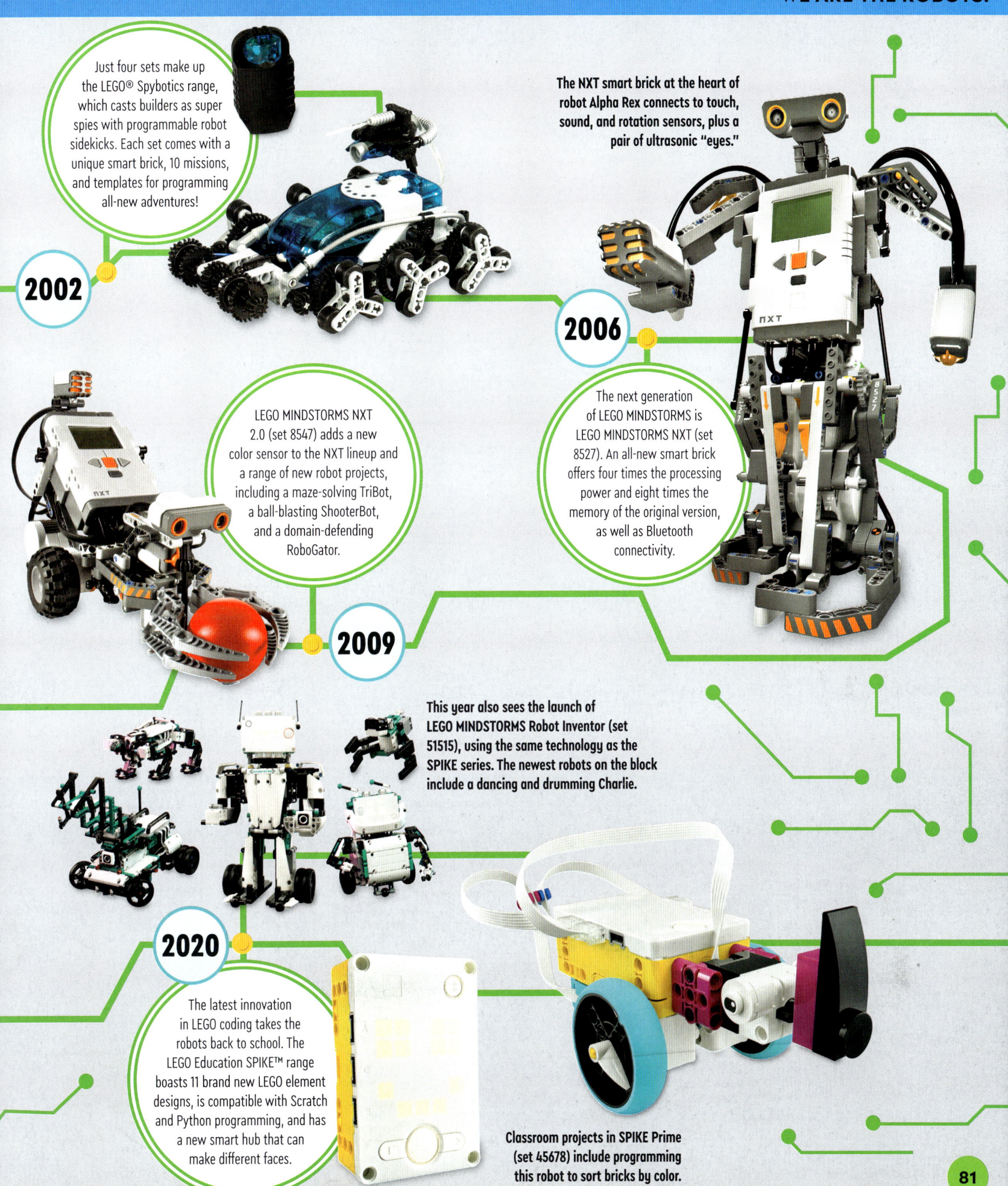

2002
Just four sets make up the LEGO® Spybotics range, which casts builders as super spies with programmable robot sidekicks. Each set comes with a unique smart brick, 10 missions, and templates for programming all-new adventures!

2006
The NXT smart brick at the heart of robot Alpha Rex connects to touch, sound, and rotation sensors, plus a pair of ultrasonic "eyes."

The next generation of LEGO MINDSTORMS is LEGO MINDSTORMS NXT (set 8527). An all-new smart brick offers four times the processing power and eight times the memory of the original version, as well as Bluetooth connectivity.

2009
LEGO MINDSTORMS NXT 2.0 (set 8547) adds a new color sensor to the NXT lineup and a range of new robot projects, including a maze-solving TriBot, a ball-blasting ShooterBot, and a domain-defending RoboGator.

This year also sees the launch of LEGO MINDSTORMS Robot Inventor (set 51515), using the same technology as the SPIKE series. The newest robots on the block include a dancing and drumming Charlie.

2020
The latest innovation in LEGO coding takes the robots back to school. The LEGO Education SPIKE™ range boasts 11 brand new LEGO element designs, is compatible with Scratch and Python programming, and has a new smart hub that can make different faces.

Classroom projects in SPIKE Prime (set 45678) include programming this robot to sort bricks by color.

DESTINATION: ADVENTURE!

Look underground, underwater, in the desert, or in the jungle, and you're sure to find a minifigure team exploring there! From the bygone days of the **LEGO® Adventurers** to the near-future world of **LEGO® Aquazone**, a whole host of themes have made memorable settings the key to characterful, quest-led escapades.

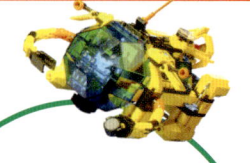

Aquazone is the first LEGO theme dedicated to underwater adventure. Its first six sets introduce the crystal-mining Aquanauts and their villainous rivals, the Aquasharks.

Sets such as Neptune Discovery Lab (set 6195) feature working magnets, moving compass pieces, and the first minifigure flippers.

1995

Hydronauts sets such as Hydro Search Sub (set 6180) can carry things using suction cups.

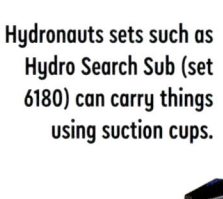

1999

LEGO® Rock Raiders goes off-world and underground as miners and monsters compete for crystals on Planet U. Closer to home, the Adventurers journey deep into the Amazon jungle.

Rock Raider Axel meets a stony-faced Rock Monster in The Loader-Dozer (set 4950).

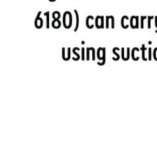

Pilot Harry Cane lifts Johnny Thunder out of the jungle in Expedition Balloon (set 5956).

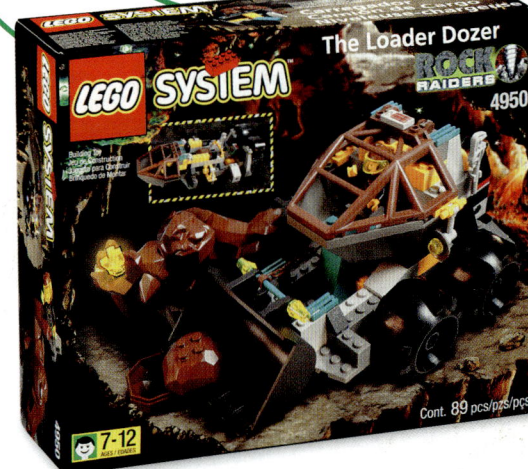

DESTINATION: ADVENTURE!

The American frontier town of Legoredo is the setting for LEGO® Western sets, where newcomers choose between a law-abiding life or jailbreaking, bank-raiding banditry!

Sheriff's Lock-Up (set 6755) is one of the first sets to feature log bricks, aka palisade bricks.

1996

Based around a team of intrepid archaeologists, the LEGO Adventurers theme visits 1920s Egypt with sets such as Sphinx Secret Surprise (set 5978). Elsewhere, Hydronauts take on Stingrays in the final Aquazone sets.

Aqua Dozer (set 2161) and other Aquaraiders sets are only available in North America.

This year's Aquazone sets are all about the Aquaraiders, who decorate their subs with scary eyes and teeth! Meanwhile, LEGO Western concludes with sets inspired by Indigenous American cultures.

1997

1998

The Adventurers face their biggest challenge yet on Dino Island. Villainous Sam Sinister is hunting down the dinosaur inhabitants, and only Johnny Thunder and co. can save them!

Sets such as **Dino Research Compound (set 5987)** feature the first LEGO® System dinosaur figures.

My best friends call me... rarely!

Like other Adventurers minifigures, Sam Sinister has different names in different countries. He is also known as Baron Von Barron and Evil Eye.

2000

DON'T STOP NOW! THERE'S MORE TO EXPLORE...

83

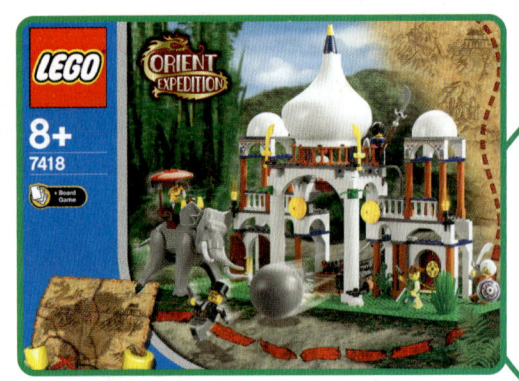

Taking the treasure chest out of Scorpion Palace (set 7418) makes a giant boulder drop down from the roof!

The LEGO Adventurers' last expedition takes them across Asia, where they meet new friends Babloo, Sangye Dorje, and Jing Lee, as well as unique elephant, yeti, and golden dragon figures.

Johnny Thunder and Dr. Kilroy make a daring Himalayan crossing in their Aero Nomad (set 7415).

2003

This mine's all mine!

The biggest rock monster in the theme is brick-built baddie The Crystal King (set 8962).

Rebooting 1999's Rock Raiders, the LEGO® Power Miners dig deep to discover all-important energy crystals and all-new rampaging Rock Monsters—this time on planet Earth!

Power miners Doc, Duke, and Brains carry a rock monster containment cage on the back of their Titanium Command Rig (set 8964).

2009

LEGO Atlantis sets overflow with fantasy creatures, such as the Shark Warrior in Typhoon Turbo Sub (set 8060).

2010

LEGO® Atlantis is the latest underwater theme, telling a tale of explorers seeking a sunken civilization. Deeper still, the final Power Miners sets approach the Earth's molten core.

Power Miner Rex wears a silver anti-heat suit inside his subterranean Magma Mech (set 8189).

84

DESTINATION: ADVENTURE!

Dino 2010's Dino Truck Transport (set 7297) tows a cage for a T-rex with glowing red eyes...

Two very similar yet very different adventure themes launch this year. In Europe, LEGO® Dino 2010 is all about recapturing escaped dinosaurs in the jungle. In the US, LEGO® Dino Attack is all about making them history!

...while Dino Attack's Iron Predator vs. T-rex (set 7476) reworks the same vehicle with a dino-busting missile launcher!

2005

The giant squid in Aquabase Invasion (set 7775) has glow-in-the-dark tentacles and a digested diver in its belly.

Not to be confused with 1997's Aquazone faction, LEGO® Aqua Raiders adds something new to submarine themes—huge, brick-built creatures including sharks, squid, and giant lobsters!

2007

The spirit of LEGO Adventurers lives on in LEGO® Pharaoh's Quest sets, pitting archaeologists against Ancient Egyptian monsters. Elsewhere, the LEGO Atlantis team find the fabled city.

City of Atlantis (set 7985) is brimming with booby traps and guarded by sea monster minifigures.

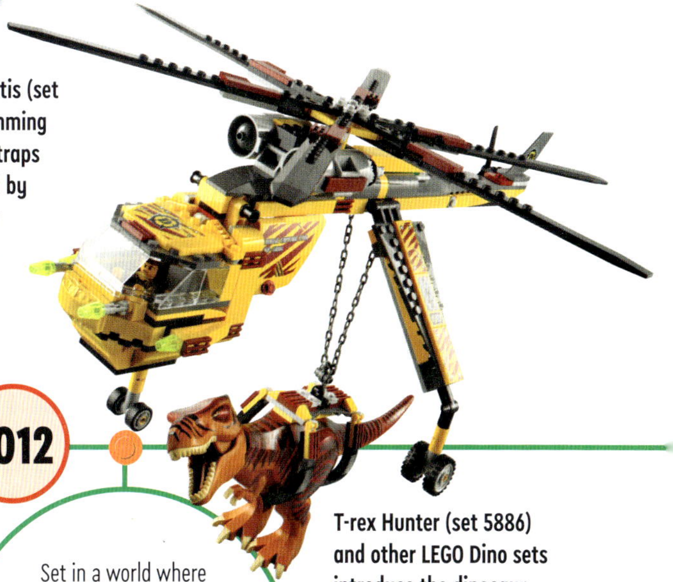

2011

The largest Pharaoh's Quest set, Scorpion Pyramid (set 7327), is defended by a giant scorpion, a flying mummy, and two Anubis Guards.

2012

Set in a world where dinosaurs threaten modern cities, LEGO® Dino stars Johnny Thunder's descendant, Josh Thunder, as leader of the team tasked with keeping the beasts at bay.

T-rex Hunter (set 5886) and other LEGO Dino sets introduce the dinosaur figures that will later star in LEGO® Jurassic World sets.

85

GALACTIC HISTORY

In the real world, **LEGO® Star Wars™** dates back to 1999, but in a brick-built galaxy far, far away, it's a century-spanning saga! Check out these key sets in story order, with dates showing the number of years before the Battle of Yavin (BBY) and after the Battle of Yavin (ABY).

Five sets explore this legendary era, first seen in 2011's *Star Wars: The Old Republic* video game, including Jedi Master Satele Shan's Republic *Striker*-class Starfighter (set 9497) and Darth Malgus' Sith *Fury*-class Interceptor (set 9500).

c. 3600 BBY

Set in the early days of the Galactic Empire, 2019 video game *Star Wars Jedi: Fallen Order* follows the adventures of a fugitive Jedi Padawan and his droid. BD-1 (set 75335) depicts that droid as an almost life-size 1,062-piece display model!

14 BBY

The largest of two sets based on live-action TV series *Star Wars: Obi-Wan Kenobi*, Inquisitor Transport *Scythe* (set 75336) comes from a time when the Empire is at its peak and the few remaining Jedi are outnumbered by their hunters.

10 BBY

Ten years before becoming the most famous hunk of junk in the galaxy, the Kessel Run *Millennium Falcon* (set 75212) is a sleek white space yacht—as seen in the film *Solo: A Star Wars Story* and its LEGO *Star Wars* subtheme.

9 BBY

86

GALACTIC HISTORY

c. 230 BBY
A fresh-faced Master Yoda trains two Jedi younglings in Tenoo Jedi Temple (set 75358). The first set based on animated TV series *Star Wars: Young Jedi Adventures*, it depicts the peaceful "golden age" of the Galactic High Republic.

32 BBY
LEGO® *Star Wars*™ launched alongside *Star Wars: Episode I The Phantom Menace* in 1999. Many sets have depicted its late Republic setting since then, including Anakin's Podracer—20th Anniversary Edition (set 75258) in 2019.

22 BBY
Begun the Clone War has! Sets inspired by the climax of *Star Wars: Episode II Attack of the Clones* include Duel on Geonosis (set 75017), which pits a highly mobile Master Yoda (on a LEGO® Technic pole) against the devious Count Dooku!

19 BBY
The year that the Republic fell is documented in LEGO sets based on *Star Wars: Episode III Revenge of the Sith* and animated series *Star Wars: The Bad Batch*. Duel on Mustafar (set 75269) re-creates the epic clash between Obi-Wan Kenobi and Anakin Skywalker/Darth Vader, just before the Sith Lord got his famous suit!

22–19 BBY
Sets based on animated series *Star Wars: The Clone Wars* and LEGO *Star Wars: The Yoda Chronicles* chart this turbulent time in galactic history. They include 2023's Coruscant Guard Gunship (set 75354) and 2014's JEK-14's Stealth Starfighter (set 75018).

5 BBY
There are rumblings of rebellion this year, as anti-Empire heroes band together in *Star Wars Rebels* and *Star Wars: Andor*. Inspired by the latter show, 2023's Ambush on Ferrix (set 75338) sees Imperial Security fighting back!

2 BBY
The Empire really starts to take the Rebellion seriously when it puts Grand Admiral Thrawn on the case! The blue bad guy makes his minifigure debut in The *Phantom* (set 75170), based on the third season of animated action series *Star Wars Rebels*.

Happy blue year, rebels!

TO THE BATTLE OF YAVIN... AND BEYOND!

87

0 BBY/ABY

It's a busy time for *Star Wars* historians, as the events of *Rogue One: A Star Wars Story* lead straight into *Star Wars: Episode IV A New Hope*! More than 50 LEGO *Star Wars* sets mark this time of civil war, including Yavin 4 Rebel Base (set 75365).

3 ABY

Star Wars: Episode V *The Empire Strikes Back* depicts a dark time for the Rebellion, as Han Solo is frozen in carbonite and Luke Skywalker learns a big secret about his father! Both classic movie moments are re-created in Betrayal at Cloud City (set 75222).

3–4 ABY

Sets based on animated series LEGO *Star Wars: The Freemaker Adventures* explore life on the edge of the Galactic Civil War. They feature all-new characters the Freemaker family, created especially for the LEGO *Star Wars* universe in 2016.

What does ABY stand for again?

Ask Baby Yoda!

12 ABY

Heroes from *The Clone Wars* and *Rebels* join forces in sets based on live-action series *Star Wars: Ahsoka*. In Ahsoka Tano's T-6 Jedi Shuttle (set 75362), Ahsoka, Sabine Wren, and droid Huyang take on all-new villain Inquisitor Marrok.

9–11 ABY

Live-action TV series *The Mandalorian* and *The Book of Boba Fett* are both set around five years into the New Republic era. Doe-eyed display model The Child (set 75318) is one of the largest sets to be based on either show.

33 ABY

Two sets are based on animated TV series *Star Wars Resistance*, which charts the growing threat from new baddies on the block the First Order. In Major Vonreg's TIE Fighter (set 75240), show hero Kaz Xiono teams up with rebel icon General Leia.

GALACTIC HISTORY

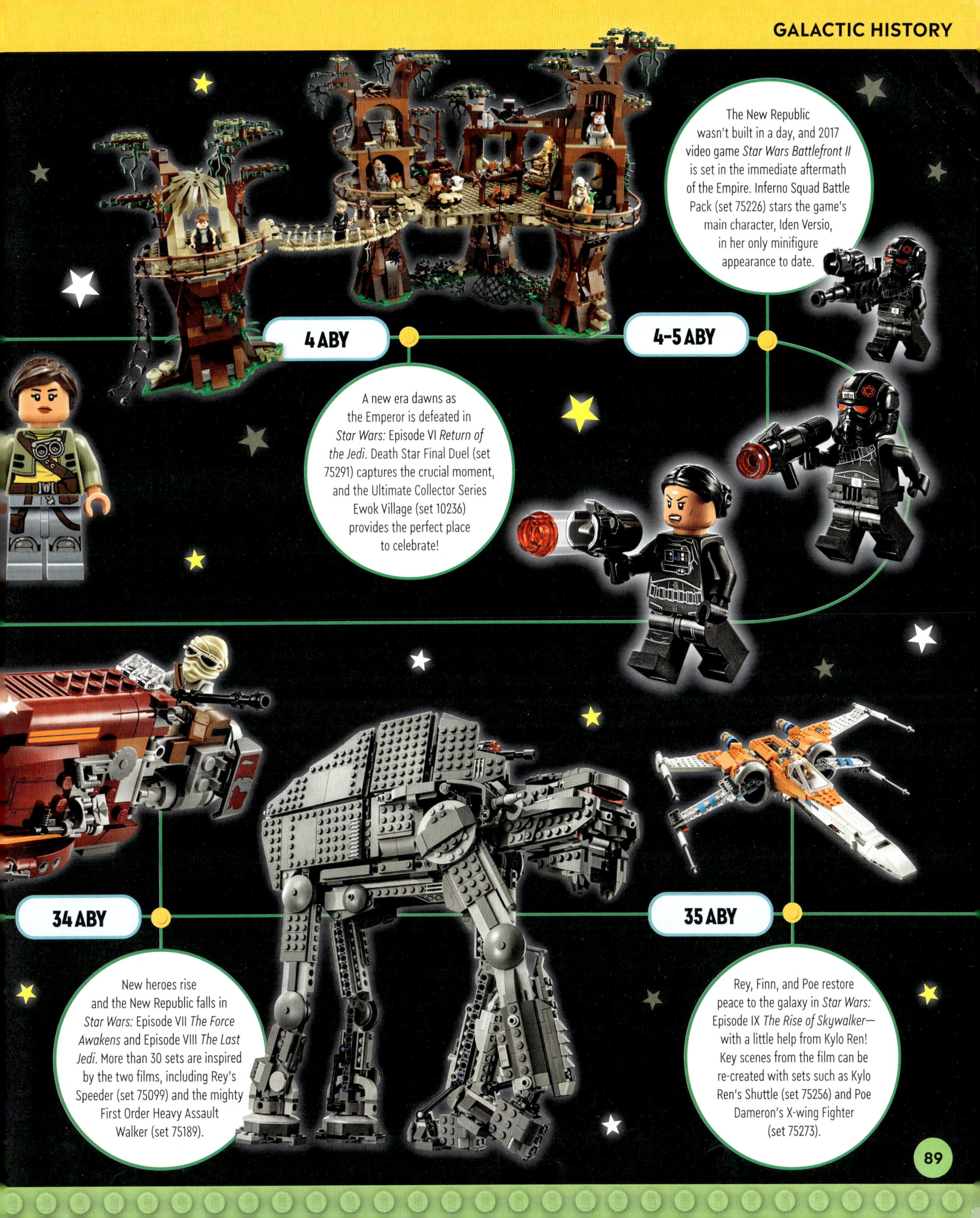

4 ABY

A new era dawns as the Emperor is defeated in *Star Wars: Episode VI Return of the Jedi*. Death Star Final Duel (set 75291) captures the crucial moment, and the Ultimate Collector Series Ewok Village (set 10236) provides the perfect place to celebrate!

4–5 ABY

The New Republic wasn't built in a day, and 2017 video game *Star Wars Battlefront II* is set in the immediate aftermath of the Empire. Inferno Squad Battle Pack (set 75226) stars the game's main character, Iden Versio, in her only minifigure appearance to date.

34 ABY

New heroes rise and the New Republic falls in *Star Wars: Episode VII The Force Awakens* and *Episode VIII The Last Jedi*. More than 30 sets are inspired by the two films, including Rey's Speeder (set 75099) and the mighty First Order Heavy Assault Walker (set 75189).

35 ABY

Rey, Finn, and Poe restore peace to the galaxy in *Star Wars: Episode IX The Rise of Skywalker*—with a little help from Kylo Ren! Key scenes from the film can be re-created with sets such as Kylo Ren's Shuttle (set 75256) and Poe Dameron's X-wing Fighter (set 75273).

SIZE MATTERS NOT!

Ever since the theme started in 1999, there have been **LEGO® Star Wars™** sets in all shapes and sizes. Ranging from the Ultimate Collector Series to Mech sets and Microfighters, every innovation has added a new way to play in that galaxy far, far away!

Be forewarned: I'm four-armed!

1999
The first minifigure-scale LEGO Star Wars sets introduce many new pieces, including alien heads, droid parts, and lightsaber hilts. In the same year, the LEGO® MINDSTORMS® Droid Developer Kit (set 9748) lets you build a programmable LEGO® Technic R2-D2!

2012
Planet Sets such as AT-ST and Endor (set 9679) pack all their parts inside a container that looks like a Star Wars world! Elsewhere, this year's LEGO® Games set Star Wars: The Battle of Hoth (set 3866) is a buildable board game with rebel and Imperial microfigures.

2014
Reimagining classic Star Wars craft as simplified single-seater rides, the LEGO Star Wars Microfighters line launches with six sets including Star Destroyer (set 75033). The 97-piece set uses 4,687 fewer elements than the largest UCS version.

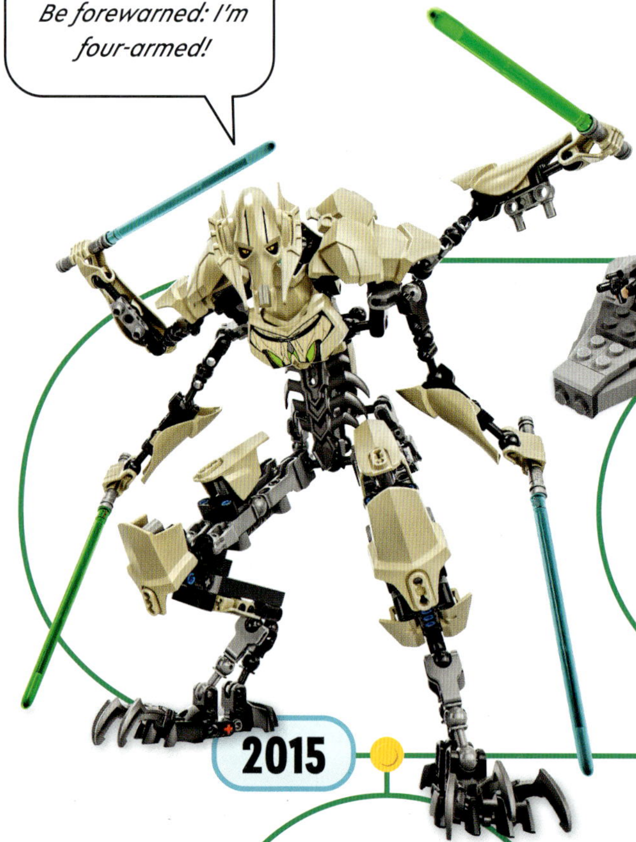

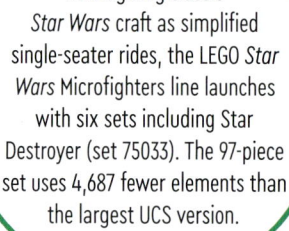

2015
The launch year's range of large LEGO Star Wars buildable figures includes six-limbed Separatist General Grievous (set 75112) and his nemesis, Obi-Wan Kenobi (set 75109), which boast LEGO® BIONICLE® style articulation. It's a perfect pairing for play or display.

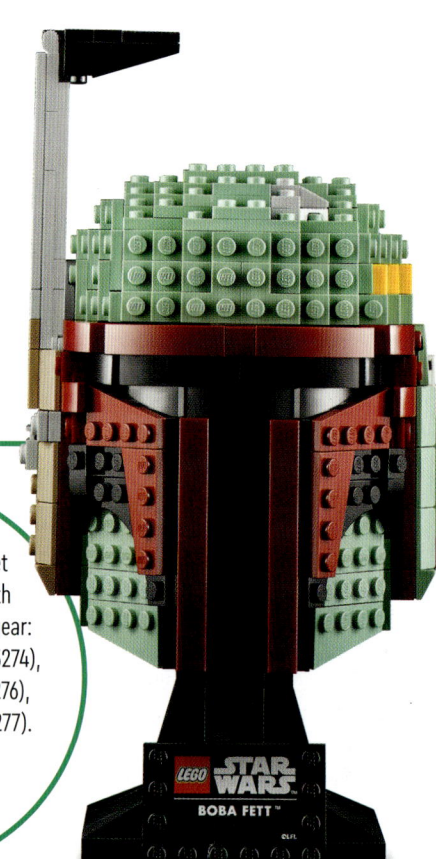

2020
The LEGO Star Wars Helmet Collection range arrives with three helpings of iconic headgear: TIE Fighter Pilot Helmet (set 75274), Stormtrooper Helmet (set 75276), and Boba Fett Helmet (set 75277). Each one stands around 8 in (20 cm) high on a brick-built stand.

SIZE MATTERS NOT!

2000
Bigger and more detailed than any LEGO sets that have gone before, the LEGO *Star Wars* Ultimate Collector Series launches with two sets, including the 1,304-piece X-wing Fighter (set 7191). The UCS range is still going strong today, with close to 40 super-size sets.

2003
The first of many Mini Building Sets capture the essence of enormous *Star Wars* starships in marvelous microscale. The MINI *Millennium Falcon* (set 4488) remains instantly recognizable when made from just 87 pieces—and is far easier to smuggle past Imperial checkpoints!

2011
The first LEGO *Star Wars* Advent Calendar (set 7958) begins an annual tradition of sets featuring a festive mix of micro builds and seasonal minifigures. Yoda plays Santa this time around, with droids and Sith Lords getting in on the act in years to come.

2007
LEGO *Star Wars* Battle Packs contain minimal parts and maximum minifigures for faction vs. faction fun! Droids Battle Pack (set 7654) and Clone Troopers Battle Pack (set 7655) are the first of more than 40 such sets to date, many including exclusive minifigures.

2022
Each Diorama Collection set captures a moment of *Star Wars* magic in a display scene measuring 34 studs wide and 18 studs deep. The first of seven sets in the range so far, Death Star Trench Run Diorama (set 75329) is a true microscale masterclass!

2023
Just when you thought the Sith couldn't get any scarier, along comes the LEGO *Star Wars* Mechs range! Darth Vader Mech (set 75368) puts the minifigure menace in his own robot-style walker, complete with an XL lightsaber for lording it over the rest of the range.

Size matters lots!

91

2017
MILLENNIUM FALCON

The biggest LEGO® Star Wars™ set of them all is also the first LEGO set of any kind to have more than 7,000 pieces. The *Millennium Falcon* can be given an Original or Sequel Trilogy look, and comes with a choice of crew. Representing *The Empire Strikes Back* are Han, Leia, Chewie, and C-3PO, while *The Force Awakens* heroes include older Han, Rey, Finn, and BB-8.

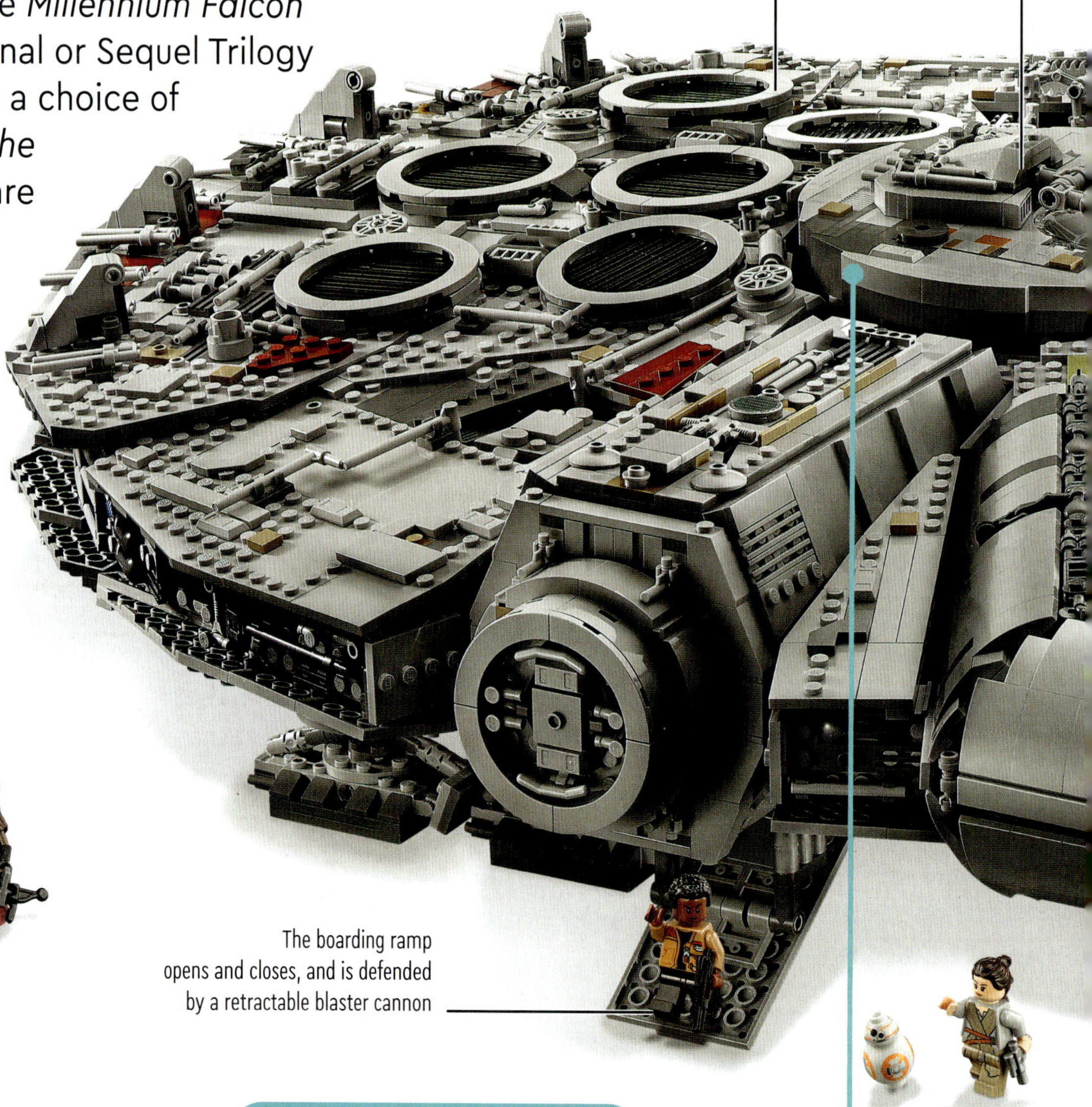

This section of hull lifts off for access to the cargo hold

The ship's top quad laser turret pairs with one on the underside

The boarding ramp opens and closes, and is defended by a retractable blaster cannon

This version of Han Solo is found in just one other set

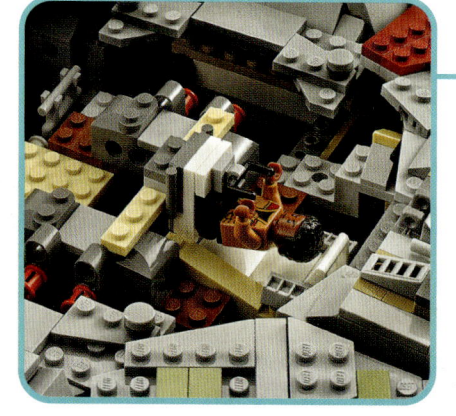

The quad laser cannons lift off to reveal a gunner's station. The seat inside is angled to provide a view out of the window beneath the cannons.

SET NUMBER	75192
PIECES	7,541
MINIFIGURES	7 + a BB-8 figure
SIZE	33 in (84 cm) long, 22 in (56 cm) wide

SIZE MATTERS NOT!

Sand yellow and olive green pieces are used to depict rust

The *Falcon* has this sensor dish when Rey and Finn find it

This circular sensor dish doesn't survive the Battle of Endor!

This top view shows the ship in its Original Trilogy configuration, with a circular sensor dish and no updated tractor beam gear on the mandible tips.

Six round heat vents keep the engines cool

Deep recesses are maintenance access points

The *Falcon* stands firm on six large landing legs

Enhanced tractor beam projectors first seen in *The Force Awakens*

The cockpit has room for four minifigures: the pilot in the front-left seat, a copilot on the right, and two passengers seated or standing behind.

A hull plate behind the sensor dish lifts away for access to the main hold. Here the crew can play dejarik around a special gaming table.

THE 2000s

2000

The LEGO® Studios Moviemaker Set (set 1349) comes with a digital camera for making stop-motion minifigure movies.

Minifigures become soccer players in 16 soccer sets.

The LEGO® Mickey Mouse theme features exclusive Disney LEGO figures.

Eleven sets based on *The Sorcerer's Stone* launch the LEGO® Harry Potter™ theme.

Action heroes the LEGO® Alpha Team spring into action against the villainous Ogel.

The first LEGO® Racers sets are tiny, monster-driven motors.

LEGO® Galidor™ action figures tie in with a sci-fi TV show.

LEGOLAND® Deutschland opens in Günzburg, Germany.

The first LEGO® Stores open in Germany, Russia, and the UK.

The first LEGO® Advanced Model with more than 2,000 pieces is the Statue of Liberty (set 3450).

The LEGO® Star Wars™ Ultimate Collector Series launches with a 703-piece TIE Interceptor and a 1,300-piece X-wing.

The LEGO Group opens a new brick factory in Kladno, Czechia.

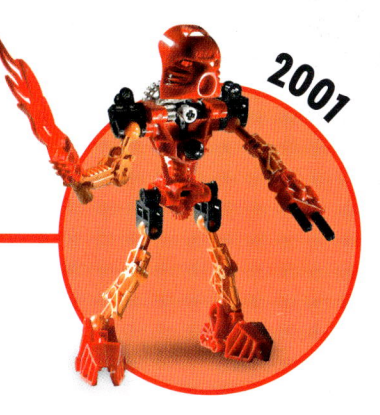

2001

The Legend of Mata Nui begins in the first year of BIONICLE®.

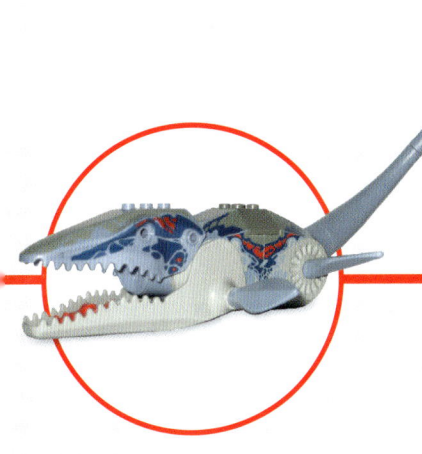

Eight buildable creatures make up the LEGO® Dinosaurs range.

LEGO® Jack Stone sets feature large figures and simple builds for children ages four and up.

2002

Minifigures perform perilous feats in the LEGO® Island Xtreme Stunts theme and video game.

LEGO® Spybotics buildable robots come with secret agent missions on CD-ROM discs.

LEGO® Serious Play® sets use LEGO building to promote creative thinking in business.

2003

LEGO® Town becomes LEGO® World City, with a focus on cops, crooks, and railroads.

The LEGO® Sports theme kicks off with soccer, basketball, and Gravity Games sets.

The first LEGO® Spider-Man™ sets are based on the 2002 movie starring Tobey Maguire.

95

2003 (cont.)

LEGO® Discovery Channel sets celebrate real-life space exploration.

LEGO® CLIKITS™ sets feature all-new parts for making jewellery and fashion accessories.

Some minifigures are depicted with realistic skin tones for the first time.

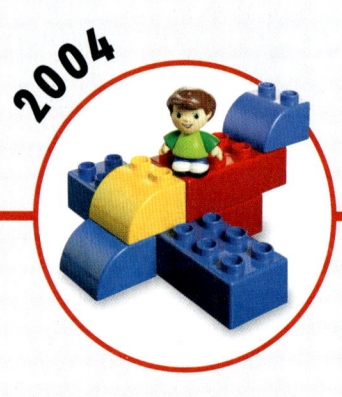

2004

LEGO® QUATRO bricks for babies are four times the height, width, and depth of standard LEGO bricks.

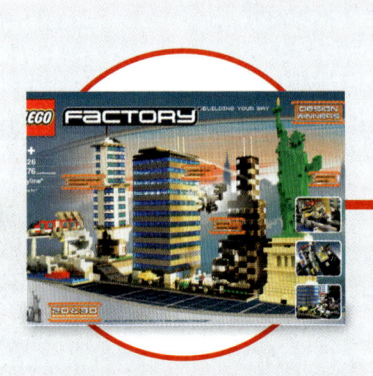

2006

Competition-winning fan builds become real sets with the LEGO® Factory range.

LEGO® DC Batman™ begins with six minifigure-scale sets and a supersize Batmobile.

Japanese manga and anime inspire the mega mechs of LEGO® EXO-FORCE™.

Two new themes are based on Nickelodeon TV shows—*SpongeBob SquarePants* and *Avatar: The Last Airbender*.

2008

LEGO® *Indiana Jones*™ sets re-create the archaeologist action hero in minifigure form.

The LEGO® Architecture series begins with models of two iconic Chicago skyscrapers.

The heroic LEGO® Agents set out to save the world from devious Dr. Inferno!

Four LEGO® Speed Racer™ sets are based on the fast-moving movie of the same name.

2005

Jørgen Vig Knudstorp becomes president and CEO of the LEGO Group.

The LEGO® City theme debuts with police, fire, construction site, and boat sets.

LEGO® Vikings sets pit warrior minifigures against brick-built mythical beasts.

The LEGO® Dino Attack and LEGO® Dino 2010 themes have similar sets but different dinosaur storylines.

2007

The first LEGO® Creator 3in1 sets make building three times as much fun!

Huge, brick-built sea creatures are the real stars of LEGO® Aqua Raiders sets.

LEGO® Creator, LEGO® Technic, and LEGO® *Star Wars*™ sets are the first to feature new Power Functions motors.

Café Corner and Market Street lay the foundations for the LEGO® Modular Buildings Collection.

2009

Former LEGO Group president and CEO Kjeld Kirk Kristiansen is inducted into the Toy Industry Hall of Fame in the US.

Minifigures take on Rock Monsters in the LEGO® Power Miners theme.

Creationary, Lunar Command, and Minotaurus are among the first tabletop LEGO® Games.

The LEGO Group opens a new factory in Monterrey, Mexico, and acquires one from Flextronics in Nyíregyháza, Hungary.

SPORTS FOR ALL

Sooner or later, the world of **sports** and LEGO® building were always going to come together. One is all about flexing your abilities, displaying your dexterity, making the most of your free time, having fun, and playing well. And the other is sports!

A handle on the side of the fan stand makes Icons of Play's crowd bob up and down!

2023 Real-life soccer stars including Megan Rapinoe and Asisat Oshoala feature in Icons of Play (set 40634). The playable pitch set-up is a nod to the very first LEGO Soccer sets!

Like the real event of the same name, Gravity Games sets feature skateboarding and snowboarding.

1998 Minifigures play soccer for the first time in LEGO® Town sets celebrating the 1998 FIFA World Cup. Players, pitch baseplates, spectator stands, and more are all available separately.

This year's sets are the first to carry the LEGO® Sports logo. They are produced in partnership with the National Basketball Association, the National Hockey League, and Gravity Games.

Players can be customized with stickers showing the flags of different nations.

2000 LEGO® Soccer gets its own theme (also known as LEGO® Football). Minifigure players can be built onto spring-loaded platforms and goalkeeping paddles to kick and deflect the ball.

2003

98

SPORT FOR ALL

Table Football (set 21337) has 2,339 pieces, including dozens of heads and hairstyle options!

LEGO® BrickHeadz™ Go Brick Me sets let builders personalize their own Manchester United (set 40541) or FC Barcelona (set 40542) player, while LEGO® Ideas scores with Table Football.

2022

Each DFB player comes with his own ball, while manager Joachim Löw comes with a tactics board.

2020

With 3,898 pieces, Old Trafford—Manchester United (set 10272) becomes the biggest sports set so far—only to be followed by two even bigger stadium models in 2021 and 2022!

A sports-themed series of collectible LEGO® Minifigures ties in with the 2016 European Football Championship. DFB Series (set 71014) re-creates 15 real players and their manager!

2016

Hockey sets feature large figures that swing for the puck piece when you hit their helmets.

2007

The LEGO Sports theme ends with Superstar Figure (set 3573). The small set includes an Adidas-branded goalkeeper with enormous gloves and equally enormous hair!

MATA NUI MATTERS

Set in "the time before time," when mighty biomechanoids wield elemental powers, BIONICLE®—later known as **LEGO® BIONICLE®**—was one of the most unusual, most influential, and most successful LEGO themes of all. With a name that's short for "Biological Chronicle," the epic story spanned books, films, comics, games, and a new LEGO building system.

LEGO Group partners with Christian Faber, who sets a challenge for LEGO designers: create a new set of elements for building LEGO action figures with realistic movements. The result is an innovative ball-and-socket connection that combines grip with flexibility.

socket

ball

1995

Many people's first glimpse of BIONICLE is in Mata Nui: The Online Game, which launches five months before the first sets.

Like other Bohrok, Lehvak (set 8564) can fire a rubbery bug from inside his head!

2002

No longer part of the LEGO Technic range, BIONICLE becomes a best-selling brand in its own right. The insectoid Bohrok are the theme's first baddies, with a bad habit of launching small Krana creatures at the upgraded Toa Nuva.

2003

Main villain Makuta (set 8593) and his Rahkshi minions menace the Matoran in this year's sets—and in the first ever LEGO feature film, BIONICLE: *Mask of Light*. A new range of novels and a video game also build on the legend.

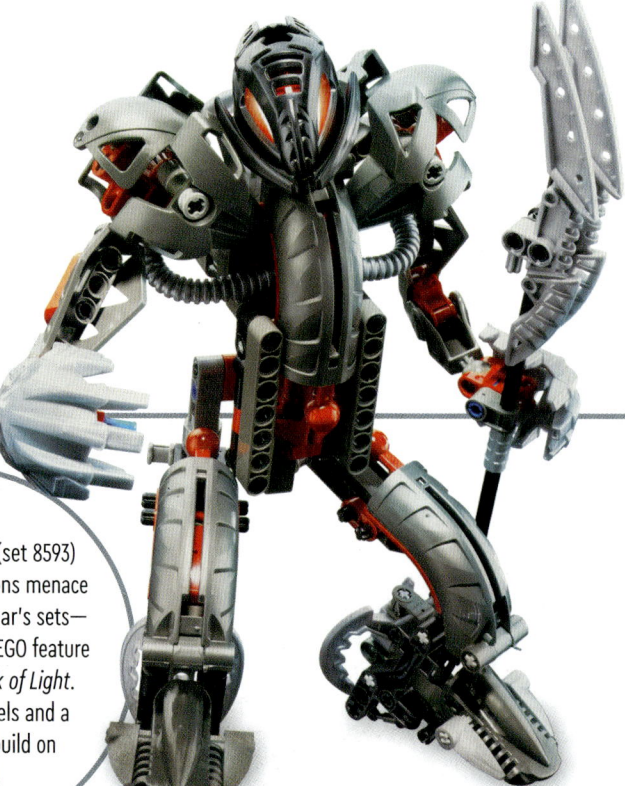

MATA NUI MATTERS

1999 — The new ball-and-socket joints find their first home in LEGO® Technic Slizer sets (known as Throwbots in the US). These small, disk-throwing robot figures come in spaceship-style packaging and tie in to a story about dueling aliens with elemental powers.

2000 — Christian and the LEGO Technic team finalize an in-depth story called BIONICLE, in which a group of biomechanical heroes called Toa defend the peaceful inhabitants of Mata Nui island. It is the most detailed storyline an original LEGO theme has ever had.

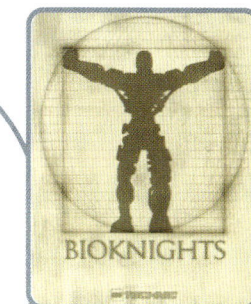

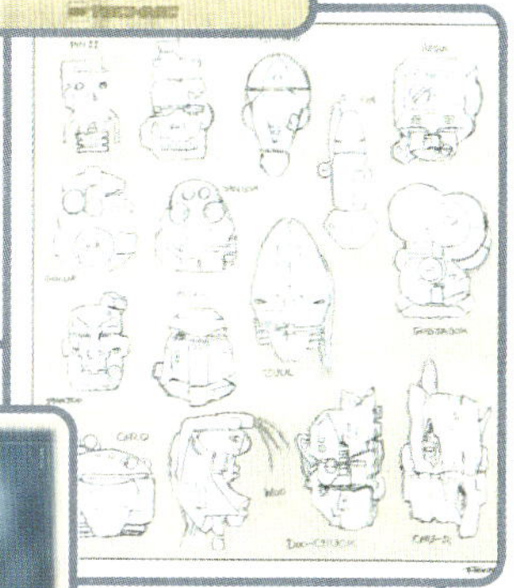

Christian's early concept art includes an unused name for the theme, character designs, and a view of Mata Nui.

2001 — The six Toa come in canisters containing a poster and a mini CD-ROM packed full of BIONICLE info. Kanohi masks can be displayed around the top of the canister.

The first LEGO Technic BIONICLE sets include Toa heroes, Turaga elders, Matoran islanders, and Rahi creatures, but no villains. Mystery bags containing exclusive Kanohi masks for the characters are sold separately, sparking an instant collectors' craze!

Each set combines new mask and joint elements with traditional LEGO Technic parts and functionality. Tahu (set 8534) has a gear on his back to send his sword arm swinging!

2004 — This year's sets and film sequel BIONICLE 2: Legends of Metru Nui turn the clock back 1,000 years to a time when high-tech heroes such as Toa Matau (set 8605) battled Dark Hunters including Slizer-disk shooting warrior Krekka (set 8623).

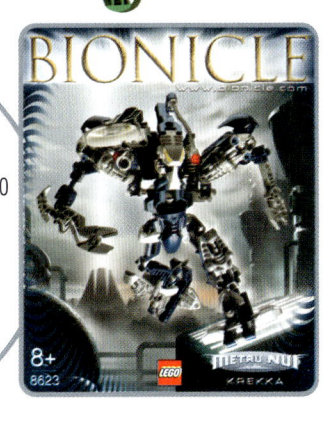

2005 — Third movie *Web of Shadows* sees the Toa transformed into beast-like Hordika by their new Visorak enemies. A new range of sets, meanwhile, has heroes and villains alike turned into small, single-piece figures defending brick-built fortresses.

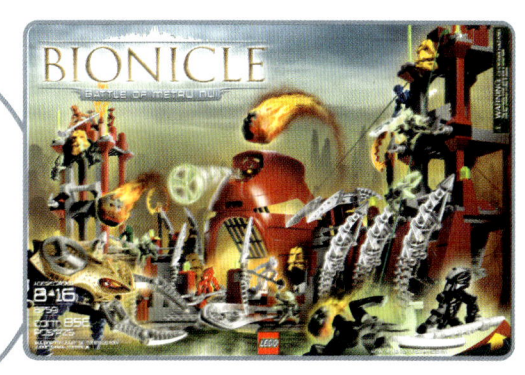

Builds such as Battle of Metru Nui (set 8759) bring BIONICLE down to minifigure scale.

Krekka can combine with two other sets to form a version of Makuta called Ultimate Dume.

THE LEGEND CONTINUES!

2006

Innovations in this year's sets include light-up eyes and weapons, flexible spiky body parts, and very little reliance on LEGO Technic functionality. New heroes, including Axonn (set 8733), battle Piraka villains such as rubber-faced Reidak (set 8900).

Piston parts in Axonn's legs give the build extra strength and stability.

2007

Toa Mahri heroes tackle squid-shooting Barraki as BIONICLE takes a deep dive into underwater adventures. Similarly subaquatic, the last wave of minifigure-scale sets includes the seabed-scuttling Toa Terrain Crawler (set 8927).

2010

After 10 years, the original run of BIONICLE comes to an end with six sets depicting all-time classic characters. Each of these "BIONICLE Stars" comes with a special bonus piece to create a set of golden armor.

The updated Tahu (set 7116) wearing all six items of golden armor.

Many of this year's figures have dials on their backs for counting hits from Thornax fruit pieces. On Agori vehicle Kaxium V3 (set 8993), the dials are beside the back wheels.

2011

LEGO Hero Factory steps out of BIONICLE's shadow with a new figure-building system. Though still based around ball-and-socket joints, the new approach uses simplified shell parts for quicker building without LEGO Technic pins.

This year also sees the launch of the LEGO® Hero Factory theme, with sets such as Preston Stormer (set 7164), using many BIONICLE elements.

Hero Factory characters such as Surge 2.0 (set 2141) are robots sworn to protect the galaxy from diabolical masterminds.

2015

After Hero Factory ends, LEGO BIONICLE makes a mythic return with reimagined Toa and all-new enemies such as Skull Slicer (set 70792). Now using the building system created for Hero Factory, the range reintroduces gear-operated arms for classic LEGO BIONICLE battles.

MATA NUI MATTERS

Ghoulish glow-in-the-dark pieces make Takadox (set 8916) and his brother Barraki extra eerie.

The six original Toa return with new looks and a new ally—the fabled Mask of Life itself, now in Toa form as Toa Ignika. Several large vehicle sets include the 21-in- (53-cm-) long Jetrax T6 (set 8942), available in blue or yellow.

The mask in Toa Ignika (set 8697) depicts a BIONICLE figure with its arms raised.

2008

The island comes alive in Toa Mata Nui (set 8998), an embodiment of the BIONICLE realm and the star of new movie BIONICLE: *The Legend Reborn*. In common with other 2009 sets, he carries a Thornax launcher for a new battle game.

2009

LEGO BIONICLE bows out for a second time as the Toa take on Umarak the Destroyer (set 71316) and his Elemental Beasts. They are aided on their mission by crystal-blue Ekimu the Mask Maker (set 71312), one of LEGO BIONICLE's most powerful heroes.

Umarak is the biggest figure in the second era of LEGO BIONICLE, and combines with his Elemental Beasts to become even bigger!

2016

Toa master Gali goes head-to-head with scary Skull Spider in Gali—Master of Water (set 70786).

103

1999 — The first release to carry the LEGO Racers name is not a set—but a video game! Players can build their own custom cars and minifigure drivers before putting them to the test on a track.

2001 — The first brick-built LEGO Racers are some of the smallest-ever LEGO sets. Most have fewer than 10 pieces, including a monster figure designed to go flying every time its race car crashes.

Shredd (set 4570) and his fellow monsters also feature in this year's video game sequel, LEGO® Racers 2.

LIFE IN THE FAST LANE

For a theme based solely on racing cars, **LEGO® Racers** proved remarkably diverse! Over the years, it featured monster-driven mini builds, magnificent models of real-life racing icons, and motorized minifigure cars from the futuristic world of 2015.

2002 — Minifigures take the wheel in remote-controlled sets. The 1,484-piece Williams F1 Team Racer (set 8461) puts the theme on a different track, with advanced builds of real-life racing cars.

This year's smaller sets have pull-back motors and unique driver figures.

The third LEGO Racers video game, *Drome Racers*, is set in 2015 and features futuristic cars such as RC Nitro Flash (set 4589).

2003 — The range expands to include motorcycles with pull-back motion; a 58-in (148-cm) race track; and "Slammer" cars, launched by slamming down on a LEGO® Technic trigger.

Extreme Power Bike (set 8371) is mostly made with LEGO Technic parts.

104

LIFE IN THE FAST LANE

2010 — New Air Blast pieces set Racers speeding with a stomp of the foot, and the 801-piece Lamborghini Polizia (set 8214) becomes the biggest LEGO police car ever.

2012 — The balloon tires of four monster trucks mark the end of the LEGO Racers theme. Each set includes an eject function to propel the minifigure drivers to new adventures!

Don't worry! I'm a professional!

Star Striker (set 9094) is driven by the daredevil Captain Stunt.

Ice Rally (set 8124) combines with other Tiny Turbos sets to make one big racetrack!

The 741-piece Lamborghini Gallardo LP 560-4 (set 8169) can be built in coupe and open-top versions. Elsewhere, foldaway race track parts double as storage cases for Tiny Turbos.

Ferrari F430 Challenge 1:17 (set 8143) comes with all the parts needed to build the Racer in red or yellow. The Tiny Turbos get ramps and a motorized bridge to leap off.

2009

2007

2004 — Four sets based on a Ferrari™ theme include Formula 1 cars built at three different scales, and a winners' podium and trophy for a pair of minifigures based on real-life F1 racing drivers.

Ferrari F1 Pit Set (set 8375) is the only Racers set built on a minifigure-scale road plate.

2005 — A new range of Tiny Turbos provides pocket-size racing action in 75 pieces or fewer. This year's largest Racers set, meanwhile, is the 1,360-piece Enzo Ferrari 1:10 (set 8653).

Flame Glider (set 8641) is one of eight Tiny Turbos released in 2005.

105

MAGIC MOMENTS

From 2001 to 2011, the **LEGO® Harry Potter™** theme charted the exploits of the world's most famous wizard as they played out on movie screens. When the movie saga ended, so did the sets. But then, the *Fantastic Beasts* films cast their own big-screen spell, and—*Accio!*—brick-built magic was back!

2002

Sets based on second movie *Harry Potter and the Chamber of Secrets* include Escape from Privet Drive (set 4728), depicting Harry's home and Ron's flying Ford Anglia car; and Dobby's Release (set 4731), featuring the first Dobby the House-Elf minifigure.

Unique printed parts make the enormous Basilisk in The Chamber of Secrets (set 4730).

2001

As *Harry Potter and the Sorcerer's Stone* hits the big screen, 11 LEGO sets re-create its key locations and characters. These include the first Hogwarts Castle (set 4709), the first Hogwarts Express (set 4708), and the first towering LEGO Hagrid figure.

The first Harry Potter minifigures mostly have yellow faces, except for gray ghost Peeves and the ghoulishly glow-in-the-dark Snape.

Sorting Hat (set 4701) is a spinner game for finding your Hogwarts house.

This year's Professor Quirrell is the first ever minifigure to have two faces!

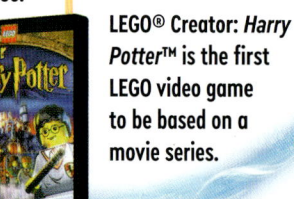

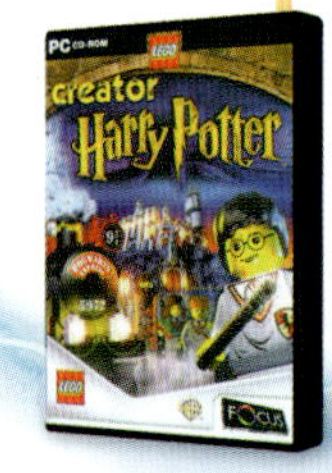

LEGO® Creator: *Harry Potter*™ is the first LEGO video game to be based on a movie series.

2004

Everything gets a refresh in sets inspired by *Harry Potter and the Prisoner of Azkaban*. Minifigures now have realistic skin tones, a larger Hogwarts Castle (set 4757) is plagued by new Dementor figures, and Motorized Hogwarts Express (set 10132) really runs!

Motorized Hogwarts Express comes with 89 in (225 cm) of track and a Hogsmeade Station build.

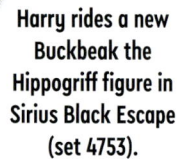

Harry rides a new Buckbeak the Hippogriff figure in Sirius Black Escape (set 4753).

MAGIC MOMENTS

2010

After a spell away, LEGO Harry Potter returns with sets based on *The Half-Blood Prince* and *The Deathly Hallows: Part 1*. Elsewhere, buildable board game Harry Potter Hogwarts (set 3862) is the first movie set in the LEGO® Games theme.

The Burrow (set 4840) is the first set to depict the Weasley family home.

The fourth version of Hogwarts Castle (set 4842) is the biggest yet, with 1,290 pieces and *Deathly Hallows* details.

2011

The first era of LEGO Harry Potter comes to an end with the biggest set in the theme so far. The 2,025-piece Diagon Alley (set 10217) includes detailed re-creations of Ollivander's Wand Shop, Borgin and Burke's Antiques, and Gringotts Wizarding Bank.

2007

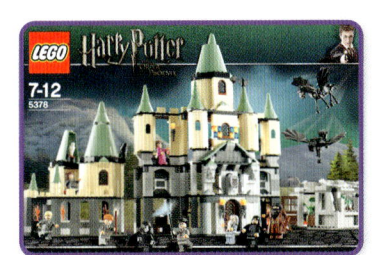

Just one set ties in with the release of *Harry Potter and the Order of the Phoenix*—but what a set! The third Hogwarts Castle (set 5378) includes eight minifigures and two Thestrals, and it unfolds to reveal the Room of Requirement and Professor Umbridge's office.

2005

New movie *Harry Potter and the Goblet of Fire* is the focus of four sets. Harry and the Hungarian Horntail (set 4767) includes the theme's first full-size dragon. Graveyard Duel (set 4766), meanwhile, is the first to feature Voldemort in minifigure form.

Harry and the Hungarian Horntail includes magnetic parts, so Harry can grab the dragon egg in one swift swoop!

THIS WAY TO THE WIDER WIZARDING WORLD!

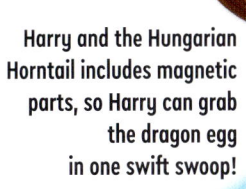

107

The 5,544-piece Diagon Alley (set 75978) is one of the biggest ever minifigure-scale sets.

2020

The Lily Potter minifigure cradles the infant Harry in one arm.

A huge new version of Diagon Alley features six shops and *The Daily Prophet* newspaper office. Forbidden Forest: Umbridge's Encounter (set 75967) includes the first LEGO centaurs, and Harry's parents become LEGO Minifigures in a new collectible series.

The first LEGO Harry Potter Advent Calendar (set 75964) comes with exclusive Harry, Ron, and Hermione minifigures.

Hogwarts Clock Tower (set 75948) links to last year's (and later years') minifigure-scale Hogwarts sets as part of one enormous castle build. Meanwhile, *Prisoner of Azkaban* set Expecto Patronum (set 75945) includes a brand new transparent-blue stag figure.

Hogwarts Clock Tower includes an extra-tall Madame Maxime minifigure.

2019

Collectible Minifigures such as Dean Thomas are the first to feature new mid-length leg pieces.

As if by magic, LEGO Harry Potter reappears after a seven-year break, accompanied by LEGO® Fantastic Beasts™ sets. Both film series feature in this year's LEGO® BrickHeadz™ range and in a series of collectible LEGO® Minifigures celebrating the entire Wizarding World.

Grindelwald's Escape (set 75951) is inspired by new film *Fantastic Beasts: The Crimes of Grindelwald*.

On its release, the 6,020-piece microscale version of Hogwarts Castle (set 71043) is the second largest LEGO set—by piece number—of all time.

2018

108

MAGIC MOMENTS

New Hogwarts™ Moment sets look like books—until they open up to reveal magical classroom scenes! Meanwhile, large-scale sculptures and gold-colored minifigures in seven sets celebrate 20 years since the start of the LEGO Harry Potter theme.

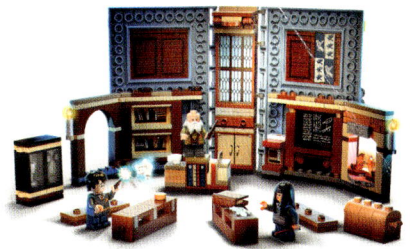

Hogwarts Moment: Charms Class (set 76385) comes with exclusive Harry, Cho Chang, and Professor Flitwick minifigures.

Hogwarts Icons—Collectors' Edition (set 76391) uses 3,010 pieces to depict Hedwig the owl, an invitation to Hogwarts, Harry's wand and glasses, and more!

2021

All four Hogwarts houses get a House Banner set that opens to reveal a minifigure common room. The Battle of Hogwarts completes the modular collection begun in 2018, combining with six other sets to form an endlessly customizable Hogwarts Castle.

Slytherin House Banner (set 76410) comes with Draco Malfoy, Pansy Parkinson, and Blaise Zabini minifigures.

The headquarters of the Order of the Phoenix emerge out of nowhere in 12 Grimmauld Place.

Two iconic London locations join the LEGO Harry Potter range—The Ministry of Magic (set 76403) and 12 Grimmauld Place (set 76408). A third, Platform 9¾ at King's Cross Station, is revisited in Hogwarts Express—Collectors' Edition (set 76405).

2022

2023

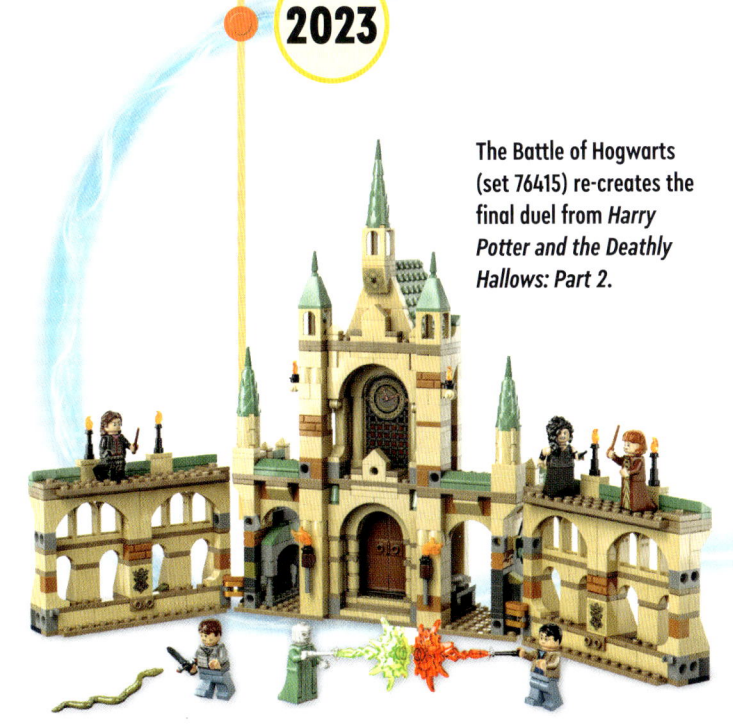

The Battle of Hogwarts (set 76415) re-creates the final duel from *Harry Potter and the Deathly Hallows: Part 2*.

Hogwarts has no end of locations to explore. This year's sets are the first to visit the Hogwarts Castle Owlery (set 76430) and the Hogwarts Castle Boathouse (set 76426). Both sets come with new, collectible Hogwarts portrait pieces.

2024

109

2023
GRINGOTTS WIZARDING BANK COLLECTORS' EDITION

This magical money house from the Harry Potter universe reveals its riches over several levels. At the very top, a Ukrainian Ironbelly dragon perches on a secret store room. At the bottom, the Lestrange family vault hides an enchanted treasure hoard. In between, Harry and Hagrid can explore a wealth of spectacular details— all closely guarded by goblins!

The main bank build detaches from its underground vaults to sit alongside the other establishments in magical shopping street Diagon Alley (set 75958).

- Advertisement for fang brushes from the Magical Menagerie
- A large chandelier hangs over the main foyer
- Connection points for building a larger street scene
- The Sorcerer's Stone is stored inside this vault
- Feeding schedule for the Ironbelly dragon
- Discarded chocolate frog

SET NUMBER	76417
PIECES	4,801
MINIFIGURES	12 + a Hagrid figure
SIZE	32 in (79 cm) tall, 13 in (32 cm) wide

MAGIC MOMENTS

Next-door store is the Magical Menagerie

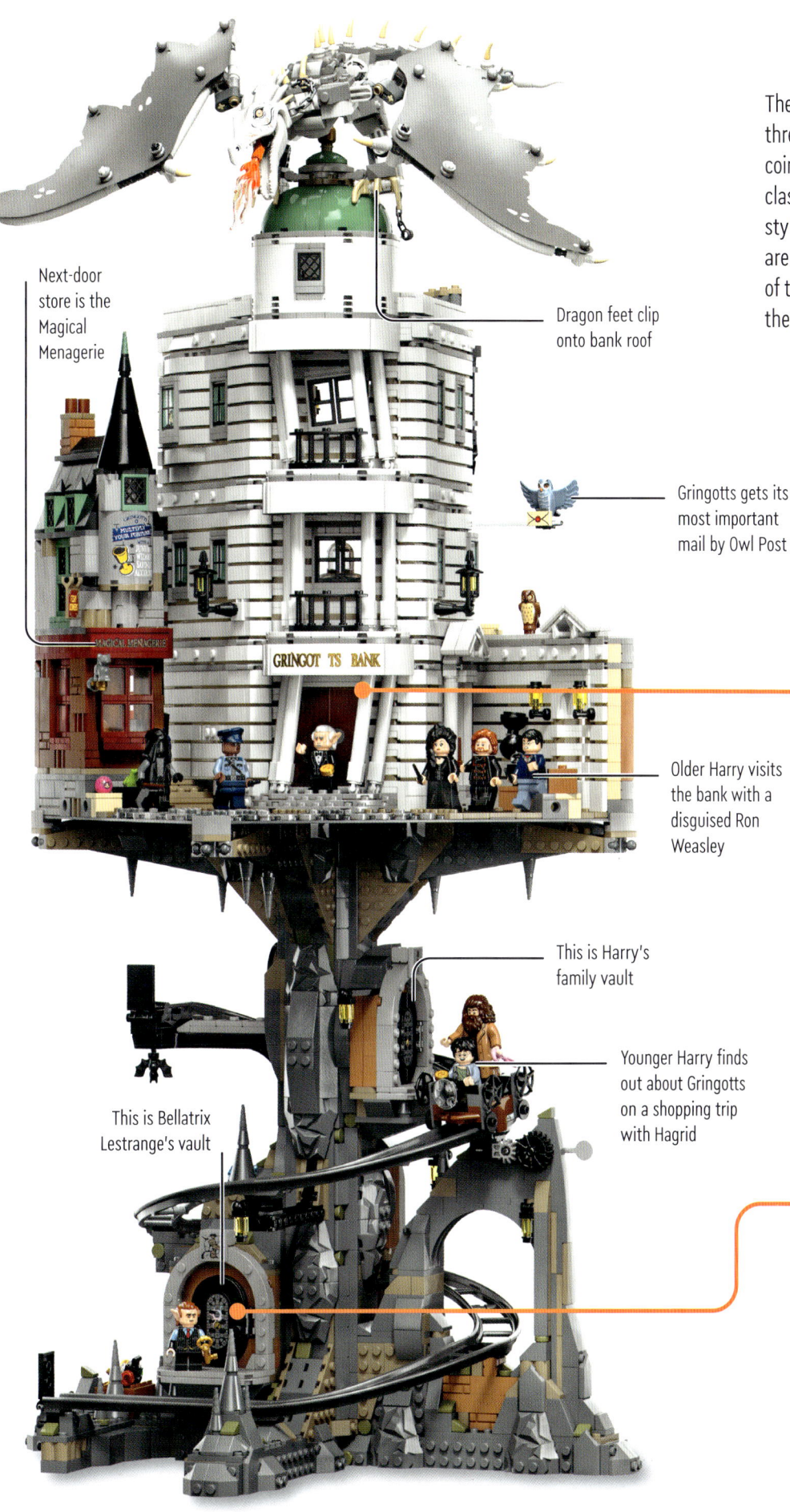

Dragon feet clip onto bank roof

The set comes with three life-size Galleon coins depicting a classic LEGO® Castle-style dragon. They aren't a part of the bank build—they're just for fun!

Gringotts gets its most important mail by Owl Post

Older Harry visits the bank with a disguised Ron Weasley

This is Harry's family vault

Younger Harry finds out about Gringotts on a shopping trip with Hagrid

This is Bellatrix Lestrange's vault

The bank's grand foyer is dominated by a tall desk with steps up for chief goblin teller Ricbert. Harry has to get past him to visit the Potter family vault.

In the underground section of the set, a mine cart runs on LEGO roller-coaster rails, stopping off at three opening bank vaults filled with magical treasure.

111

THE CREATOR MASTER PLAN

Best known for its 3in1 sets (which come with instructions for building three different things with one set of bricks), the **LEGO® Creator** theme has been going for more than 20 years. Over that time it has included dinosaurs, dragons, houses, hovercraft, Ferris wheels, and even fish tanks.

2001 — The first sets bearing the LEGO Creator name follow earlier LEGO® Basic sets, with buckets of bricks intended for creative building without step-by-step instructions.

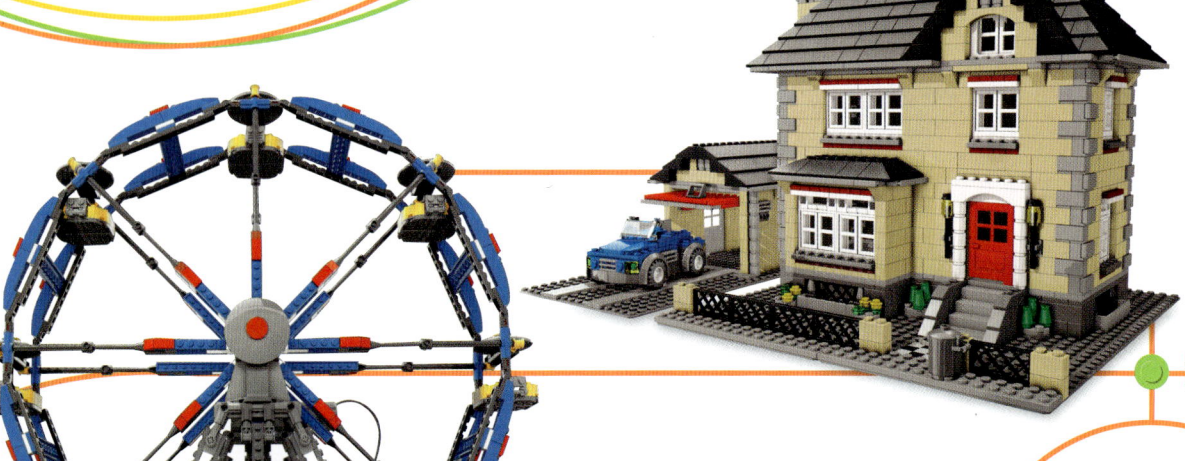

A Power Functions motor turns this 18.5-in (47-cm) Ferris Wheel.

2007 — Creator 3in1 sets go supersize with a 1,174-piece Model Town House (set 4954) that can be rebuilt in two other house styles, and a 1,063-piece Ferris Wheel (set 4957) that can be rebuilt as a bridge or a crane.

2008 — Stegosaurus (set 4998) has light-up eyes and can be rebuilt as two different dinosaurs. Transport Ferry (set 4997), meanwhile, can become a hovercraft or a cargo plane.

Call this a timeline? Where's the Jurassic Period!?

112

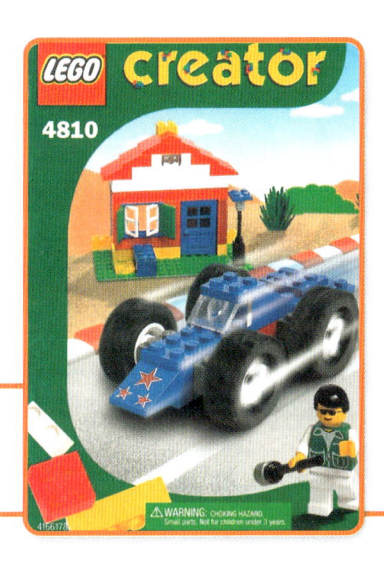

THE CREATOR MASTER PLAN

2003 — The LEGO® Inventor range sits alongside brick buckets, with sets such as Motor Movers (set 4094) coming with instructions to make models that walk, climb, and even stir drinks!

2004 — X-Pod sets introduce the three-models-in-one concept. Each set comes packaged inside a large, round "pod" piece, which also forms part of one of the three builds.

X-Pod Creatures (set 4349) can be built as a pterodactyl, a chicken, or a dragonfly!

2006 — Sets such as Roaring Roadsters (set 4896) feature LEGO Creator 3in1 branding for the first time, while others, such as Revvin' Riders (set 4893), promise an 8in1 experience!

2009 — With a car transporter and two cars, the main build of Highway Transport (set 6753) is made up of three models itself. The huge set can also become a tow truck or a mobile crane.

2011 — Creator 3in1 sets such as Hillside House (set 5771) and Lighthouse Island (set 5770) feature minifigures for the first time. The former also boasts doorbell and dog bark sound effects!

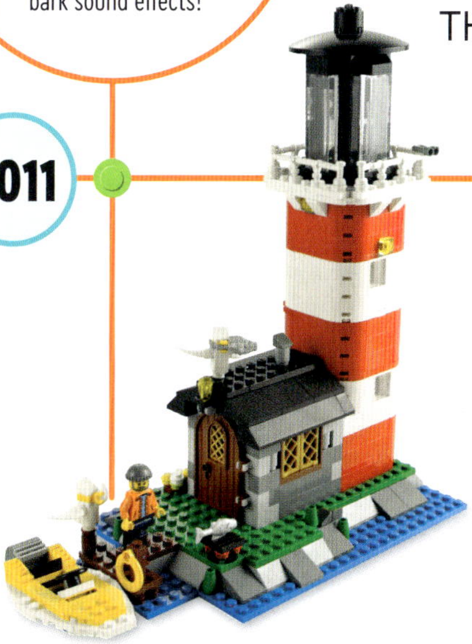

MORE CREATIVE CREATOR BUILDS THIS WAY!

113

2013

The 166-piece Fierce Flyer (set 31004) is a bald eagle that can be rebuilt as a scorpion or a beaver. Little Eagle (set 30185), meanwhile, re-creates the same bird in just 48 pieces.

2015

Rainforest Animals (set 31031) boasts a unique feeding function. Pop tile pieces into the parrot's bill, then lift its tail to see these "seeds" come out at the other end!

2019

The minifigure-scale Townhouse Pet Shop & Café (set 31097) includes several brick-built pets, while Deep Sea Creatures (set 31088) offers a range of much bigger beasts.

This shark can be rebuilt as a squid, an anglerfish, or a whale.

2020

Cool Creator vehicles for 2020 include the Space Rover Explorer (set 31107) with its brick-built monster, and Monster Burger Truck (set 31104) with its brick-built dog.

2021

The five colorful species in Fish Tank (set 31122) make effortless and eye-catching pets, as do 2017's Mighty Dinosaurs, now reissued in two new color schemes.

114

THE CREATOR MAS[TER]

2016

Small but perfectly formed, London Bus (set 40220) and Ocean Explorer (set 31045) foretell much larger sets with the same names and subject matter to be released the following year.

The LEGO C[reator] Expert London Bus has 1,568 more pieces than this 118-piece build.

The LEGO® Technic Ocean Explorer has 1,327 pieces, while this Creator version has just 213.

2018

This skater's dream home can be rebuilt as a skate park and an arcade.

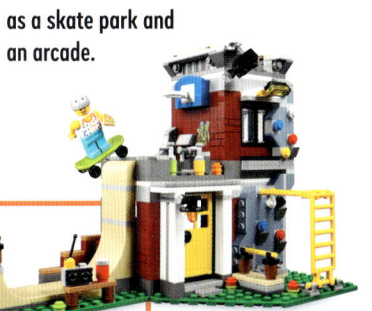

Minifigures feature in 10 of this year's 17 sets, enjoying the thrills of the Pirate Roller Coaster (set 31084) and a Modular Skate House (set 31081) among other things.

ROARRRR!!

Yikes! Time to withdraw!

2017

Mighty Dinosaurs' (set 31058) main build is a T-rex with 13 points of articulation. Mini Piggy Bank (set 40251), meanwhile, is a cuter companion with a tilting face and ears.

2022

Viking Ship and the Midgard Serpent (set 31132) reimagines a classic LEGO® Vikings set from 2005, while Paris Postcard (set 40568) is part of a new range of souvenir city scenes.

2023

Main Street (set 31141) becomes the biggest ever 3in1 Creator set, with 1,459 pieces for building two very different street scenes or a four-story apartment building!

115

TEAMS AND SCHEMES

From **Time Cruisers** to **Ultra Agents**, the LEGO Group has had a long history of pitting teams of goodies with top-flight tech against equally well-equipped baddies. The battles between these action factions can play out however you want them to, but the losing side will always rebuild to come back fighting another day!

Seven sets chart the adventures of the LEGO® Time Cruisers as they skip through the centuries in their Hypno Cruiser (set 6492). At first, Dr. Cyber and his sidekick Timmy have no rival faction, but then the Time Twisters arrive to turn history on its head.

1996–1997

EXO-FORCE upgrade to even more impressive mechs in 2007, but so do their robot foes. The Combat Crawler X2 (set 7721) is a six-legged robo-ride, with a working cannon on top and a detachable walker with huge claws at the front.

New robot parts are used to make EXO-FORCE's enemies.

2007

This year's EXO-FORCE sets venture deep into the jungle, after which the theme is never seen again. The disappearance could be a case for new heroes the LEGO® Agents... if they weren't so busy foiling the schemes of devious Dr. Inferno!

Team leader Agent Chase escapes from Dr. Inferno's base in LEGO Agents Mission 5: Turbocar Chase (set 8634).

2008

EXO-FORCE mechs like Hikaru's Chameleon Hunter (set 8114) are designed to blend in with, and cut through, jungle greenery.

2009

Dr. Inferno turns up the heat in the second and final year of LEGO Agents. In Robo Attack (set 8970), he is at the controls of a giant walker, and it's up to agents Chase and Trace to keep innocent citizens out of his clutches.

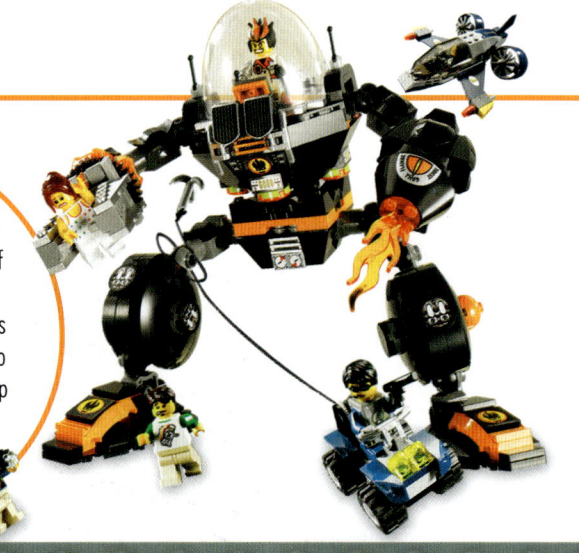

TEAMS AND SCHEMES

2001

In LEGO® Alpha Team, Dash Justice and his squad of special agents use a fleet of futuristic vehicles to combat evil Ogel and his army of skeleton drones. What's so bad about Ogel? Why, he's the very opposite of "LEGO"!

Alpha Team assemble!

But I'm already assembled!

Radia • Cam • Tee Vee • Dash • Crunch

2002

Alpha Team returns in Mission Deep Sea, tracking down Ogel's ocean lair and saving sea creatures from becoming his mutated minions! Ogel Underwater Base and AT Sub (set 4795) is the biggest set in the entire Alpha Team range.

2006

Inspired by Japanese anime and manga, this year's new minifigure heroes are the LEGO® EXO-FORCE™. The team members pilot mighty mechs in their battles against a robot army, and never let anything mess with their all-new hair pieces!

This year's Stealth Hunter (set 7700) and Grand Titan (set 7701) mechs combine to make Takeshi's massive Mountain Warrior.

2004

For its final mission, Alpha Team straps on skis to save a world frozen by Ogel's Ice Orbs! This year's sets have an "Alpha Mode" transformation feature—Flex's Chill Speeder (set 4742), for example, can change from a snowmobile into a walker.

2014

What could be cooler than LEGO Agents? A whole new range of LEGO® Ultra Agents! This team's cutting-edge tech includes carbon-infused AppBricks that unlock digital missions when touched against a smartphone or tablet.

It's a foolish villain who attacks Ultra Agents Mission HQ (set 70165), and that villain is called Terabyte!

2015

All-new Super Villains for the final year of Ultra Agents include highly hazardous Toxikita; brainwashed Professor Brainstein; and their big, bad boss, AntiMatter! Three agents take on the criminal kingpin in UltraCopter vs. AntiMatter (set 70170).

Gray-haired team leader Solomon Blaze also appears in LEGO® Space Galaxy Squad sets.

117

SPACE IS THE PLACE

Real-world space exploration has inspired many **LEGO® Space** sets—and the partnerships between the LEGO Group and NASA and other space agencies have inspired many young scientists. Over the years, those partnerships have seen astronauts build LEGO sets in space and metal minifigures travel much, much farther than any human being!

Mission to Mars is based on NASA's 2001 Mars Odyssey mission, which put a satellite in orbit around the Red Planet.

Six sets in partnership with NASA and Discovery Channel include a new Lunar Lander (set 10029), the first LEGO model of the International Space Station (set 7467), and Mission to Mars (set 7469).

Space Module with Astronauts (set 367) predates the partnership between the LEGO Group and the US's National Aeronautics and Space Administration (NASA), but is inspired by their moon missions between 1969 and 1972.

NASA launches the first Space Shuttle in 1981, and a LEGO® Town Space Shuttle (set 1682) follows soon after. Sold exclusively in the US, it is the first LEGO set to feature NASA insignia.

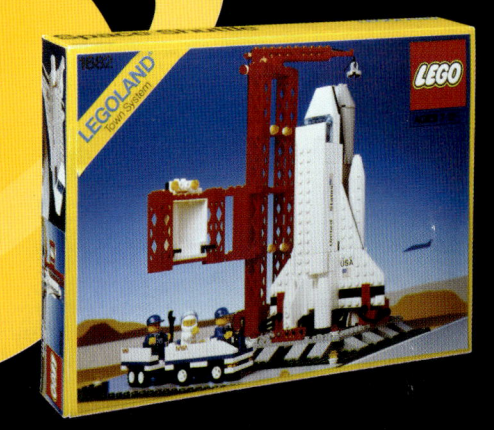

In the US, Space Module with Astronauts is known as Moon Landing (set 565), and does not touch down in stores until 1976.

SPACE IS THE PLACE

SHOOT OVER THE PAGE

Japanese astronaut Satoshi Furukawa becomes the first person to play with LEGO bricks in space. He builds a model of the International Space Station on board the International Space Station!

Denmark's first astronaut, Andreas Mogensen, travels to the International Space Station with 20 unique minifigures. On his return, the minifigures are given away in a competition for Danish schoolkids.

Shortly after working on the real NASA rover *Curiosity*, which reached Mars in 2012, engineer Stephen Pakbaz designs a LEGO version for fun. In 2014, a model based on his build becomes an official LEGO set.

Two NASA rovers arrive on Mars carrying special aluminum LEGO bricks and pictures of minifigure astronauts Biff Starling and Sandy Moondust, helping raise awareness of the mission and its aims.

2004 · 2011 · 2014 · 2015

Mogensen's minifigures are decorated with European Space Agency logos.

NASA Mars Science Laboratory Curiosity Rover (set 21104) is the fifth set from LEGO® CUUSOO (later LEGO® Ideas).

Two of this year's LEGO Ideas sets celebrate NASA's achievements. NASA Apollo Saturn V (set 21309) re-creates the rocket that first took astronauts to the moon. Women of NASA (set 21312), meanwhile, pays tribute to four pioneers of science, technology, engineering, and mathematics.

Women of NASA includes minifigures of astronauts Mae Jemison and Sally Ride, computer scientist Margaret Hamilton, and astronomer Nancy Grace Roman.

Mae Jemison and Sally Ride

Margaret Hamilton

Nancy Grace Roman

Three metal minifigures make it all the way to the planet Jupiter! The aluminum adventurers set off from Earth on NASA's *Juno* spacecraft in 2011, on a mission to inspire the next generation of space scientists.

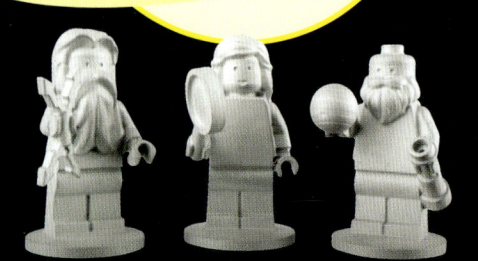

The *Juno* minifigures represent the Roman god and goddess Jupiter and Juno, and scientist Galileo Galilei, who discovered Jupiter's moons in the 1600s.

This year's LEGO® City Mars Exploration sets are inspired by the latest NASA tech and by projects that are still on the drawing board. NASA Apollo 11 Lunar Lander (set 10266) meanwhile, is the most detailed LEGO lunar module yet.

NASA Apollo Saturn V stands 39 in (100 cm) tall, and commemorates the 1969 moon landing with 1,969 pieces!

LEGO City's Rocket Assembly & Transport (set 60229) is based on NASA's real-life launch and ground control systems.

120

SPACE IS THE PLACE

The ISS is a joint project between NASA, Russia's Roscosmos, the Japan Aerospace Exploration Agency, the European Space Agency, and the Canadian Space Agency.

LEGO® Education and NASA team up for new schools STEM program Build to Launch, and the latest LEGO International Space Station (set 21321) is perfectly timed to celebrate 20 years of continuous human habitation on the ISS.

The LEGO® Friends get their own NASA Space Shuttle in this year's Olivia's Space Academy (set 41713).

The minifigure stars of the Build to Launch program (see 2020) head into space for real on a crucial test flight for the Artemis program. The next stage of the program will take humans back to the moon for the first time since 1972!

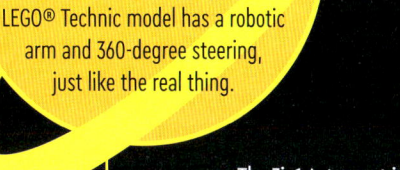

The latest Martian rover and its onboard drone, *Ingenuity*, are the subject of NASA Mars Rover Perseverance (set 42158). The 1,132-piece LEGO® Technic model has a robotic arm and 360-degree steering, just like the real thing.

The 3in1 Astronaut in Space can be rebuilt as a spaceship or a space dog!

The 2,354-piece NASA Space Shuttle Discovery (set 10283) is two outer-space icons in one: its payload is a detailed model of the Hubble Space Telescope, launched by *Discovery* in 1990.

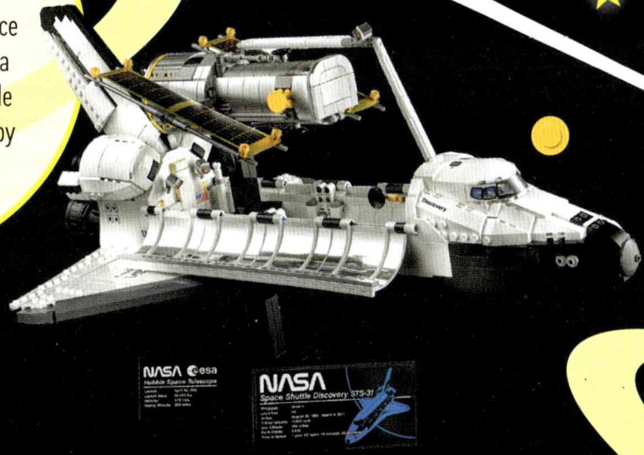

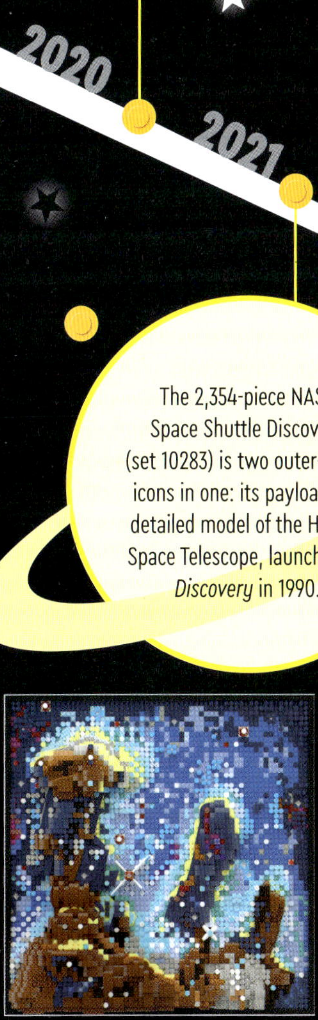

This year also sees huge, brick-built versions of photos taken by the real Hubble Space Telescope go on display at LEGO stores around the world.

This year's NASA-inspired sets span several themes, from the LEGO® Creator Space Astronaut (set 31152) to the LEGO® Icons NASA Artemis Space Launch System (set 10341) and the LEGO Technic NASA Apollo Lunar Roving Vehicle—LRV (set 42182).

STREETS AHEAD

First there was Town Plan. Then there was LEGO® Town. But by 2005, the everyday magic of minifigure life demanded a **LEGO® City**! Now approaching its 20th anniversary, this evergreen theme gets ever greener—with electric cars, recycling trucks, and even wildlife conservation teams.

Bridging the gap between LEGO Town and LEGO City, World City sets include a Police HQ (set 7035), a High-Speed Train (set 4511), and a Rescue Chopper (set 7044).

2003

The City gets not only its first Farm (set 7637), complete with cow figures, but also its first wind farm, courtesy of Octan Energy's Wind Turbine Transport (set 7747).

The tram in Public Transport Station (8404) has room for eight minifigures.

2010

2009

Hard-working City minifigures finally have somewhere to go home to with the arrival of City House (set 8403). They can even travel there on the City's first tram!

Have you seen a wind turbine anywhere?

2011

A 494-piece Space Center (set 3368) sends City minifigures to the stars in a realistic rocket. Back on Earth, a crafty crook sets his sights on the City's first ever bank.

Bank & Money Transfer (set 3661) has an opening bank vault beneath an opening skylight.

122

STREETS AHEAD

"I'm told I can light up any room!"

2005

LEGO City launches with more than 20 sets, including a police station, a fire station, and supersize construction vehicles such as XXL Mobile Crane (set 7249).

Police Station (set 7237) includes a minifigure with a working flashlight.

Coast Guard Helicopter & Life Raft (7738) has a working rescue winch.

2006

Hospital (set 7892) adds to the emergency services, while working trains, an airport, and a police boat that really floats prove that all vehicles are welcome in LEGO City.

2007

An Octan-branded Service Station (set 7993) keeps the City moving, and LEGO City Harbor (set 7994) includes the largest-ever LEGO element: a 22-in (58-cm) ship's hull.

2008

With 953 pieces, Police Headquarters (set 7744) claims the record for the biggest LEGO City police station. Farther afield, Coast Guard sets keep City residents safe at sea.

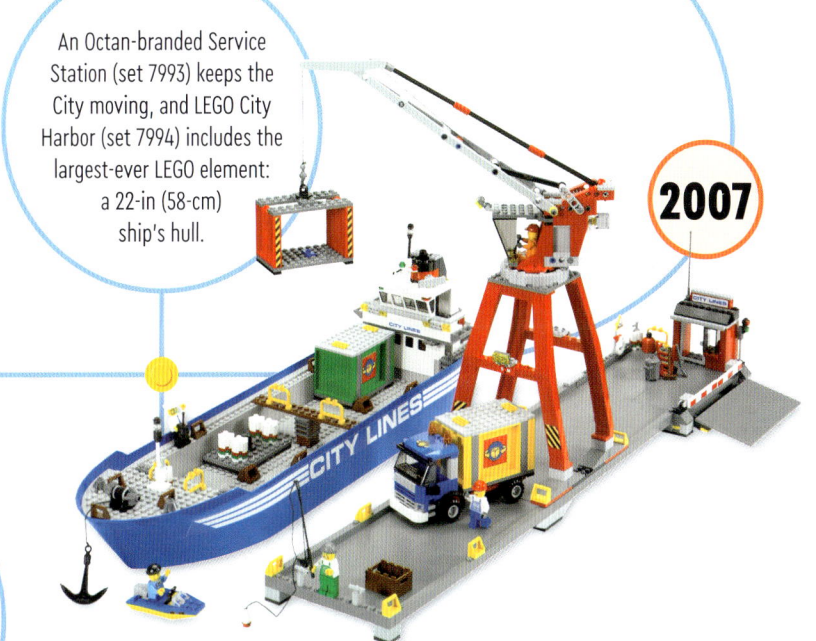

Fire Plane (set 4209) has a trapdoor function for dropping "water" on forest fires.

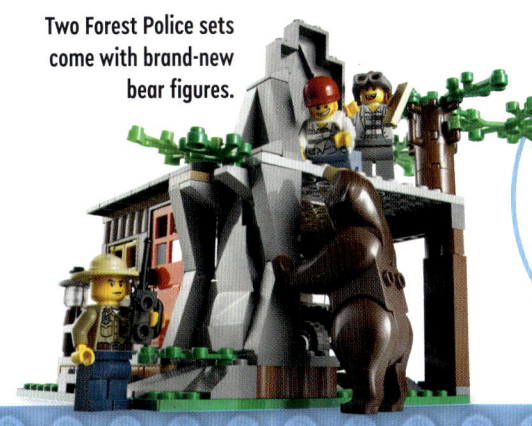

2012

Two Forest Police sets come with brand-new bear figures.

Big-hatted cops meet bears and bad guys in Forest Police sets, hard-hatted miners strike gold in The Mine (set 4204), and newly red-hatted fire teams take to the air.

THIS WAY TO EXPLORE MORE OF THE CITY

123

2013

The LEGO® City Undercover video game introduces the world to minifigure hero Chase McCain™, who also appears in this year's High-Speed Chase (set 60007).

Chase McCain is the first City minifigure to have a name!

We all have names, but some of us aren't telling!

2014

The Arctic exploration begun in LEGO Town continues in sets such as Arctic Base Camp (set 60036), complete with seven intrepid minifigures, four huskies, and a polar bear.

2019

TV star Freya McCloud drives the Fire Chief Response Truck (set 60231)

Mars Exploration sets are inspired by real-life NASA space programs, and other sets start to feature the stars of a new TV series, LEGO® City *Adventures*.

Capital City includes the theme's first double-decker bus and an electric car charging point.

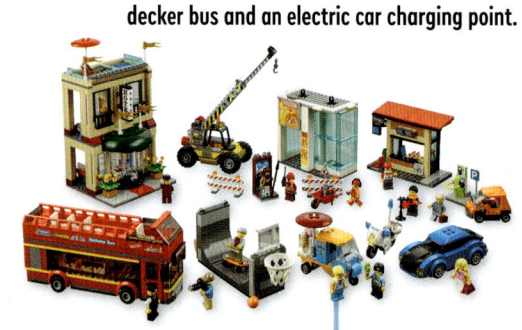

2018

The Mountain Police take on crooks dressed as tree trunks, while a caveman also drops into Capital City (set 60200) as part of the still-under-construction City museum.

2017

Pizza Van (set 60150) starts a tasty trend for street-food sets, and the City Jungle range sends explorers in search of ancient ruins and minifigure-eating plants.

2020

Pulling a ripcord launches these City 'copters whirring into the sky!

Sets such as Air Race (set 60260) include helicopters that really fly. Ocean Exploration Ship (set 60266) becomes the biggest LEGO boat to really float.

This seaworthy ship measures 25 in (64 cm) from bow to stern.

2021

Wildlife Rescue sets introduce new animal figures, Town Center (set 60292) is home to the City's first guide dog, and Stuntz sets feature pull-and-go motorcycles.

Wildlife Rescue Camp (set 60307) includes new elephant, lion, monkey, and eagle figures.

124

STREETS AHEAD

Swamp Police and Deep-Sea Explorers sets add airboats, alligators, submarines, and sawfish to City sets. The theme's biggest set so far includes its very own LEGO Store.

Swamp Police Starter Set (set 60066) packs lots of story into just 78 pieces.

2015

Fun in the Park (set 60134) introduces a wheelchair element and a baby figure. Two of this year's Volcano Explorers sets boast builds that really erupt!

The 1,683-piece City Square (set 60097) is the biggest LEGO City set of the 2010s.

2016

Town Center is one of several sets to feature new road plates in 2021.

Mobile Police Dog Training (set 60369) includes a trainer in a bite-proof suit!

This year's Police sets focus on training—for officers and police dogs. Civilian minifigures, meanwhile, put their skills to the test at the Ski and Climbing Center.

2022

There's healthy food for everyone at the City's first ever Grocery Store (set 60347). School Day (set 60329) boasts the City's first ever school building.

Ski and Climbing Center (set 60366) has a working lift to the top of its slope.

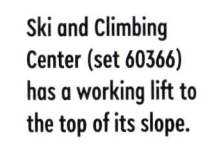

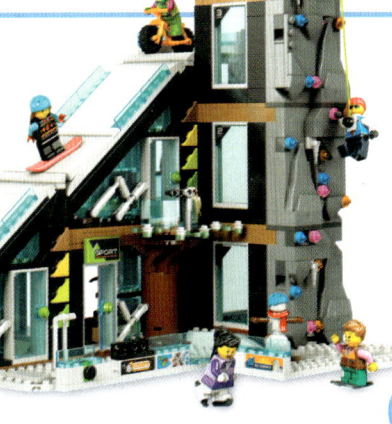

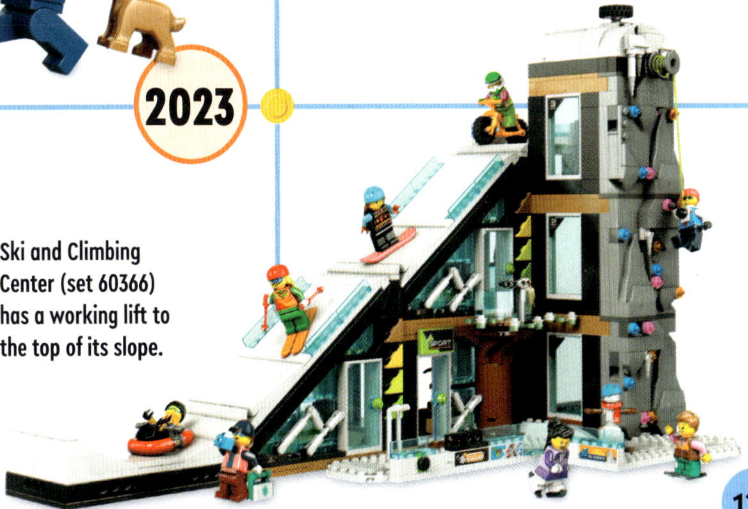

2023

125

2023

DOWNTOWN

The biggest-ever LEGO® City set captures all the buzz of an ultramodern urban neighborhood. At street level, very busy minifigures can check out the comics shop, get a haircut, and enjoy a bowl of noodles or a slice of pizza. The upper levels include a hotel, a vet's office, and a recording studio, while the rooftops are given over to green energy and an open-air dance floor.

Wind turbines and solar panels generate energy for the city

Balcony is part of the hotel's penthouse suite

Billboard promoting an action-packed movie

The comics shop is packed full of pop-culture memorabilia, including the scary monster suit that matches the monster in the movie poster.

Minifigures can sit and eat at the pizzeria counter, or take their meal to go in a box

The blue line along the road is a cycle path

A string of colorful lights draws customers to the noodle stand

Smoothie wagon can sell delicious fruit drinks—any time, any place!

126

STREETS AHEAD

- **SET NUMBER** 60380
- **PIECES** 2,010
- **MINIFIGURES** 14
- **SIZE** 17 in (42 cm) tall, 18 in (45 cm) wide

Speakers and lights hang over the rooftop dance floor

Pedestrian bridge is one floor lower in this layout

The modular buildings and road sections can be rearranged to create different city layouts. This one gives the vet a roof terrace and puts the pizza parlor at the foot of a tower.

When dogs jump down from the examination table at the City vet, they can tuck into the twin bowl of dog food and water found on the floor beside it.

When the DJ visits the barber, his confident smile and green hair can be swapped for an alarmed look and a hairstyle he clearly doesn't like!

A gardener sweeps up fallen leaves in this pocket park

Striped pole is a traditional sign for a barber's shop

127

NEW HEIGHTS

What makes a LEGO® modular building? First of all, it's modularity—meaning that each story can easily be lifted off and each building can slot seamlessly into a larger street scene. Then there's its creativity. Since 2007, **LEGO® Modular Buildings Collection** has been associated with advanced building techniques, highly imaginative use of parts, and truly incredible levels of detail.

LEGO designer Jamie Berard is inspired by fan builders to create Café Corner (set 10182). The set includes more ambitious build techniques than any previous official LEGO set—such as the café sign made out of minifigure skis threaded onto a flexible LEGO tube!

2007

Pet Shop (set 10218) is the first modular set to split into two buildings, meaning that the shop can be placed on the left or the right of the townhouse - or displayed separately. To the relief of residents, the set is the first in the range to include a toilet.

With 22 windows including skylights, it's no surprise that Grand Emporium (set 10211) comes with its own window-cleaning minifigure! Another four minifigures can pass through the range's first revolving door, while two more are frozen in place as mannequins.

Pet Shop features a goldfish in a tank and a new dog in a new color.

2011

2010

Town Hall is the first modular building in the main range not designed by Jamie Berard.

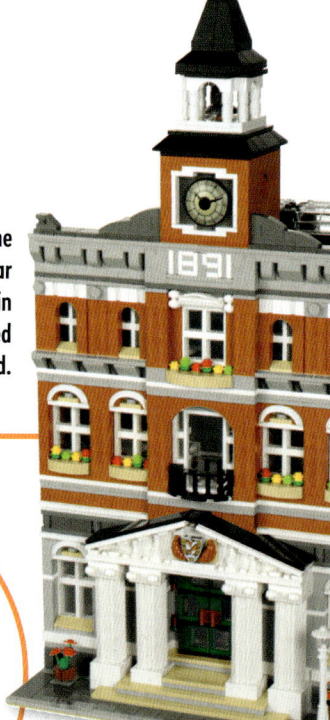

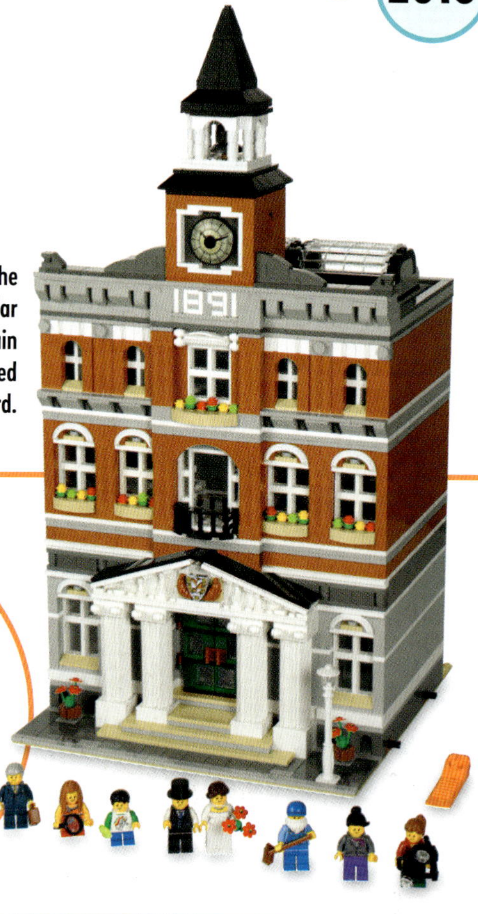

Let's go and paint the town red!

2012

Standing 20 in (50 cm) tall, the 2,766-piece Town Hall (set 10224) has a working elevator! The year inscribed on its parapet marks the 1891 birth of LEGO Group founder Ole Kirk Kristiansen, and, in reverse, the 1981 birth of the model's designer, Astrid Graabæk.

NEW HEIGHTS

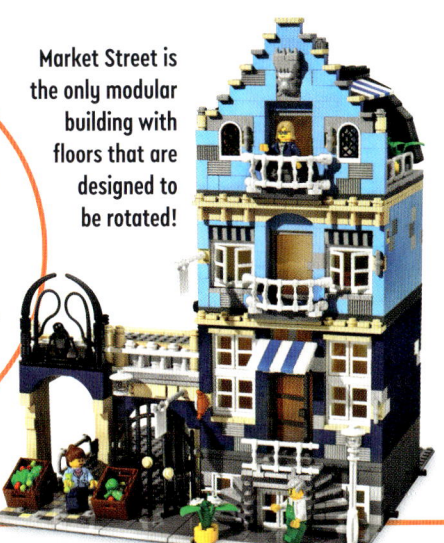

Market Street is the only modular building with floors that are designed to be rotated!

Designed by Dutch fan builder Eric Brok, Market Street (set 10190) is released as a LEGO® Factory set—a forerunner of LEGO® Ideas. Though not part of Jamie Berard's original plan for the modular series, it is swiftly welcomed into the up-and-coming collection.

Green Grocer (set 10185) is the first modular building with a furnished interior. Details such as chilled display cabinets, a radiator, a grandfather clock, and an open fireplace push the element count up to 2,352 pieces, making it the largest set in the range until 2012.

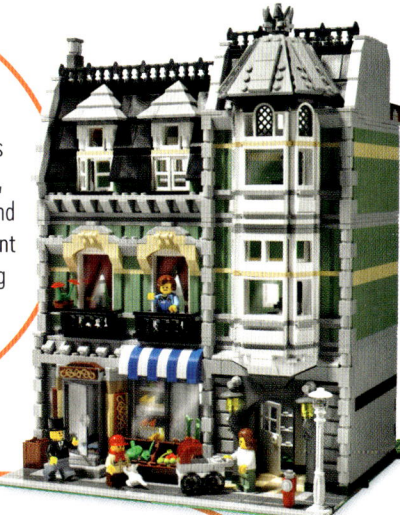

2008

Grand Emporium, like many other department stores, features a revolving door and escalators.

Jamie Berard designed Café Corner and Green Grocer at the same time as Fire Brigade (set 10197), though the latter is not released until 2009. It is the first set in the series to feature a motor vehicle—in the form of a fire engine that fits inside the station house.

Fire Brigade has a trapdoor in the roof for access to the lower floor.

2009

Palace Cinema is the first set to include a red 32×32 baseplate since 1978.

2013

Palace Cinema (set 10232) is the first modular building released under the LEGO® Creator Expert banner. Designed by Astrid Graabæk and Jordan Schwartz, it includes a classic limo, spotlights for staging movie premieres, and a red baseplate for a red carpet.

THE COLLECTION CONTINUES...

129

2014 — Parisian Restaurant (set 10243) is an especially personal project for returning designer Jamie Berard, as he names the eatery "Chez Albert" after his grandfather and bases the minifigure couple enjoying a romantic meal on his brother and his fiancée.

2015 — There's more story than ever before in Detective's Office (set 10246). Cookie smugglers bake their wares on the top floor before sneaking them through the back of the barbershop and into the pool hall—right below sleuth Ace Brickman's office!

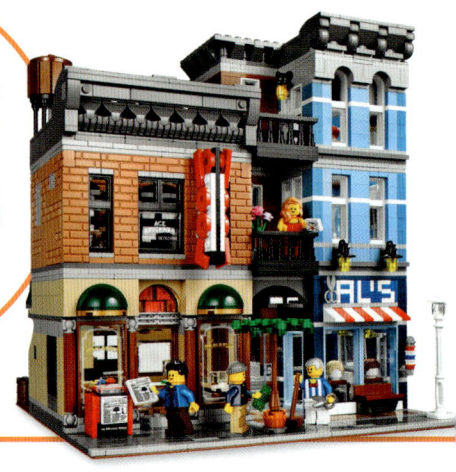

2019 — The first modular building since Fire Brigade with room to park a vehicle, Corner Garage (set 10264) features a forecourt as well as a drive-in workshop. Designer Florian Müller uses the Octan brand colors first seen in LEGO® Town, but in the more muted shades of a bygone era.

2020 — Like the Pet Shop before it, Bookshop (set 10270) includes one business and one home, built on separate baseplates so they can be rearranged. Model designer Wes Talbott based two of its minifigures on his parents and parts of the build on dollhouses made by his mother.

2021 — While the cops in Police Station (set 10278) hang out at the doughnut shop, any crooks in the cell can work on the escape tunnel hidden under the floor! This set, designed by Chris McVeigh, is the first modular building released as part of the LEGO® Icons range.

I dough-nut know which one to choose!

The railings along the Boutique Hotel roof are made from black snake pieces.

130

NEW HEIGHTS

2016

Designed by Jamie Berard and Nick Vas, Brick Bank (set 10251) boasts a grand main entrance and two secret ways in. The first is a chimney with room for a minifigure crook, and the second is a cash-size slot in the neighboring laundromat!

2017

To celebrate 10 years of Modular Buildings, Jamie Berard asked fellow LEGO model designers for help furnishing the eight rooms that make up Assembly Square (set 10255). They soon filled his desk with builds for sofa beds, dentist chairs, bakery shelves, and more.

2018

Inspired by the streamlined styles of the 1950s, Downtown Diner (set 10260) is a modular building like no other. Model designer Mike Psiaki even updates the minifigures, swapping the classic LEGO smile seen throughout the main range so far for varied facial expressions.

Assembly Square is made up of 4,002 pieces.

2022

Boutique Hotel (set 10297) looks at modular buildings from a new angle—a 53-degree angle, to be exact! Model designer Anderson Ward Grubb uses ingenious techniques to create its diagonal wall, making space for an art gallery filled with brick-built masterpieces.

2023

The second modular building designed by Anderson Ward Grubb, Jazz Club (set 10312) finds room for a pizzeria and a tailor's shop alongside an intimate music venue. There's even a greenhouse filled with fresh produce on the roof of the pizzeria!

Jazz Club is the first set to come with a minifigure double bass!

131

2023

NATURAL HISTORY MUSEUM

SET NUMBER	10326
PIECES	4,014
MINIFIGURES	7
SIZE	13 in (31 cm) tall, 16 in (39 cm) wide

This temple of knowledge is the widest and grandest edifice in the Modular Buildings range. It is packed full of amazing artifacts—from historical hats to outer space scenes—with a star dinosaur skeleton exhibit that can be displayed inside or outside the building.

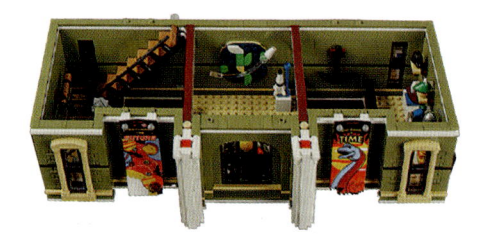

Like all the Modular Buildings, the museum splits into sections for easy access to the interiors.

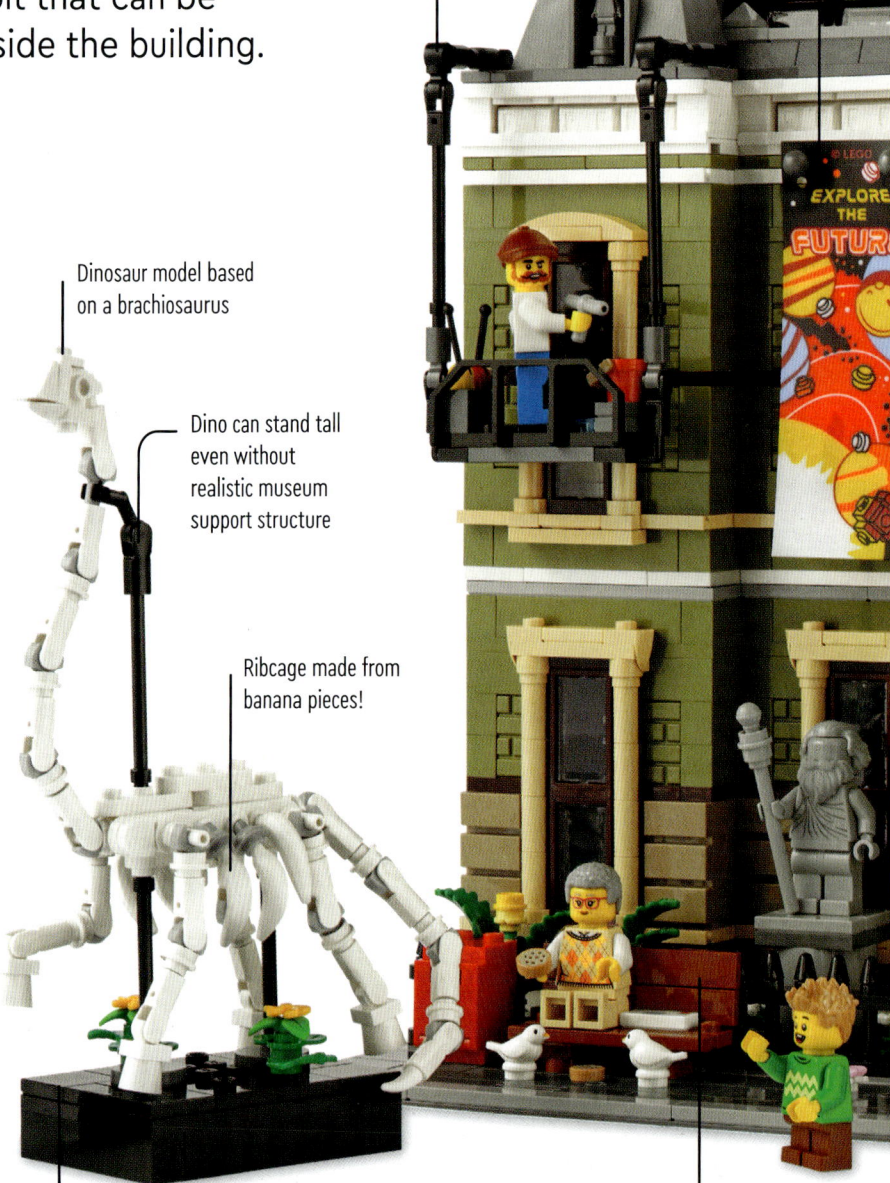

Window cleaner's cradle clips onto roof

Banners advertise latest exhibitions

Dinosaur model based on a brachiosaurus

Dino can stand tall even without realistic museum support structure

Ribcage made from banana pieces!

Dinosaur and display base can be built into ground floor of museum

This bench is a perfect place to feed the birds

Fallen flower on the sidewalk

NEW HEIGHTS

Domed roof space houses the chief curator's office

A "glass" roof lets light in to the upper level

Springtime tree in full blossom

Out-of-this-world exhibits include this realistic model of the solar system, complete with a ring around Saturn.

There is space for the dino inside the museum—with its body on the ground floor and its head and neck upstairs!

Archaeological finds on display include animal skulls and a fossil made out of a tightly coiled minifigure whip piece.

Statue made from all-gray minifigure parts

Runaway dog has a dinosaur bone!

133

LANDMARK ACHIEVEMENTS

LEGO® Architecture sets bring real-life landmarks down to size, forming a compact collection of the world's most celebrated sites. The range dates back to 2008, but its subject matter spans a much bigger history, starting four-and-a-half-thousand years ago!

By far the most ancient building in the LEGO Architecture range is The Great Pyramid of Giza (set 21058). Lifting the top off the set reveals a scene of the pyramid under construction.

2600 BCE

A marvel of 1930s engineering, the Golden Gate Bridge seems to recede into the distance thanks to the forced-perspective building technique used in San Francisco (set 21043).

1937

The largest LEGO Architecture set is the 2,276-piece Robie House (set 21010). The Chicago home is one of three sets celebrating the work of American architect Frank Lloyd Wright.

1909

Home to Australia's highest observation deck, Sydney Tower was completed in 1981. It dominates 2017's skyline of Sydney (set 21032), soaring high above the opera house and bridge.

1959

In a city of distinctive buildings, New York's Solomon R. Guggenheim Museum is one of the most distinctive. The 2017 LEGO version (set 21035) includes two yellow taxis.

1981

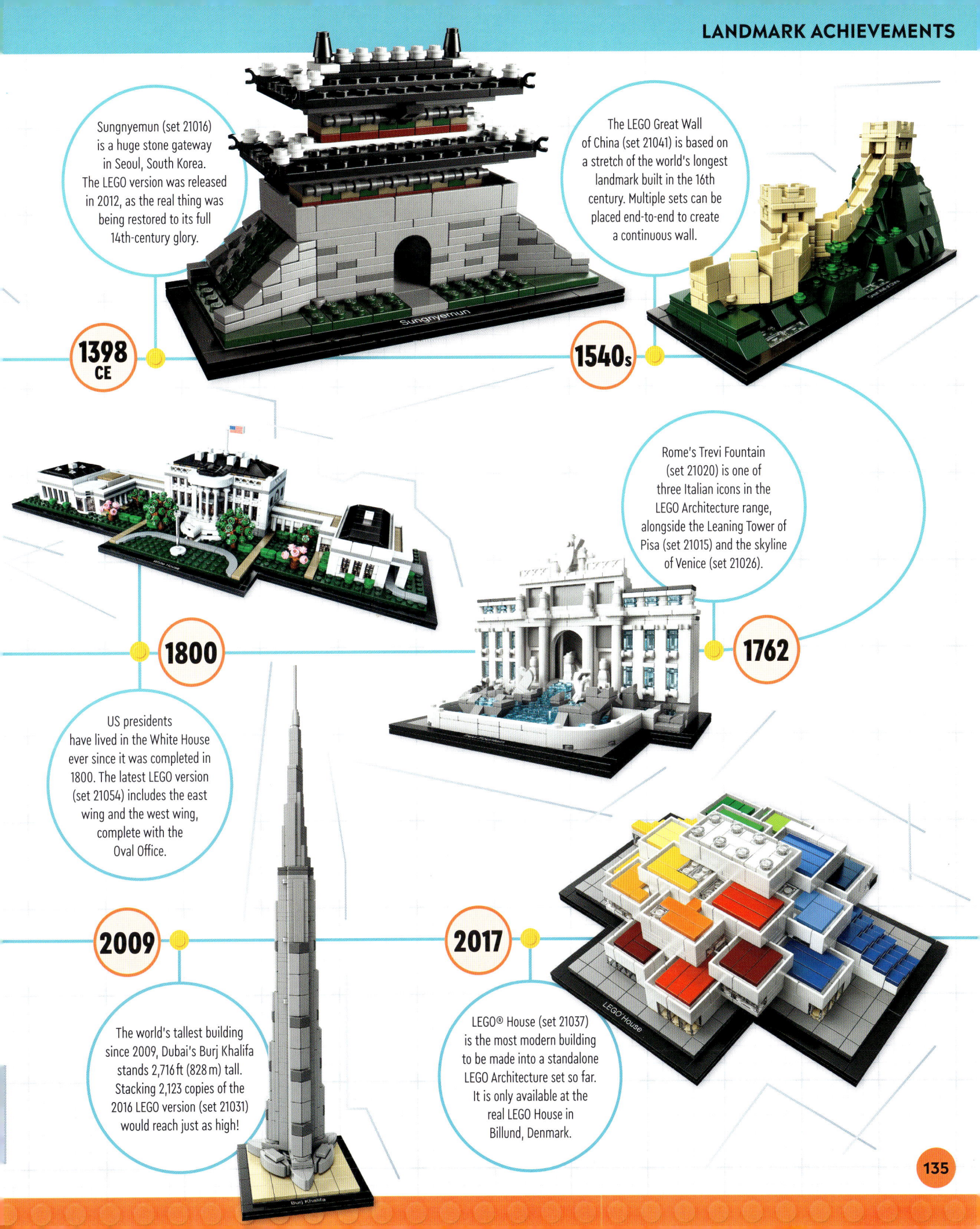

LANDMARK ACHIEVEMENTS

Sungnyemun (set 21016) is a huge stone gateway in Seoul, South Korea. The LEGO version was released in 2012, as the real thing was being restored to its full 14th-century glory.

1398 CE

The LEGO Great Wall of China (set 21041) is based on a stretch of the world's longest landmark built in the 16th century. Multiple sets can be placed end-to-end to create a continuous wall.

1540s

Rome's Trevi Fountain (set 21020) is one of three Italian icons in the LEGO Architecture range, alongside the Leaning Tower of Pisa (set 21015) and the skyline of Venice (set 21026).

1762

US presidents have lived in the White House ever since it was completed in 1800. The latest LEGO version (set 21054) includes the east wing and the west wing, complete with the Oval Office.

1800

The world's tallest building since 2009, Dubai's Burj Khalifa stands 2,716 ft (828 m) tall. Stacking 2,123 copies of the 2016 LEGO version (set 21031) would reach just as high!

2009

LEGO® House (set 21037) is the most modern building to be made into a standalone LEGO Architecture set so far. It is only available at the real LEGO House in Billund, Denmark.

2017

HAPPY HOLIDAYS!

There are LEGO® sets for all kinds of annual celebrations, but **Christmas sets** are the gift that keeps on giving! Since 1977, there have been more than 300 winter holiday sets, including advent calendars, collectible Minifigures, gingerbread houses, decorations, and brick-built trees.

2019
Marking 10 years of the Winter Village Collection, Gingerbread House (set 10267) takes the range in a new direction, with a frosted fairytale home for a Gingerbread couple and their Gingerbread Baby.

2018
This year's LEGO® BrickHeadz sets have a holiday vibe, with an Easter Bunny (set 40271), a Thanksgiving Turkey (set 40273), and a double helping of Christmas cheer with Mr. & Mrs. Claus (set 40274).

2009
An idyllic festive scene by itself, Winter Toy Shop (set 10199) is the start of a still-growing Winter Village Collection. Every year brings another snow-capped set for seasonal play and display.

2006
Holiday Train (set 10173) is the first large-scale seasonal set. Measuring more than 40in (1m) long, the 965-piece locomotive is loaded with Christmas trees, presents, passengers, and pets.

2020 — Even Ebeneezer Scrooge can be a Christmas decoration in the LEGO world! Charles Dickens Tribute (set 40410) is based on *A Christmas Carol*, and features minifigures of Scrooge, Bob Cratchit, and Tiny Tim.

2021 — The latest Santa's Sleigh (set 40499) is the biggest ever. Its 343 pieces include four realistic reindeer figures, gifts including a guitar and a teddy bear, and snacks for a round-the-world journey.

2022 — There have been plenty of brick-built Christmas trees over the years, but none as majestic as this one! Christmas Tree (set 40573) stands 12in (30 cm) tall and can be rebuilt as two smaller trees.

1977 — You wait years for a LEGO Santa, and then three come along at once! Between them, Two Santas (set 245) and Santa and Sleigh (set 246) have the honor of being the first festive sets.

1995 — The first minifigure Santa makes his rounds in Santa Claus and Sleigh (set 1807). He shares his beard with a LEGO® Castle wizard and his hat with several LEGO® Pirates. Yo-ho-ho!

2005 — The first LEGO® City Advent Calendar (set 7324) comes with eight minifigures, including Santa. There has been a LEGO City advent calendar every year since, plus many more for other themes.

137

KEEPING UP WITH THE JONESES

In the real world, the **LEGO® Indiana Jones™** theme launched alongside the fourth Indy film in 2008. It re-created scenes from the whip-cracking movie series for two years and then hung up its hat until 2023. For LEGO Indy himself, however, the story begins in 1930s China...

This set belongs in a museum!

Indiana Jones and the Temple of Doom

1935

Two LEGO sets are based on the second Indiana Jones movie, which is set before the first one, in 1935. It starts with Indy and his friends narrowly escaping danger in Shanghai, China, only to discover all-new dangers on the way to New Delhi in India! Both sets were released in 2009.

Shanghai Chase (set 7682) sees a smartly dressed Indy on the run with his sidekick Short Round and singer Willie Scott.

The Temple of Doom (set 7199) puts Indy and his pals on a wild mine cart ride measuring more than 36 in (90 cm) long.

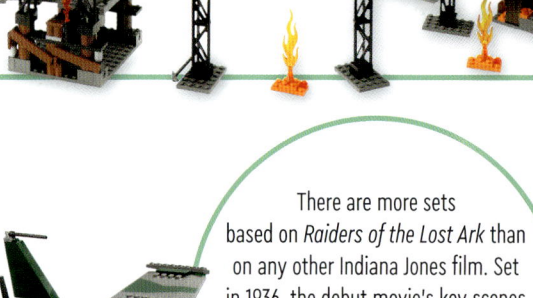

There are more sets based on *Raiders of the Lost Ark* than on any other Indiana Jones film. Set in 1936, the debut movie's key scenes are all re-created in LEGO form, taking Indy from a booby-trapped temple in Peru to the wings of an experimental aircraft in Egypt.

Designed for play and display, 2023's Temple of the Golden Idol (set 77015) is the biggest LEGO Indiana Jones set. Its 1,545 pieces include a rolling brick-built boulder and an illuminated idol.

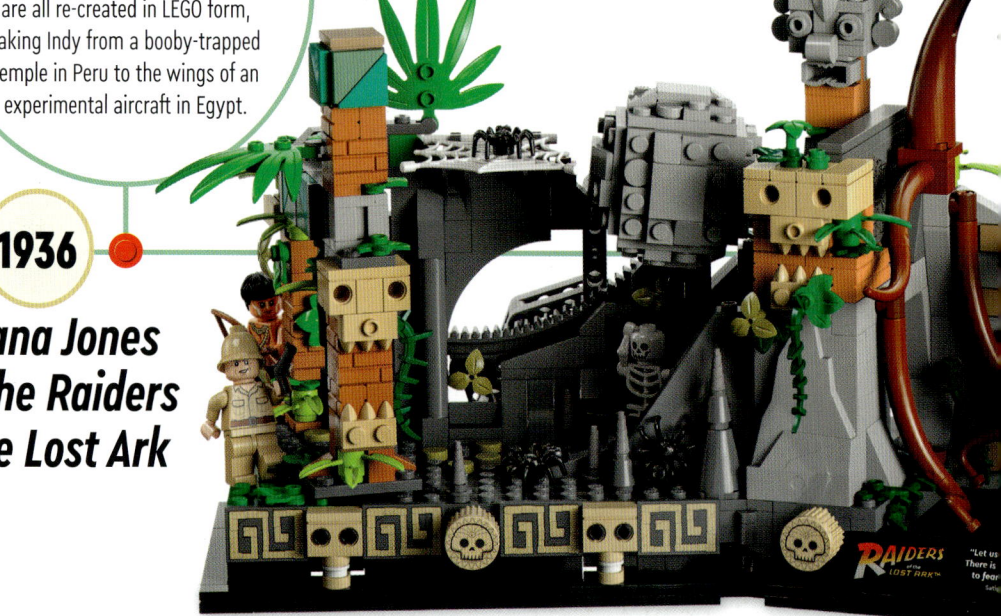

Fight on the Flying Wing (set 7683) from 2009 pits heroes Indy and Marion Ravenwood against a pair of villains and their enormous airplane.

1936

Indiana Jones and the Raiders of the Lost Ark

138

KEEPING UP WITH THE JONESES

Just three sets include this transparent skull element, made especially for the Indiana Jones theme.

All six sets based on the fourth Indiana Jones film focus on its scenes in South America. The largest, Temple of the Crystal Skull (set 7627), pairs Indy with Mutt, his long-lost son, as they dodge spear shooters, spinning stairs, and baddie Irina Spalko to discover the temple's secrets.

With 929 pieces, 2008's Temple of the Crystal Skull remained the theme's biggest set until 2023.

1957
Indiana Jones and the Kingdom of the Crystal Skull

Aah, Venice!

Venice Canal Chase (set 7197) from 2009 boasts breaking boat, exploding engine, and collapsing bridge functions.

In the third movie, Indy dallies with the double-crossing Dr. Elsa Schneider in Venice, Italy; then teams up with his dad for a hair-raising race to Berlin in Germany. Four sets follow the film's late '30s action, with three focusing on the fast-paced father and son reunion.

1938
Indiana Jones and the Last Crusade

Fighter Plane Chase (set 77012) from 2023 includes an exclusive Henry Jones Sr. minifigure and a plane with breakaway wings.

"That's what scares me"
—Indiana Jones

139

THE 2010s

2010

LEGO® Minifigures get their own range of collectible characters.

Sets featuring characters from *Toy Story*, *Cars*, and *Prince of Persia* are the first to be based on Disney films.

Minifigures seek out adventure over land and underwater in LEGO® World Racers and LEGO® Atlantis sets.

The latest LEGO pirates are Disney's *Pirates of the Caribbean*™.

A second LEGOLAND® Park in the US opens in Florida.

2012

LEGO® Friends launches as the first ever mini doll theme.

2013

Tribes of advanced animals bring the action in LEGO® Legends of Chima™.

LEGO® Minecraft® sets use many new pieces to re-create the game's blocky world.

The Teenage Mutant Ninja Turtles burst out of the sewers and into LEGO sets!

2011

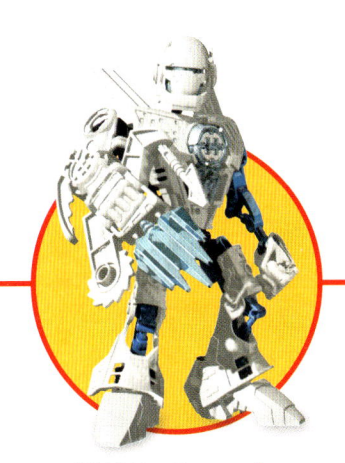

LEGO® Hero Factory takes over the buildable figures baton from BIONICLE®.

LEGO® NINJAGO® introduces the world to the Masters of Spinjitzu.

Fan-designed sets are released under the LEGO® CUUSOO banner (the theme is renamed LEGO® Ideas in 2014).

It's minifigures versus flying mummies in the LEGO® Pharaoh's Quest theme.

Super Heroes sets star movie and comic-book characters from the worlds of Marvel and DC.

Minifigures go to Middle-earth in LEGO® *The Lord of the Rings*™ and LEGO® *The Hobbit*™ sets.

New action themes include LEGO® Monster Fighters and LEGO® Dino.

LEGOLAND® Malaysia is the first LEGOLAND attraction in Asia.

2014

New Creator Expert branding is introduced for the largest, most complex sets.

THE LEGO® MOVIE™ is a box-office smash, with an amazing range of sets to boot.

Mini dolls visit the Magic Kingdom in the LEGO® *Disney Princess*™ range.

More than 20 brick-built monsters launch the collectible LEGO® Mixels™ theme.

141

2014 cont.
Super-spy missions are more super than ever with the LEGO® Ultra Agents.

2015
LEGO® Speed Champions re-creates real-life supercars at minifigure scale.

Fantasy adventure theme LEGO® Elves is the latest to star mini dolls.

Movie monsters tower over minifigures in LEGO® Jurassic World sets.

The first LEGO® BrickHeadz™ are highly stylized sculptures of Super Heroes.

Six sets with unique figures re-create the action from *The Angry Birds Movie*.

LEGOLAND® Dubai becomes the first LEGOLAND® resort in the Middle East.

Ole Kirk Kristiansen's great-grandson Thomas Kirk Kristiansen becomes deputy chairman of the LEGO Group.

Niels B. Christiansen becomes CEO of the LEGO Group.

2018
The LEGO® UniKitty theme features 12 new variants of the brick-built star of THE LEGO MOVIE.

Special sets mark 60 years of the LEGO brick and 40 years of the LEGO minifigure.

Bio-based LEGO elements made from Brazilian sugarcane debut. Made from bio-polyethylene, a flexible plastic, the range includes trees, leaves, and bushes.

LEGO® DIMENSIONS sets blend building with the latest video game technology.

TV's famous Mystery Inc. gang chase creepy crooks in LEGO® Scooby-Doo™ sets.

The LEGO Group opens a new brick factory in Jiaxing, China.

2016
Scannable shields with in-app abilities power up the LEGO® NEXO KNIGHTS™ theme.

2017
THE LEGO® BATMAN MOVIE and THE LEGO® NINJAGO® MOVIE™ go big in sets as well as on screen.

LEGO® BOOST combines coding and building for kids aged seven and up.

LEGOLAND Japan opens in Nagoya, Japan, welcoming one million visitors in its first six months.

The LEGO® House visitor attraction opens as the "Home of the Brick" in Billund, Denmark.

2019
Everything is awesomely apocalyptic in THE LEGO® MOVIE 2™ and its tie-in sets.

LEGO® Hidden Side™ sets are haunted by ghosts that can only be seen with a special app.

The LEGO® Overwatch® theme features play sets and display sets based on the hit video game.

A pilot program for LEGO® Braille Bricks launches to help children learn the writing system used by visually impaired people. The kit launches the following year.

143

MEET THE MINIFIGURES

LEGO® minifigures have always been sought-after, and since 2010, the **LEGO® Minifigures** series has made them individually available. Every collectible character comes with accessories, a display stand, and lots of personality. Each one is a surprise—with no clue who is inside the packaging!

Cheerleader is the first Minifigure to carry pom poms.

Demolition Dummy

Super Wrestler

Zombie

2010

Series one includes a Super Wrestler, a Demolition Dummy, and the first ever LEGO Zombie. The Cheerleader is the first minifigure to have legs with detailing on the sides.

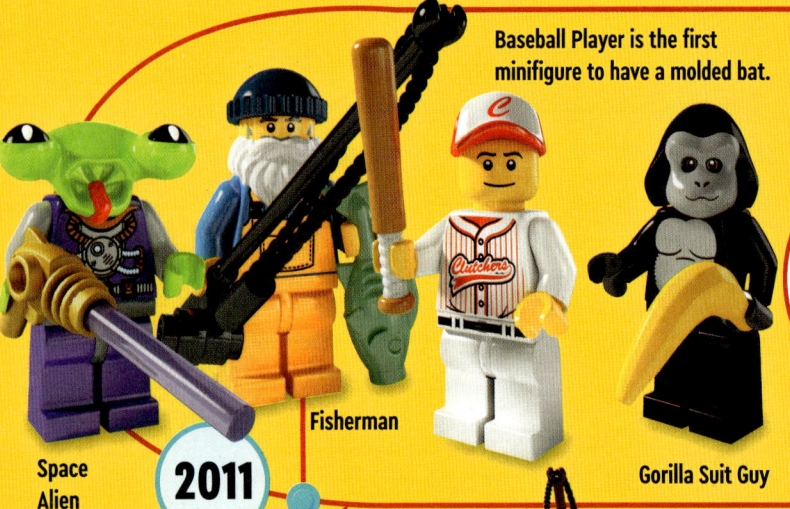

Baseball Player is the first minifigure to have a molded bat.

Space Alien

Fisherman

Gorilla Suit Guy

2011

Series two offers thrills with a Skier and a Surfer, and chills with a Witch and a Vampire. The Mime is the first minifigure to come with a choice of three different heads.

Series four introduces minifigure ice skates for the Figure Skater and the Hockey Player and pink spiky hair for the Punk Rocker.

Series three's Gorilla Suit Guy starts a trend for collectible Minifigures dressed as their favorite animals, while the Space Alien is the first with an all-new head piece.

144

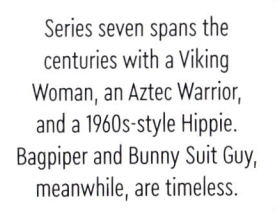

MEET THE MINIFIGURES

Series seven spans the centuries with a Viking Woman, an Aztec Warrior, and a 1960s-style Hippie. Bagpiper and Bunny Suit Guy, meanwhile, are timeless.

Bunny Suit Guy
Aztec Warrior
Viking Woman
1960s-style Hippie

Bagpiper holds the first minifigure bagpipes.

Series eight is released in time for Christmas 2012, and includes a Santa Minifigure alongside the slightly less lovable Evil Robot, Alien Villainess, and Vampire Bat.

THE CHARACTERS KEEP ON COMING!

Series five's accessories include a chimp for the Zookeeper, a fish for the Ice Fisher, a pie for the Small Clown, and a head and tail for the Lizard Man.

2012

Small Clown carries the first LEGO pie.

Ice Fisher
Zookeeper
Lizard Man

Series six introduces brand-new head pieces for the Minotaur, the Clockwork Robot, and the Classic Alien, as well as the first teddy bear accessory for the Sleepyhead.

145

Roller Derby Girl
Chicken Suit Guy
Mermaid
Judge is the only minifigure to wield a gavel element.

2013

Series nine's Roller Derby Girl is the first minifigure to wear roller skates. Chicken Suit Guy, on the other not-quite-hand, is the first to have wings instead of arms!

Spider Lady
Zombie Pirate 
Monster Rocker
Wolf Guy

Series 10 boasts something extra special among its cast of characters— the ultra-rare Mr. Gold, who was limited to 5,000 Minifigure bags around the world.

Scallywag Pirate
Penguin Boy
Ice Queen

Series 15 is packed with new pieces, including the Faun's legs, the Ballerina's tutu, the Animal Control Officer's escaped skunk, and Shark Guy's entire suit.

Series 14 is all about the monsters, with the likes of Wolf Guy, Spider Lady, Monster Rocker, and the Zombie Pirate all creeping into stores in time for Halloween!

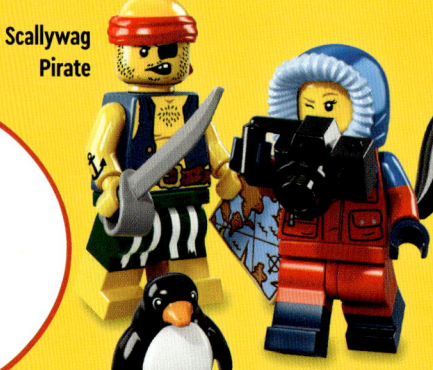

Wildlife Photographer's new penguin is later seen in a THE LEGO® BATMAN MOVIE set.

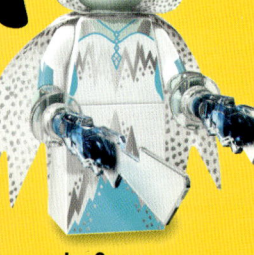

2016

Series 16 starts off scary with the likes of Ice Queen and Scallywag Pirate, but then Penguin Boy and Wildlife Photographer's penguin turn everything super cute.

MEET THE MINIFIGURES

Series 12 launches alongside an online game that lets collectors unlock virtual Minifigures such as Genie Girl, Swashbuckler, Battle Goddess, and Piggy Guy.

2014

Evil Wizard

Classic King

Sheriff

Battle Goddess

Swashbuckler

Series 11 has a fairytale flavor with its smiling Scarecrow, ice-pop-loving Yeti, and happy Holiday Elf. Not to mention a gingerbread flavor with its spicy Gingerbread Man!

Hot Dog Guy is the first minifigure to wear a food-themed suit.

Genie Girl

Piggy Guy

2015

Series 13 boasts some fantastic facial hair—on the Classic King, the Sheriff, and the Evil Wizard. But this wave's undisputed star is the clean-shaven Hot Dog Guy.

Series 17 cranks up the cuteness factor again with the Connoisseur's French bulldog, the Veterinarian's rabbit, and adorable Butterfly Girl and Rocket Boy.

2017

2018

Rocket Boy carries a "hand-drawn" flag.

Series 18 has a party vibe, celebrating the 40th anniversary of the minifigure. Classic Police Officer has even come dressed as one of the first minifigures from 1978!

THE CHARACTERS KEEP ON COMING!

147

Series 21 proves that this theme still has legs, in fact the Centaur Warrior has four all for herself! Violin Kid plays one of the world's smallest violins… a brand-new element.

Shipwreck Survivor's new hermit crab comes with a buildable shell.

Series 20 marks 10 years of collectible Minifigures with Brick Costume Guy, while Space Fan, Pirate Girl, and Tournament Knight are throwbacks to earlier LEGO themes.

Series 22 boasts more exclusive accessory parts including a toucan, a pony, and a racing wheelchair. The Troubadour even carries a lute and some loot!

2021

2022

Marine Biologist holds an all-new LEGO turtle.

Series 19 is full of surprises, with its nearly naked Shower Guy, a Mountain Biker with a massive mountain bike accessory, and the first ever LEGO® Monkey King.

2020

2019

Bear Costume Guy carries this exclusive rainbow tile.

148

MEET THE MINIFIGURES

Sugar Fairy carries a unique candy cane.

Series 24 makes history with T-rex Costume Fan and headlines with Newspaper Kid. But the biggest news is surely that Brown Astronaut has an adorable new Spacebaby!

Series 25 is all about awesome animal accessories, including a goat for the Goatherd, an Afghan hound for the Pet Groomer, and a red herring for the Film Noir Detective.

Series 23's festive seasonal selection includes a Snowman and an Elf, as well as costumed Reindeer and Cardboard Robot characters. The latter clearly preferred the box to the gift!

2023

Train Boy's train has "25" printed on the smokebox door.

2024

Series 26 is out-of-this-world! Space characters include Alien Space Tourist, Robot Butler, Flying Saucer Costume Fan, and Nurse Android, who is holding an all-new pink Spacebaby.

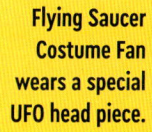

Flying Saucer Costume Fan wears a special UFO head piece.

149

DISNEY TIME

The relationship between the LEGO Group and the Walt Disney Company dates back to the 1950s, but the bond has been at its strongest since 2010. Nowadays, there are new **LEGO® Disney** sets every year, delighting young and old with builds based on brand-new blockbuster movies and all-time classics from across the Magic Kingdom.

The links between the LEGO Group and Disney begin with wooden toys based around 1955 film *Davy Crockett: King of the Wild Frontier*, a pull-along wooden Pluto (set 427), and inflatable Mickey Mouse bathing rings.

1956

New vehicle parts are used to make *Cars* stars such as Lightning McQueen and Sally Carrera.

The first LEGO® *Disney Princess*™ sets form part of the DUPLO range. They include DUPLO figure versions of Cinderella, Sleeping Beauty, and Snow White, all of whom come with new fabric skirt pieces.

2012

2013

Live-action adventure *The Lone Ranger* inspires six minifigure sets, while the latest LEGO DUPLO sets celebrate *Cars* spin-off *Planes* and animated TV adventure series *Jake and the Never Land Pirates*.

The first of several Disney-themed LEGO® Ideas sets is a 677-piece tribute to Disney Pixar's WALL•E (set 21303).

Jasmine from *Aladdin*, Anna and Elsa from *Frozen*, and Aurora from *Sleeping Beauty* join the LEGO *Disney Princess* lineage, while TV stars Sofia the First and Doc McStuffins become the latest LEGO DUPLO figures.

I have a new "tail" to tell...

2014

2015

LEGO *Disney Princess* becomes a magical mini doll theme, with sets based on *Brave*, *Cinderella*, *Tangled*, and *The Little Mermaid*. New pieces designed for the range include flower petal bricks and a mermaid tail for Ariel.

Elsa's Sparkling Ice Castle (set 41062) is the first of many LEGO® Disney® *Frozen* sets.

DISNEY TIME

1999 — The first ever brick-built sets to be based on existing characters re-create the timeless world of Winnie the Pooh in LEGO® DUPLO® form. Unique Pooh, Piglet, Eeyore, and Tigger figures star in the first seven sets.

2000 — The first Mickey and Minnie Mouse figures feature in this year's LEGO® Baby and LEGO® System sets. Builds such as Minnie's Birthday Party (set 4165) make use of many parts first found in LEGO® FABULAND™.

2011 — As the swashbuckling movie saga reaches its fourth installment, LEGO® Pirates of the Caribbean™ sets sail into stores. Meanwhile, LEGO® Cars becomes a theme in its own right after debuting in last year's LEGO DUPLO range.

The LEGO® Pirates of the Caribbean The Black Pearl (set 4184) has 804 pieces—more than half are black!

2010 — This year's Toy Story range includes LEGO DUPLO sets and minifigure sets such as Western Train Chase (set 7597).

Disney sets return to the LEGO lineup—and this time they're here to stay! The LEGO® Prince of Persia™ theme is the first to be based on a live-action Disney movie, while Toy Story and Cars sets fly the flag for animation.

Miles' Exo-Flex Suit (set 10825) is one of three 2016 LEGO DUPLO sets based on TV show Miles From Tomorrowland.

2016 — Eighteen classic characters including Donald Duck, Maleficent, Mr. Incredible, and the Cheshire Cat become collectible LEGO® Minifigures, and the 4,080-piece Disney Castle (set 71040) becomes the biggest LEGO Disney set to date!

SEE MORE FROM MICKEY, MOANA, AND MULAN!

151

Belle (set 41595) and the Beast (set 41596) are instantly recognizable, even as LEGO BrickHeadz.

Mulan is the latest LEGO *Disney Princess*; LEGO BrickHeadz of Jack Skellington & Sally (set 41630) star in the first set based on *The Nightmare Before Christmas*; and *Incredibles 2* sets include an Elastigirl minifigure like no other.

Elastigirl's Rooftop Pursuit (set 10759) uses a single element for her long arms first used for Ms. Marvel in the LEGO® Marvel Super Heroes theme.

2017

2018

This year's LEGO *Disney* Moana's Ocean Voyage (set 41150) is the first LEGO set to combine mini dolls and big figures. Elsewhere, the first Disney-themed LEGO® BrickHeadz™ include the title characters from *Beauty and the Beast*.

Mini doll sets based on new movies *Encanto* and *Raya and the Last Dragon* include The Madrigal House (set 43202), while new minifigure subtheme Mickey and Friends sends Mickey and Minnie into outer space!

2021

Four sets based on 2009 blockbuster *Avatar* feature long minifigure arms and legs first designed for LEGO® Toy Story™ sets in 2010. Sets based on new movie *Lightyear*, meanwhile, create an all-new Buzz of their own!

Mickey Mouse & Minnie Mouse's Space Rocket (set 10774) includes new rocket ship parts with a stowaway alien print.

Six legs are better than four.

2022

Minifigure versions of Buzz Lightyear and Izzy Hawthorne star in Zyclops Chase (set 76830).

152

Scrooge McDuck and Hercules are among the diverse second Disney Series of collectible LEGO® Minifigures, while Mickey, Minnie, Goofy, and Chip 'n' Dale ride the rails in the 2,925-piece Disney Train and Station (set 71044).

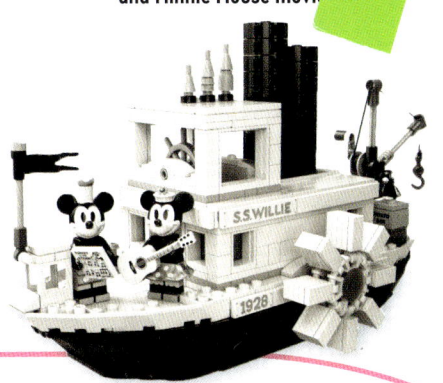

2019

Based on rides at Disney Parks, the app-controlled Disney Train and Station measures over 30 in (70 cm) long.

LEGO Ideas set Steamboat 21317) harks back to the and Minnie Mouse movi

Anna and Elsa's Storybook Adventures (set 43175) opens like a book and includes four microfigures.

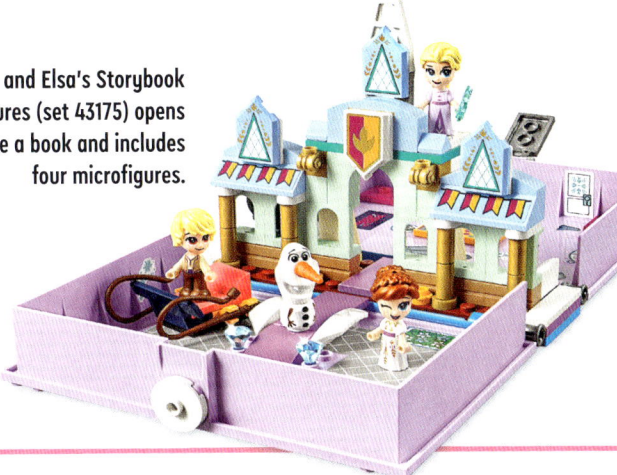

New Storybook Adventures sets open to reveal the smallest LEGO *Disney* figures so far, while display set Mickey Mouse and Minnie Mouse (set 43179) boasts the largest brick-built LEGO *Disney* figures to date.

2020

2023

Celebrating a century of the Magic Kingdom, Disney 100 sets include the "Up" House (set 43217) and Walt Disney Tribute Camera (set 43230). The Disney 100 Series of collectible Minifigures includes Pinocchio and Pocahontas.

Walt Disney Tribute Camera includes Bambi and Dumbo figures and the first ever minifigure of Walt himself.

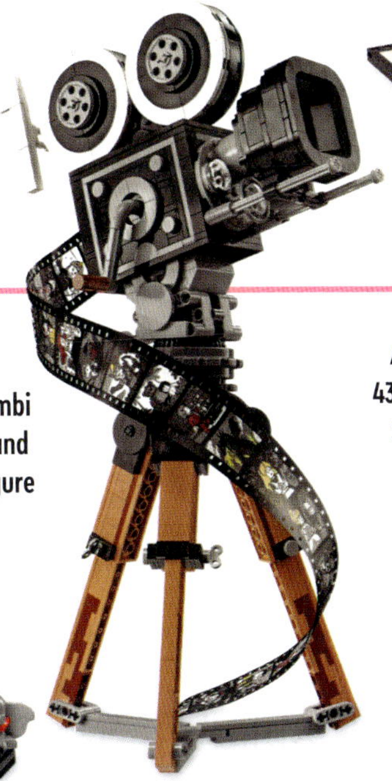

Asha's Cottage (set 43231) is one of three 2023 sets based on new movie *Wish*.

153

DISNEY CASTLE

The largest set in the LEGO® *Disney 100* range, Disney Castle celebrates a century of Disney movies in style. It is inspired by the Cinderella Castle at Walt Disney World in Florida (itself based on the fairytale palace in the 1950 *Cinderella* movie). Here, Cinders shares the castle with her LEGO® *Disney Princess*™ pals Rapunzel, Snow White, and Tiana.

SET NUMBER	43222
PIECES	4,835
MINIFIGURES	8
SIZE	32 in (80 cm) tall, 24 in (59 cm) wide

- Flag shows the real-life Disney family coat of arms
- Fireworks made from colorful transparent pieces
- Cinderella's pumpkin before it becomes a carriage
- 1,133 pearl gold parts are used to decorate the Castle
- Raised portcullis is a unique printed part
- The enchanted clock approaches midnight—the time when fairy magic wears off
- Mulan's sword
- Ten printed tiles are used as arrow slit "windows"
- Dinglehopper from *The Little Mermaid*
- This might just be an enchanted frog prince!

DISNEY TIME

Glass slipper from *Cinderella*

Sleeping Beauty's bed

Enchanted rose from *Beauty and the Beast*

Tiana | Cinderella | Rapunzel | Snow White

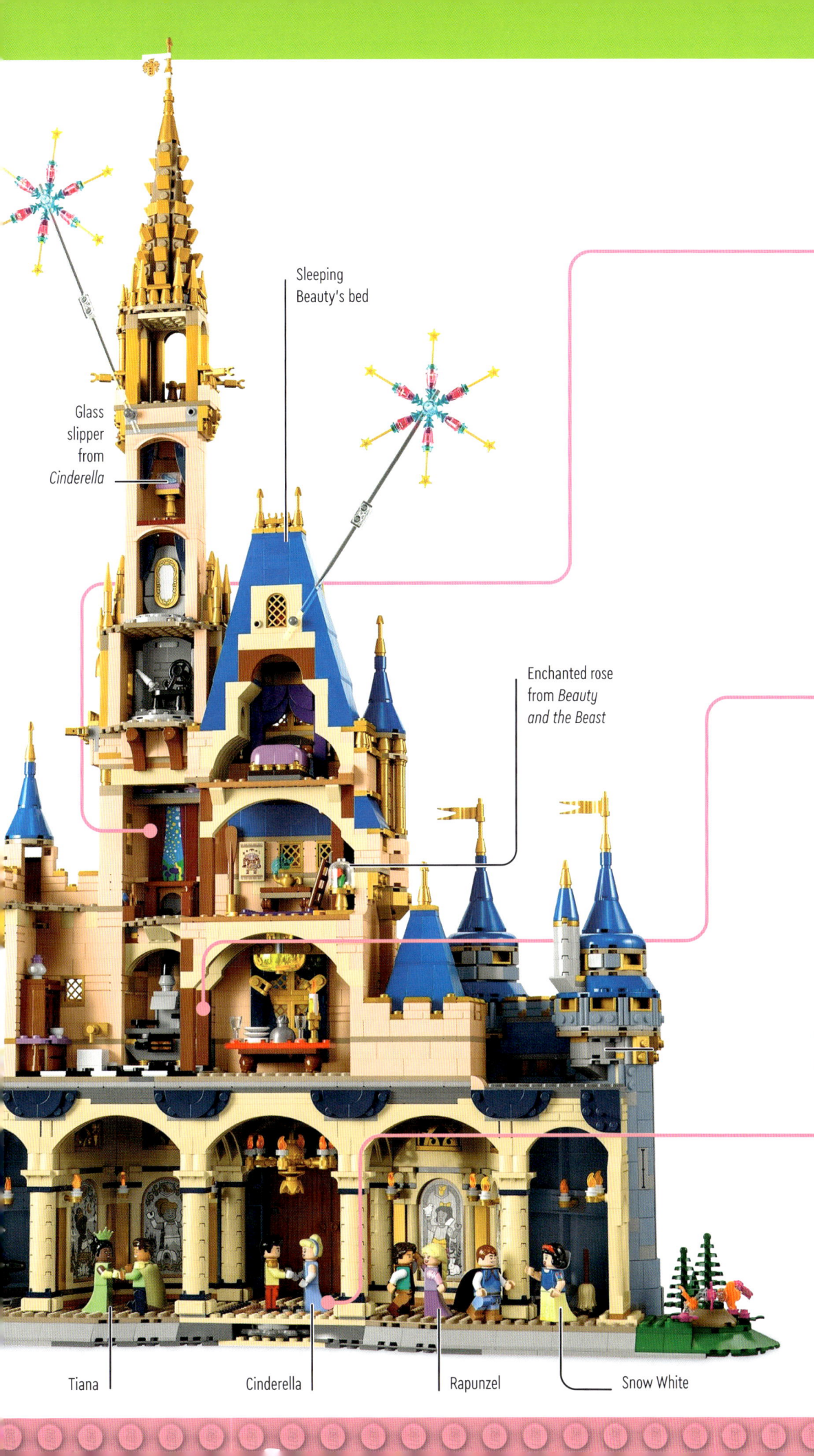

Rapunzel's room includes the painting she makes in *Tangled*, showing the lanterns that her parents launch into the sky every year on her birthday.

This room is based on *Beauty and the Beast*, but it is Prince Naveen and Tiana from *The Princess and the Frog* who have come to dinner!

Turn the wheel hidden beneath the dance floor to see Cinderella and Prince Charming take a spin in the magnificent royal ballroom.

155

NINJA, GO!

For more than a decade, LEGO® NINJAGO® has told heroic tales of an elementally empowered ninja team and their martial arts mentor, Wu. Every year has brought new sets, new minifigure friends and foes, and new animated TV adventures, with latest TV show LEGO® NINJAGO®: *Dragons Rising* taking ninja action to the next level!

The first NINJAGO set to have more than 2,000 pieces is Temple of Airjitzu (set 70751).

Zane and P.I.X.A.L. take on flying Nindroids in NinjaCopter (set 70724).

There's more NINJAGO than ever in 2015, with two seasons of the TV show, and sets based on both. *Tournament of Elements* introduces villainous Master Chen, while *Possession* sees Nya become the official sixth ninja.

2015 — TOURNAMENT OF ELEMENTS AND POSSESSION

It's a whole new, high-tech world for the ninja as they battle the Digital Overlord and get a new Nindroid team member called P.I.X.A.L. This year also sees Lloyd get his familiar Green Ninja look and Garmadon turn into a good guy.

2014 — REBOOTED

Lloyd wears Golden Ninja gear to battle his bad dad in Temple of Light (set 70505).

The third year of LEGO NINJAGO is planned to be the last, with a storyline pitting the ninja against Garmadon and his Stone Army. But the tale of Lloyd becoming the fifth ninja proves so popular that the theme cannot be stopped!

2013 — THE FINAL BATTLE

2016
SKYBOUND AND DAY OF THE DEPARTED

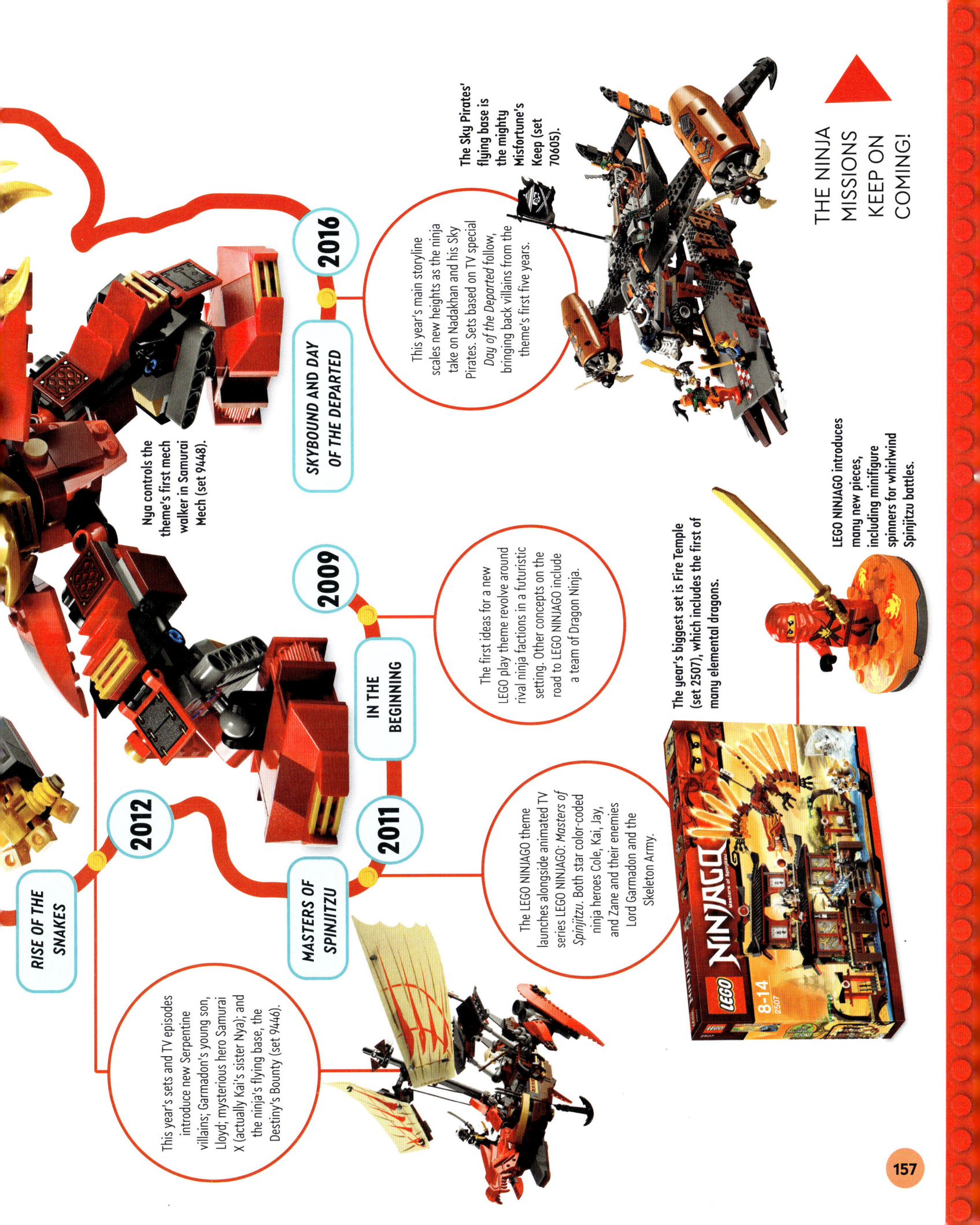

This year's main storyline scales new heights as the ninja take on Nadakhan and his Sky Pirates. Sets based on TV special *Day of the Departed* follow, bringing back villains from the theme's first five years.

The Sky Pirates' flying base is the mighty Misfortune's Keep (set 70605).

2012
RISE OF THE SNAKES

This year's sets and TV episodes introduce new Serpentine villains; Garmadon's young son, Lloyd; mysterious hero Samurai X (actually Kai's sister Nya); and the ninja's flying base, the Destiny's Bounty (set 9446).

Nya controls the theme's first mech walker in Samurai Mech (set 9448).

2009
IN THE BEGINNING

The first ideas for a new LEGO play theme revolve around rival ninja factions in a futuristic setting. Other concepts on the road to LEGO NINJAGO include a team of Dragon Ninja.

2011
MASTERS OF SPINJITZU

The LEGO NINJAGO theme launches alongside animated TV series LEGO NINJAGO: *Masters of Spinjitzu*. Both star color-coded ninja heroes Cole, Kai, Jay, and Zane and their enemies Lord Garmadon and the Skeleton Army.

The year's biggest set is Fire Temple (set 2507), which includes the first of many elemental dragons.

LEGO NINJAGO introduces many new pieces, including minifigure spinners for whirlwind Spinjitzu battles.

THE NINJA MISSIONS KEEP ON COMING!

2017 — THE HANDS OF TIME

The year begins with the ninja tackling the Time Twins and their Vermillion servants on TV and in sets such as Dawn of Iron Doom (set 70626). Then things take a broader, blockbuster turn in THE LEGO® NINJAGO® MOVIE™.

The 4,867-piece NINJAGO City (set 70620) is the first in a new series of mammoth modular NINJAGO buildings.

PRIME EMPIRE AND MASTER OF THE MOUNTAIN — 2020

Skull Sorcerer's Dungeons (set 71722) is one of several board-game-style sets with spinners that work like dice.

The ninja become in-game avatars with health bars above their heads in *Prime Empire* sets such as Kai's Mech Jet (set 71707).

The *Prime Empire* storyline and sets trap the ninja in a video game world ruled by unlovable Unagami. Then *Master of the Mountain* introduces the scary Skull Sorcerer and sets that can be played as actual board games!

New villains the Snake Warriors slither into a new range of LEGO NINJAGO sets that are not based on a TV show.

Nya becomes one with the ocean in the epic Temple of the Endless Sea (set 71755)!

2021 — THE ISLAND AND SEABOUND

There's nonstop aquatic action in this year's sets, based on the *Seabound* TV season and its lead-in miniseries, *The Island*. Both revolve around a sacred Storm Amulet, sought by a sea-monster-loving tribe and the cruel underwater king, Kalmaar.

Gold-colored minifigures in seven sets mark 10 years of LEGO NINJAGO. They include this metallic Master Wu in NINJAGO City Gardens (set 71741).

2022 — CRYSTALLIZED

Old enemies including the Overlord and the Skull Sorcerer return in the final season of the LEGO NINJAGO TV series! It takes all the ninja's combined powers to form Lloyd's Golden Ultra Dragon (set 71774) and defeat them!

158

NINJA, GO!

Two TV seasons per year is the new normal, as the ninja battle a biker gang in the *Sons of Garmadon* storyline and Dragon Hunters in *Hunted*. Sets based on both see wise old Master Wu turned into a baby and a teenager.

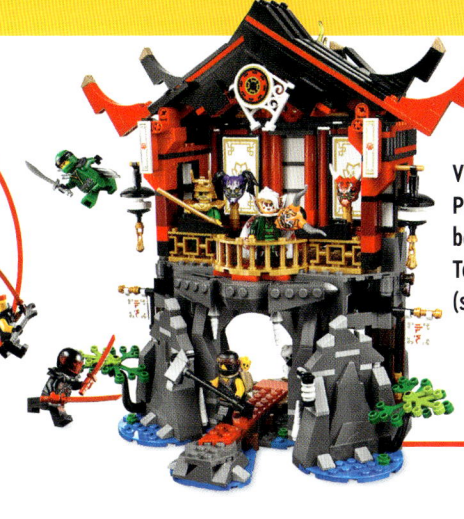

Villainous gang leader Princess Harumi brings back bad Garmadon in Temple of Resurrection (set 70643).

Teen Wu and the ninja take on the Dragon Hunters' rolling base in Dieselnaut (set 70654).

2018 — SONS OF GARMADON AND HUNTED

This year's new NINJAGO: Legacy range celebrates past seasons with sets such as Jay's Storm Fighter (set 70668), based on 2012's *Rise of the Snakes*.

Forbidden Spinjitzu sets such as Fire Fang (set 70674) feature a new kind of ninja spinner.

MARCH OF THE ONI AND SECRETS OF THE FORBIDDEN SPINJITZU — **2019**

Oni Battle Pack (set 853866) is the only set to tie in with short TV season *March of the Oni*, while nine sets depict the ninja's clashes with Pyro Vipers and Blizzard Warriors in full-length season *Secrets of the Forbidden Spinjitzu*.

This year's new "core" baddies are the Bone King and his Green Bone Warriors.

2023 — DRAGONS RISING — **2024** — DRAGONS RISING II

It's all change as brand-new animated series LEGO NINJAGO: *Dragons Rising* arrives with a fresh look and two extra ninja. New team members Sora and Arin star in sets such as Sora's Transforming Mech Bike Racer (set 71792).

In the second year of *Dragons Rising*, we meet the theme's first ever Master Dragon. Egalt the Master Dragon (set 71809) has a Master Wu-style hat and beard and the wisdom to help the ninja battle new villain Lord Ras.

2023
NINJAGO CITY MARKETS

The fourth in a range of giant Ninjago City sets is the biggest and most ambitious so far. Its working cable car links an ancient marketplace to ultramodern ninja hangouts above, including a phone store, a sushi bar, and a karaoke club. A total of 21 minifigures populate the bustling scene—nearly all of them exclusive to this set.

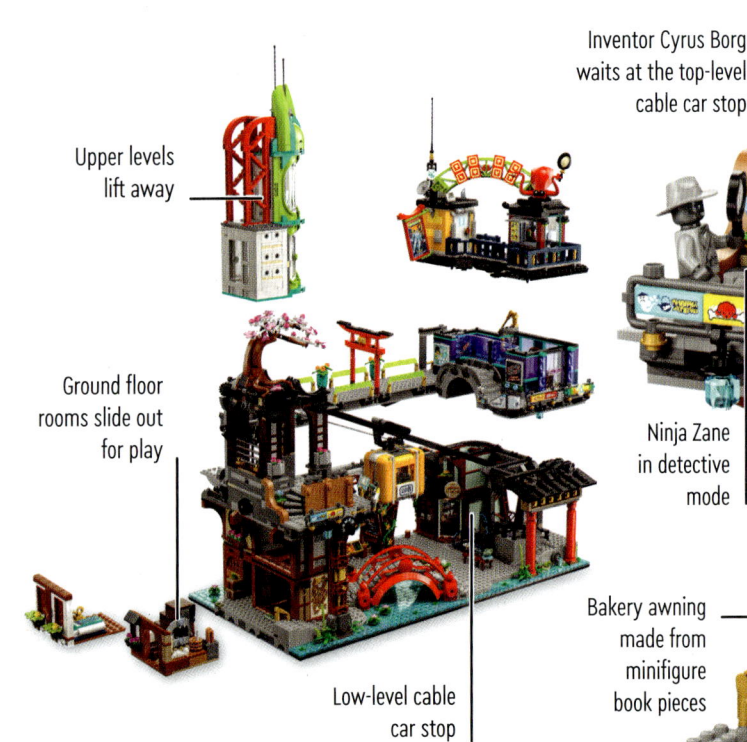

- Borg Store is the place to go for tech advice
- Cable car mechanism relies on a simple thread
- Sheriff Hounddog McBrag is on the case!
- Inventor Cyrus Borg waits at the top-level cable car stop
- Upper levels lift away
- Ground floor rooms slide out for play
- Ninja Zane in detective mode
- Low-level cable car stop
- Bakery awning made from minifigure book pieces
- Bridge made from LEGO® Technic wheel arches
- Kai's blacksmith shop

SET NUMBER	71799
PIECES	6,163
MINIFIGURES	21
SIZE	19 in (46 cm) tall, 21 in (51 cm) wide

NINJA, GO!

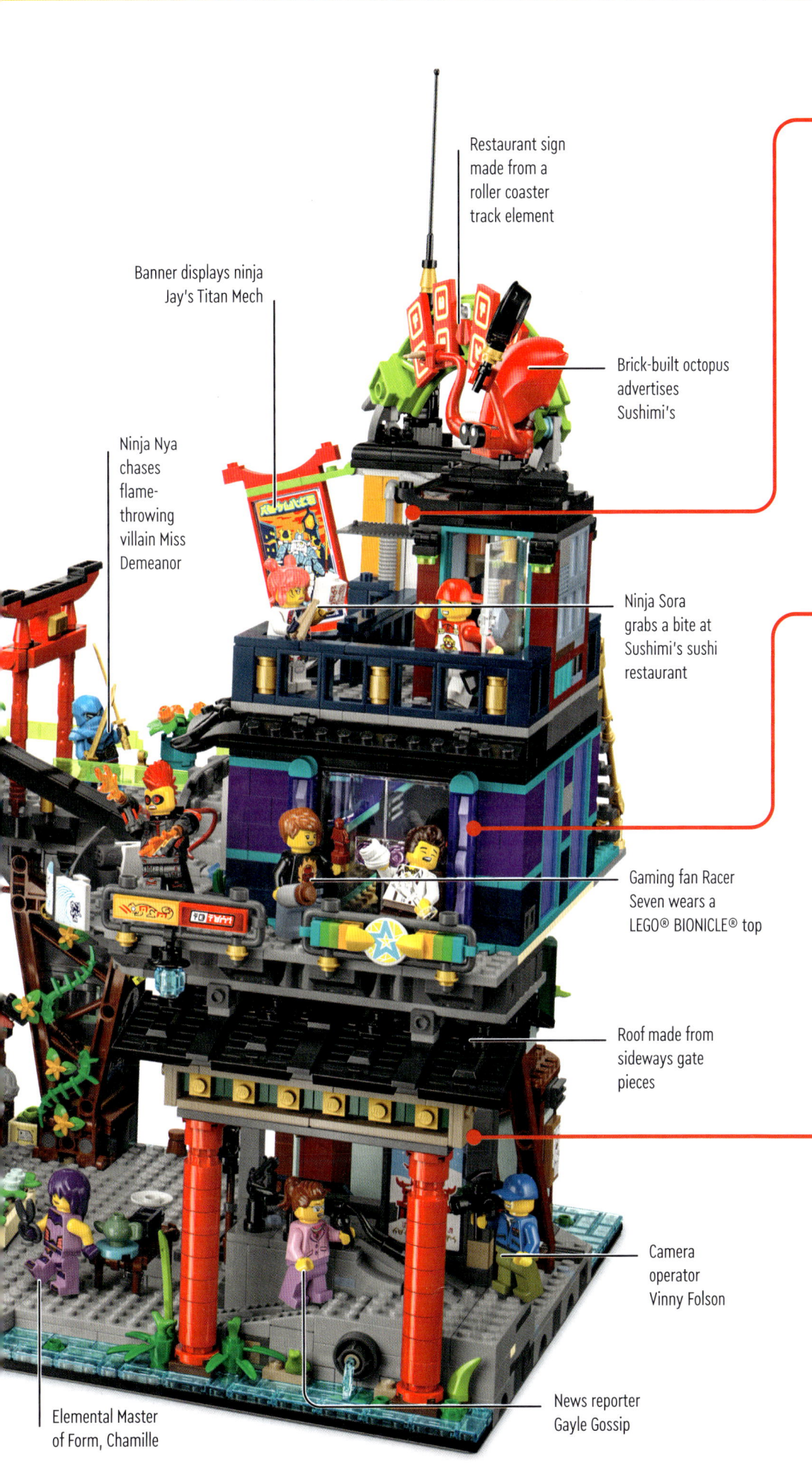

- Restaurant sign made from a roller coaster track element
- Banner displays ninja Jay's Titan Mech
- Brick-built octopus advertises Sushimi's
- Ninja Nya chases flame-throwing villain Miss Demeanor
- Ninja Sora grabs a bite at Sushimi's sushi restaurant
- Gaming fan Racer Seven wears a LEGO® BIONICLE® top
- Roof made from sideways gate pieces
- Camera operator Vinny Folson
- News reporter Gayle Gossip
- Elemental Master of Form, Chamille

The top-floor toilet has a working flush! Pressing the handle ejects 1×1 round tiles from the bowl and out through the back of the set.

In Laughy's Karaoke Club, the ninja can play pool and darts with owner Dareth before spinning some disks on the retro jukebox.

The youngest ninja, Arin and Sora, share a small apartment decorated with ninja memorabilia. Check out Arin's microfigures of Cole and Jay!

161

IDEAS WELCOME

LEGO® building has always been about ideas, but turning fans' creations into official sets is a relatively recent development. Today, the **LEGO® Ideas** website is home to hundreds of fan-made builds, all submitted in the hope that they will become real LEGO sets for sale in the stores.

The first ever fan-designed set is Blacksmith Shop (set 3739), released as a "My Own Creation" set. It is sold exclusively on the brand-new "LEGO Shop at Home" website!

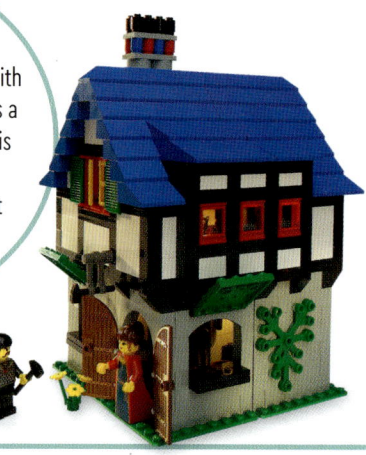

2002

The Grand Piano is 14 in (36 cm) long and made from 3,662 pieces.

Grand Piano (set 21323) is the first motorized LEGO Ideas set and the most ambitious so far. It pairs with an app to play actual piano music, while the keys move by themselves!

The 39-in (100-cm) NASA Apollo Saturn V (set 21309) becomes the tallest LEGO set of the decade, while Old Fishing Store (set 21310) is the first Ideas set with more than 2,000 pieces.

2020

2017

Guitar fans thrill to the Fender Stratocaster (set 21329), which can be built with a red or black body, while movie fans can get festive with the house from Home Alone (set 21330).

2021

With 3,955 pieces, Home Alone is the biggest LEGO Ideas set to date.

162

IDEAS WELCOME

LEGO CUUSOO

A forerunner of LEGO Ideas, the LEGO® Factory website lets fan builders design their own sets and submit them for production. Eight LEGO Factory sets are released over the next four years.

Fans voted for Airport (set 5524) to become one of the first LEGO Factory sets.

With a name meaning "fantasy," the LEGO® CUUSOO website launches in Japan. Fan builders in that country can upload their own build ideas and vote for the ones they want to see as real sets.

2005

2008

In space, no one can wear more green!

LEGO CUUSOO becomes LEGO Ideas, and the submission rules are changed so people under the age of 18 can join in too! Exo Suit (set 21109) is one of the first sets to carry the LEGO Ideas logo.

The 412-piece Shinkai 6500 is based on a real-life Japanese submarine.

LEGO CUUSOO goes worldwide, giving anyone the chance to submit and vote on potential sets. The first set to be released under the CUUSOO banner is Shinkai 6500 (set 21100).

Exo Suit is the only set to feature classic-style LEGO astronauts in green.

2014

2011

The Globe (set 21332) and Jazz Quartet (set 21334) offer two very different display pieces—one glows in the dark and really spins, while the other blows after dark and really swings!

Proving that there are no limits when it comes to LEGO Ideas, this year's sets include one based on enormous insects and another based on the world's biggest boy band, BTS!

The Insect Collection (set 21342) includes life-size butterfly, beetle, and mantis models.

2022

2023

BTS Dynamite (set 21339) is based on one of the band's most famous music videos.

163

FRIENDS FOREVER

FRIENDS FOREVER

In 2012, the brand-new LEGO® Friends theme introduced the world to the mini doll. Larger and more realistic than minifigures, each one was an individual who added something new to the idyllic brick-built world of Heartlake City. Today, there are more LEGO Friends than ever.

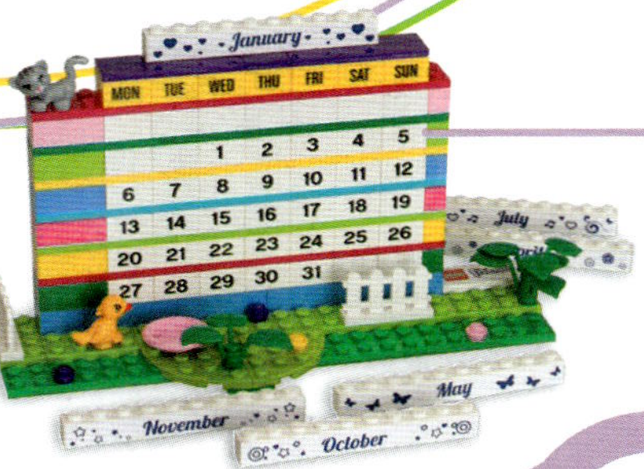

The first life-size accessories for Friends fans include a buildable calendar.

Sets such as Hedgehog's Hideaway (set 41020) are all about the animals, with no mini dolls at all.

Emma is the DJ at a jungle rescue charity fashion show in Heartlake Shopping Mall.

New Jungle Rescue sets such as First Aid Jungle Bike (set 41032) take the Friends out of Heartlake City—before the huge Heartlake Shopping Mall (set 41058) brings them back for a well-deserved day out.

Andrea plays the grand piano in the 1,552-piece Heartlake Grand Hotel (set 41101).

There's a superstar in Heartlake City, as singing sensation Livi arrives in her Pop Star Tour Bus (set 41106). Meanwhile, the Heartlake Grand Hotel gets five-star reviews as the biggest Friends set of the decade.

An animated LEGO Friends TV series debuts in the US, and the girls explore new interests in sets such as Mia's Magic Tricks (set 41001), Emma's Karate Class (set 41002), and Stephanie's Soccer Practice (set 41011).

2013

2014

2015

Emma and Stephanie tackle climbing walls and a twisting bridge in Adventure Camp Tree House (set 41122).

This year's Amusement Park range includes bumper cars, a hot-dog-shaped food truck, and the first ever full-loop LEGO roller coaster! Thrill-seeking mini dolls can also enjoy the wild life in five Adventure Camp sets.

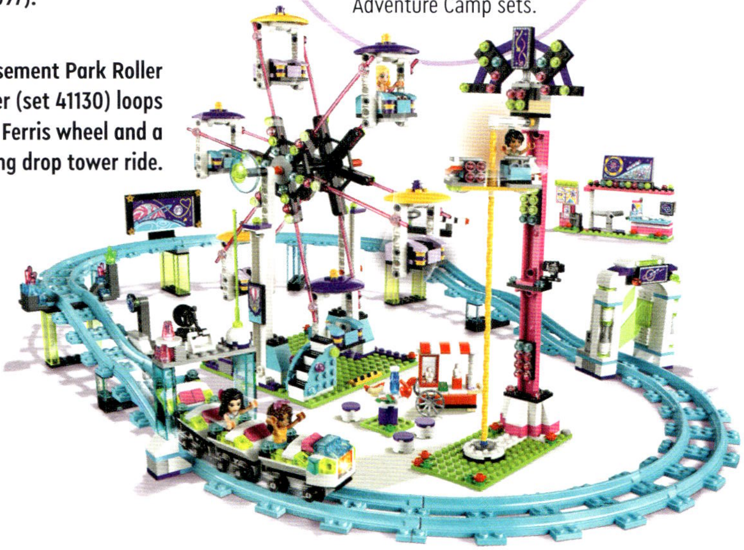

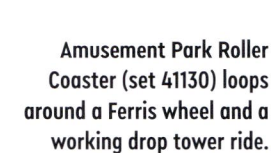

2016

Amusement Park Roller Coaster (set 41130) loops around a Ferris wheel and a working drop tower ride.

SEE MORE SETS AND MEET NEW FRIENDS!

New curved pieces? The sky's the limit!

Huge new curved pieces make this year's Heartlake Hot Air Balloon (set 41097).

2008

Work begins to create a new kind of LEGO figure, compatible with minifigure-scale parts and accessories but geared toward a different kind of role play. It takes four years to perfect the LEGO mini doll!

2012

LEGO Friends launches as the first mini doll play theme. It stars musical Andrea, arty Emma, animal-loving Mia, scientist Olivia, and sporty Stephanie—five teenage besties making the most of life in idyllic Heartlake City.

Olivia's House (set 3315) is the first in a series of sets based on the Friends' happy homes.

Sets such as Heartlake Vet (set 3188) introduce new animal figures and new element colors.

165

2017

It's all fun and games in new Snow Resort sets, but just to be on the safe side there is also Heartlake Hospital (set 41318)—the year's largest set—complete with ambulance, air ambulance, X-ray room, and the first Friends baby figure.

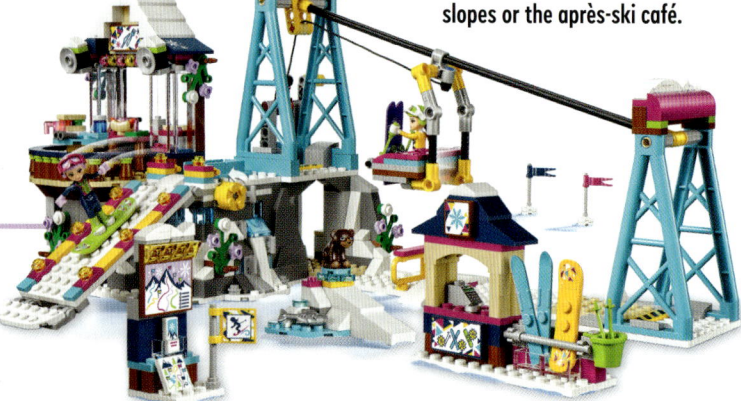

Snow Resort Ski Lift (set 41324) can take Mia and Olivia to the slopes or the après-ski café.

2021

Heartlake City gets its first wind turbine in Olivia's Electric Car (set 41443), its first fortune teller in Magical Caravan (set 41688), and its first micro doll figures representing small children in sets such as Flower Cart (set 30413).

2020

There's always room for one more adventure on the Friendship Bus (set 41395) and one more showstopping treat in Baking Competition (set 41393). Meanwhile, there are mystery animals to be found in Play Cube sets.

This year's new animal figures include alpacas, sloths, flamingos, and elephants. But which one is the mystery creature in Stephanie's Summer Play Cube (set 41411)?

2022

The first era of LEGO Friends comes to an end with epic sets such as Friendship Tree House (set 41703), Andrea's Theater School (set 41714), and the 1,682-piece Main Street Building (set 41704).

The biggest set in the original era, Main Street Building includes a hair salon, a food market, and a book café.

FRIENDS FOREVER

All five Friends get updated looks in 2018 sets such as Friendship House.

Cool new Heartlake hangouts include converted fire station Friendship House (set 41340) and holiday hot spot Heartlake City Resort (set 41347). But the go-kart track is where it's at in five fast and fabulous racing sets.

Heartlake City Resort visitors can ride a monorail from their room straight to the water slides.

2018

Rescue Mission sets send the Friends out to sea to protect dolphins, seals, and other wildlife. The latest Amusement Park sets also have an ocean vibe, while pocket-size Heart Box sets showcase the girls' many hobbies.

Rescue Mission Boat (set 41381) includes a cute and unique narwhal figure.

2019

Emma's Heart Box (set 41355) highlights her love of drawing, photography, customizing clothes, and cupcakes.

This year's sets welcome a whole new group of LEGO Friends: Aliya, Nova, Zac, Liann, Paisley, Leo, Autumn, and Olly. They study together at Heartlake International School (set 41731) and hang out at the colorful Heartlake City Community Center (set 41748).

Heartlake City Community Center includes an art studio, a music room, and first-generation Friends star Stephanie as the ribbon-cutting mayor!

2023

167

2024

ANDREA'S MODERN MANSION

•	SET NUMBER	42639
•	PIECES	2,275
•	MINI DOLLS	9 + 1 micro doll
•	SIZE	12 in (29 cm) tall, 18 in (45 cm) wide

Two generations of LEGO® Friends come together in this designer dream home. All five of the original Friends are here as grown-ups, alongside newer characters Autumn, Leo, and Paisley. Completing the party are Andrea's husband Ji-Won and their daughter, Imani.

This dial works the elevator that links all three floors

Waterfall flows from the rooftop garden

Andrea's bedroom has a rotating bed so she can turn to greet the sunrise

Grand piano overlooks a dining area

Andrea's license plate reads "POP-ST4R"

This basement recording studio doubles as a guest bedroom

Andrea drives a dark turquoise sports car with coral wheels

Leo snaps a selfie with astronaut Olivia

Stephanie and Mia make the most of the pool area

168

FRIENDS FOREVER

Every singer's home needs a karaoke machine

Ji-Won, Andrea, and Imani admire a bird on the rooftop terrace

Paisley and Autumn enjoy the hot tub

This dial opens and closes the garage door

Emma readies her camera to capture reunion memories

Andrea is now a superstar singer and entrepreneur, while Stephanie is mayor of Heartlake City. Andrea's family photos help the pair catch up.

Visitors can't get enough of Andrea's hot tub! Like the rest of the mansion, it has an ultramodern design that seems to defy the laws of gravity.

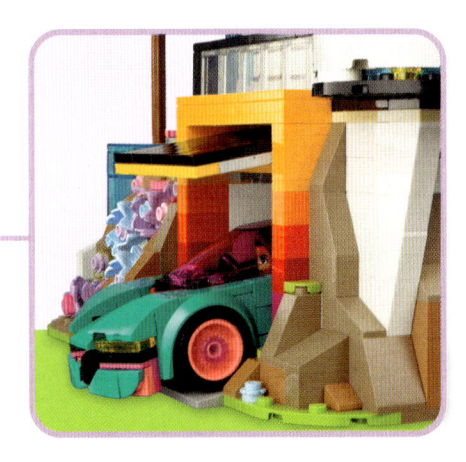

Turning a dial operates the garage door and tilts the floor so the car rolls out as the door lifts up.

SUPER SETS AND BAT-TASTIC BUILDS!

It began with LEGO® DC Batman™, but today's league of **LEGO® DC Comics™ Super Heroes** goes far beyond Gotham City. As well as all-time greats Superman and Wonder Woman, there's a Super Hero—and Super Villain—for everyone among these mighty minifigures!

First and best!

The first minifigure Super Hero from the DC Universe is LEGO® Batman™, who stars in his own theme, starting this year. Six sets pit him against iconic enemies such as the Joker, Catwoman, and the Riddler.

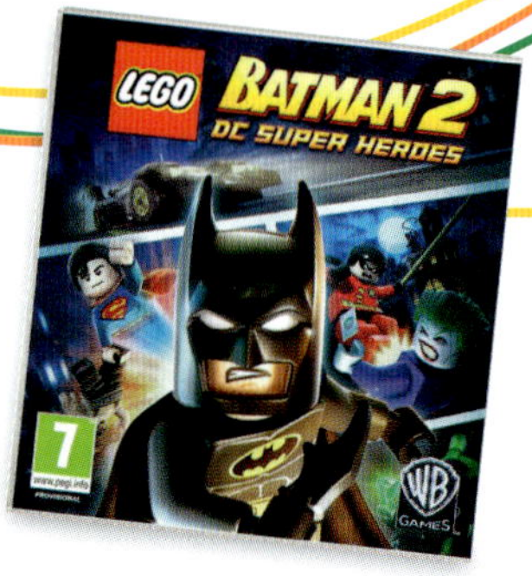

2006

Video game LEGO *Batman 2: DC Super Heroes* ties in the new Super Heroes theme with its predecessor, LEGO *Batman*.

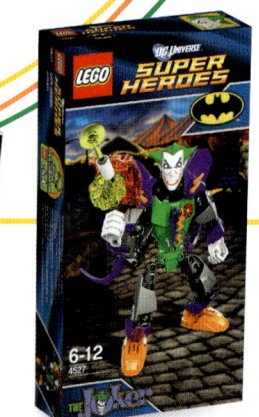

The Joker (set 4527) is the first villain to be made as a large-scale figure.

Both heroes in Superman vs. Power Armor Lex (set 6862) come with a choice of serious or smiling facial expressions.

The first Aquaman minifigure features in Arctic Batman vs. Mr. Freeze: Aquaman on Ice (set 76000).

New movie *Man of Steel* inspires three Superman sets, while a key scene from 2012 Batman film *The Dark Knight Rises* is re-created in The Bat vs. Bane: Tumbler Chase (set 76001).

A new version of The Tumbler (set 76023) is the largest set in the theme so far, with 1,869 pieces. The display model measures 17 in (43 cm) long, and comes with a fact-filled plaque.

2013

Kryptonian villain General Zod stars in Superman: Metropolis Showdown (set 76002).

2014

SUPER SETS AND BAT-TASTIC BUILDS!

The Batmobile: Ultimate Collectors' Edition (set 7784) is the only LEGO Batman set bigger than minifigure scale.

The Batcave: The Penguin and Mr. Freeze's Invasion (set 7783) is the first set to feature Robin, Alfred Pennyworth, and Bruce Wayne minifigures.

The LEGO Batman theme bows out with the first Harley Quinn minifigure, the first LEGO model of the Tumbler (from *The Dark Knight* movie trilogy), and a smash-hit video game.

2008

Harley is a big hit in The Batcycle: Harley Quinn's Hammer Truck (set 7886).

The first wave of LEGO DC Comics Super Heroes sets includes buildable action figures, six minifigure-scale Batman sets, and the first minifigures of Wonder Woman and Lex Luthor.

Comics fans get a preview of the LEGO DC Comics Super Heroes theme when limited edition Batman, Superman, and Green Lantern minifigures are given away at events in the US.

This New York Comic Con exclusive Green Lantern minifigure is mounted on a newspaper-style backing card.

2012

2011

The Flash and Batgirl team up with Batman for the first time in 2014's minifigure-scale sets.

Super Heroes arrive in LEGO® DUPLO® sets such as Batwing Adventure (set 10823).

A new series of LEGO DC Super Heroes DVD movies begins with *Justice League vs. Bizarro League*.

2015

Darkseid Invasion (set 76028) is the first full set to include a Green Arrow minifigure.

Justice League sets introduce Super Heroes Cyborg, Hawkman, and Supergirl, "big fig" Super Villains Gorilla Grodd and Darkseid—and new Super Jumper pieces that make minifigures fly!

TO THE BATCAVE!

LEGO *Batman 3: Beyond Gotham* completes the LEGO Batman video game trilogy.

171

There's all-new action in sets based on *Batman V Superman: Dawn of Justice*, and all-old action in Batman® Classic TV Series Batcave (set 76052), inspired by the 1966 Bat-show.

The 2,526-piece Batman Classic TV Series Batcave tops 2014's Tumbler set as the biggest DC Comics Super Heroes set so far.

New Mighty Micros sets such as Robin vs. Bane (set 76062) put a cartoon-style spin on classic characters.

Super Heroes launch the LEGO® BrickHeadz™ theme in event-exclusive sets such as Superman & Wonder Woman (set 41490).

2016

Each Minifigure in the DC Super Heroes series comes with a buildable stand for mid-air action poses.

The LEGO® Minifigures theme launches its own DC Super Heroes series, giving love to some lesser known characters such as Bumblebee, Metamorpho, Bat-Mite, and Stargirl. There are set releases for both iconic and new movies too.

Super Hero Shazam! features in two 2019 sets, including Batman Batwing and The Riddler Heist (set 76120).

Wonder Woman vs. Cheetah (set 76157) ties in with new movie *Wonder Woman 1984*.

2020

From the 1989 *Batman* movie, 1989 Batwing (set 76161) is the latest large-scale display set released, boasting 2,363 pieces.

2021

Batman Cowl (set 76182) stands an imposing 8.5 in (22 cm) tall and is made from 410 pieces.

Buildable Batman cowls are the latest way to display your Caped Crusader love! Two very different designs show how the World's Greatest Detective has changed his look over time.

Classic TV Series Batman Cowl (set 76238) is based on the mask worn by Batman actor Adam West in the 1960s.

172

SUPER SETS AND BAT-TASTIC BUILDS!

2017

Blockbuster films *Wonder Woman* and *Justice League* inspire this year's biggest sets, while LEGO Batman gets his own theme for the second time, thanks to THE LEGO® BATMAN MOVIE.

A new-look Aquaman launches new Power Blast pieces in Battle of Atlantis (set 76085).

Wonder Woman Warrior Battle (set 76075) includes a brick-built Ares with giant minifigure proportions.

2018

App-Controlled Batmobile (set 76112) has room inside for Batman, two motors, and a Bluetooth hub.

As Aquaman gets his own movie, Superman gets a Super Dog; the Flash gets an archenemy; and Batman gets a new ally in Batwoman, an app-controlled Batmobile, AND a dog!

2019

Named after the year of the Batman film that inspired it, 1989 Batmobile (set 76139) is the first Super Heroes set with more than 3,000 pieces. It is 24 in (60 cm) long from tip to tail fins.

Superman & Krypto Team-Up (set 76096) comes with a special Super Dog collar and cape.

2022

New movie *The Batman* is the basis for three minifigure-scale sets and the first ever LEGO® Technic Super Heroes set. Elsewhere, the LEGO® Art theme celebrates classic comic books.

LEGO Technic's The Batman—Batmobile (set 42127) has working lights and steering, and a spinning exhaust flame.

Inspired by the famous comic artist, Jim Lee™ Batman Collection (set 31205) is a LEGO Art project that can be built as a mosaic of Batman, the Joker, or Harley Quinn.

2023

For the first time since 2012, LEGO DC Comics Super Heroes gets a new buildable action figure. Meanwhile, Batcave—Shadow Box (set 76252) becomes the theme's biggest set.

Batman Construction Figure (set 76259) has 22 points of articulation, including individually posable fingers.

2022 BATCAVE—SHADOW BOX

This stunning display set is a Batman movie in a brick-built box! Inspired by 1992's *Batman Returns*, it shows the Caped Crusader's secret base as seen through a giant, bat-symbol-shaped window. The window opens up for full access to the epic interior, complete with its ultra-realistic Batmobile.

Garage door opens and closes at the touch of a button

It wouldn't be a Batcave without bats hanging from the ceiling!

Turning a dial on the back of the build switches the Batcomputer's main display between images of Catwoman and the Penguin.

This Batsuit stands in front of a chamber with a drawbridge-style door. The Batsuit can be stored inside, illuminated by a light brick.

An armory of Batarangs can be sealed behind heavy-duty sliding doors, operated by another dial on the back of the set.

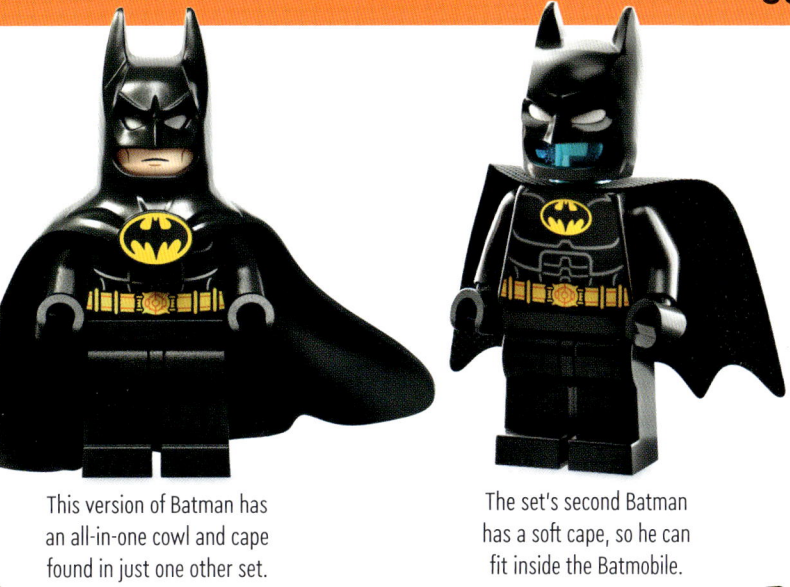

SUPER SETS AND BAT-TASTIC BUILDS!

This version of Batman has an all-in-one cowl and cape found in just one other set.

The set's second Batman has a soft cape, so he can fit inside the Batmobile.

Bruce Wayne has a similar smirk to Batman. Could they be related?

Butler Alfred wears a suit, white gloves, and a stern expression.

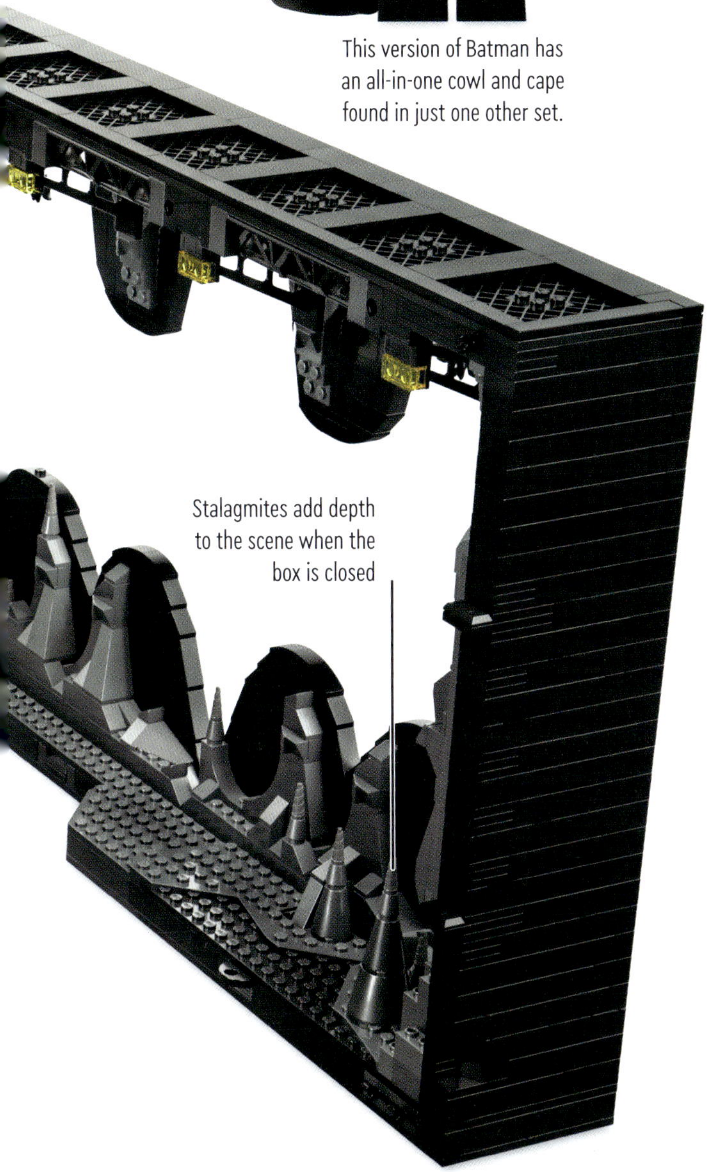

Stalagmites add depth to the scene when the box is closed

The Penguin's huge hat makes him as tall as standard minifigures.

Max Shreck looks like a respectable businessman but is really a bad guy.

Catwoman's costume shows off the stitching she used to sew it.

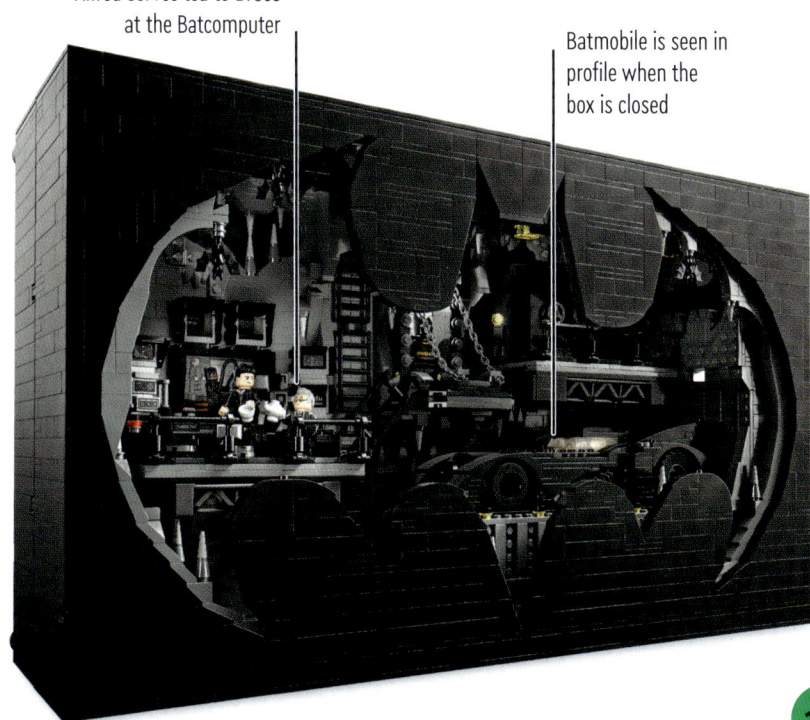

Alfred serves tea to Bruce at the Batcomputer

Batmobile is seen in profile when the box is closed

SET NUMBER	76252
PIECES	3,981
MINIFIGURES	7
SIZE	12 in (29 cm) tall, 21 in (51 cm) wide

MAKE MINE MARVEL!

First there were Marvel Comics. Next there was the Marvel Cinematic Universe (MCU). Then there was the **LEGO® Marvel Super Heroes** theme! Since 2012, it has delved into comic books, movies, and animated series to assemble sets from across the Marvel Multiverse. Most sets are sized for minifigures—others are incredible Hulks!

The first LEGO Marvel minifigures appear in three LEGO® Studios sets depicting the making of a Spider-Man movie.

2002

LEGO® Spider-Man™ becomes a play theme in its own right, with sets such as Spider-Man and Green Goblin—The Origins (set 4851) based on scenes from the 2002 film Marvel Studios' *Spider-Man*.

2003

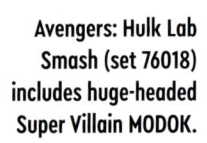

Avengers: Hulk Lab Smash (set 76018) includes huge-headed Super Villain MODOK.

Guardian of the Galaxy Groot is a brick-built giant in Knowhere Escape Mission (set 76020).

When Marvel Studios' *Guardians of the Galaxy* film takes the MCU into outer space, LEGO Marvel Super Heroes sets are quick to follow! Back on Earth, two sets celebrate the animated *Avengers Assemble* TV show.

2014

This year's Marvel Cinematic Universe sets go suitably small with Ant-Man Final Battle (set 76039), and bigger than ever with 2,996-piece The SHIELD Helicarrier (set 76042), measuring 31 in (80 cm) long.

The larger than life-size Ant-Man Final Battle includes a new Super Jumper launcher for flying minifigure fun.

2015

The SHIELD Helicarrier comes with microfigures of Captain America, Iron Man, Hawkeye, and Nick Fury.

176

MAKE MINE MARVEL!

To announce the launch of LEGO Marvel Super Heroes, 125 limited-edition Iron Man and Captain America minifigures are given away at a New York event in February. The first full sets follow in May.

The theme launches with three large buildable figures, including The Hulk (set 4530).

Four minifigure-scale sets are based on Marvel Studios' *The Avengers* film, with a fifth, Wolverine's Chopper Showdown (set 6866), inspired by the X-Men.

2012

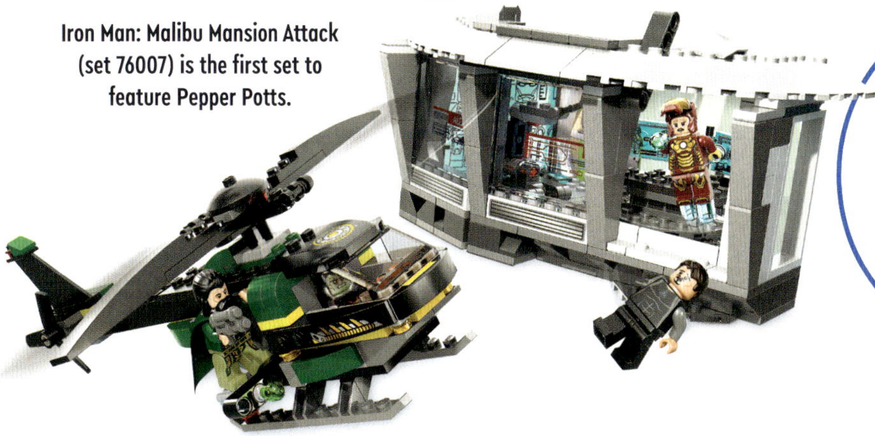

Iron Man: Malibu Mansion Attack (set 76007) is the first set to feature Pepper Potts.

This year's sets take their cues from blockbuster new movie Marvel Studios' *Iron Man 3* and the animated TV series *Ultimate Spider-Man*. Meanwhile, video game LEGO® Marvel Super Heroes becomes a smash hit in its own right!

Spider-Man: Spider-Cycle Chase (set 76004) puts Nick Fury in a flying S.H.I.E.L.D. car.

2013

The Sorcerer Supreme is one of the first characters to get the LEGO® BrickHeadz™ treatment in event-exclusive set Black Panther & Doctor Strange (set 41493).

It's an epic year for LEGO Marvel Super Heroes, with movie sets based on Marvel Studios' *Captain America: Civil War* and *Doctor Strange*, the biggest Spider-Man set of the decade, the first BrickHeadz, and the first wave of Mighty Micros cars.

Three Spider-Heroes take on three villains in the 1,092-piece Spider-Man: Web Warriors Ultimate Bridge Battle (set 76057).

2016

Classic characters become diminutive drivers in Mighty Micros sets such as Hulk vs. Ultron (set 76066).

SEE MORE FROM THE LEGO MARVEL MULTIVERSE!

177

2017

Sets based on Marvel Studios' *Guardians of the Galaxy Vol. 2*, *Spider-Man: Homecoming*, and *Thor: Ragnarok* rub super-shoulders with animation-inspired sets featuring heroes She-Hulk and Ms. Marvel.

Captain America Jet Pursuit (set 76076) comes with new Power Blast pieces and a Ms. Marvel minifigure with extraordinary arms!

Thor vs. Hulk: Arena Clash (set 76088) comes with all-new versions of its two heroes in Sakaaran armor.

2021

In another epic year, collectible Minifigures, an advent calendar, and an enormous *Daily Bugle* building vie for attention with movie sets based on Marvel Studios' *Shang-Chi and The Legend of The Ten Rings*, *Spider-Man: No Way Home*, and *Eternals*.

This festive version of Tony Stark is exclusive to the Avengers Advent Calendar (set 76196).

Bucky Barnes (aka the Winter Soldier) is one of 12 characters in the LEGO® Minifigures Marvel Studios Series.

LEGO® Art mosaic Marvel Studios Iron Man (set 31199) can be made into three different Iron Man armor portraits.

Iron Man Helmet (set 76165) is the first in a new series of LEGO Marvel busts.

2022

This year's display sets include a 2,961-piece bust of Black Panther and a mighty Thor's Hammer (set 76209), while minifigure MCU sets celebrate Marvel Studios' *Doctor Strange in the Multiverse of Madness*, *Thor: Love and Thunder*, and *Black Panther: Wakanda Forever*.

Made from 3,772 pieces and standing 32 in (82 cm) high, Daily Bugle (set 76178) is the biggest, tallest LEGO Marvel set so far.

This 18-in (46-cm) bust of Black Panther (set 76215) can be displayed with or without its vibranium gauntlets.

Sets based on animated series *Spidey and His Amazing Friends* include the colorful Spider-Man at Doc Ock's Lab (set 10783).

MAKE MINE MARVEL!

2018

Massive display model The Hulkbuster: Ultron Edition (set 76105) celebrates 10 years of the MCU, while minifigure-scale sets depict Marvel Studios' *Black Panther*, *Avengers: Infinity War*, and *Ant-Man and The Wasp*.

Okoye rides to the rescue on a brick-built rhino in *Black Panther* set Rhino Face-Off by the Mine (set 76099).

2019

Sets inspired by Marvel Studios' *Captain Marvel*, *Avengers: Endgame*, and *Spider-Man: Far from Home* mark the end of the MCU's Infinity Saga, while heroes from across the Spider-Verse star in the latest comics-inspired sets.

The Miles Morales version of Spider-Man teams up with Peter Parker in Spider-Man Bike Rescue (set 76113).

The Thanos Mech (set 76141) wears a gauntlet loaded with all six Infinity Stones.

New mech sets put heroes and villains in robot walkers, Iron Man becomes a bust and a mosaic, and Black Widow's Helicopter Chase (set 76162) re-creates a key scene from Marvel Studios' *Black Widow*.

Black Widow, Hawkeye, Thor, and Rocket wear time travel suits in Avengers Ultimate Quinjet (set 76126).

2020

New movie sets based on Marvel Studios' *Ant-Man and The Wasp: Quantumania*, Marvel Studios' *Guardians of the Galaxy Vol. 3*, and Marvel Studios' *The Marvels* are joined by more collectible Minifigures and an all-new biggest Super Heroes set ever.

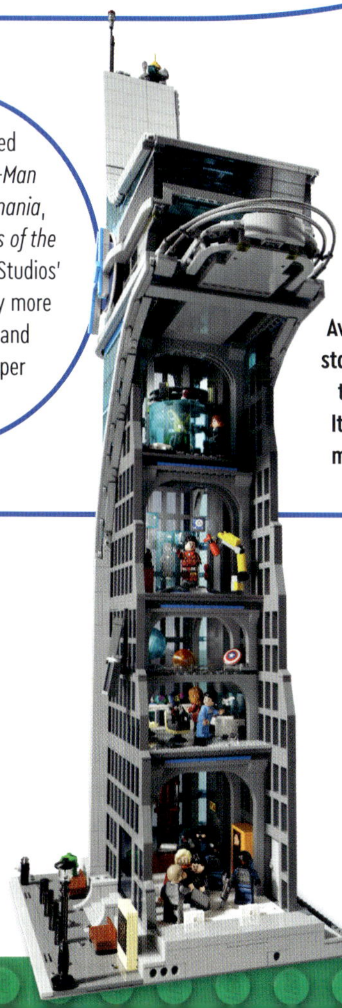

Avengers Tower (set 76269) stands 3 in (8 cm) taller than the *Daily Bugle* building! Its 5,201 pieces include 29 minifigures, a Hulk figure, and an Ant-Man figure.

2023

There's room for Captain Marvel, Ms. Marvel, Captain Monica Rambeau, and three Flerkens in The Marvels' ship, *The Hoopty* (set 76232).

Agatha Harkness and Beast from the X-Men are among this year's collectible Minifigures.

179

2022

HULKBUSTER

The mightiest LEGO® Marvel set of all is this towering take on Tony Stark's Mark 44 Iron Man armor. Launched as the largest-ever Super Heroes set, this striking display piece remains the tallest LEGO mech and boasts more metallic gold pieces than any other set. The head, chest, and shoulder pieces open up to make room for a supersize Iron Man figure!

Helmet and shoulders are hinged for easy access to cockpit

Light-up repulsors built into hands

Brick-built plaque lists vital statistics

THE INFINITY SAGA
IRON MAN
MARK 44: HULKBUSTER

ARMOUR CLASS: Special Iron Man Suit
ARMOUR TYPE: Extra Heavy Duty, Modular Armour
ARMOUR HEIGHT: 24 ft.
SPECIAL FEATURES: Multiple Repulsors, Add-Ons (from Veronica)
ARMOUR CAPABILITIES: Super Durability, Super Strength
POWER CORE: Arc Reactor

Exclusive Tony Stark minifigure in partial Iron Man armor

Unique printed helmet piece

A light brick illuminates the all-important arc reactor

Glow-in-the-dark repulsor kneepads

MAKE MINE MARVEL!

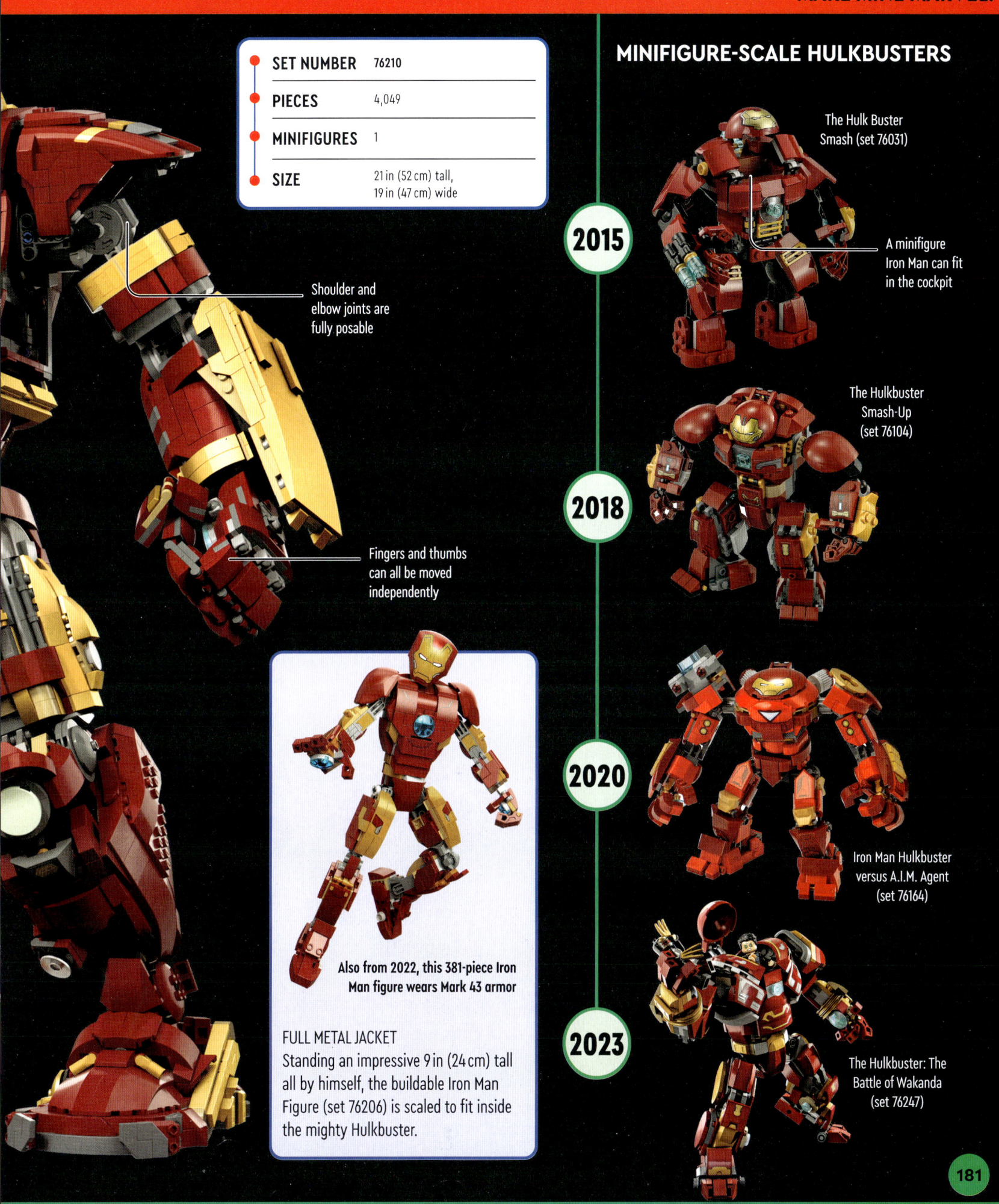

SET NUMBER	76210
PIECES	4,049
MINIFIGURES	1
SIZE	21 in (52 cm) tall, 19 in (47 cm) wide

MINIFIGURE-SCALE HULKBUSTERS

Shoulder and elbow joints are fully posable

Fingers and thumbs can all be moved independently

Also from 2022, this 381-piece Iron Man figure wears Mark 43 armor

FULL METAL JACKET
Standing an impressive 9 in (24 cm) tall all by himself, the buildable Iron Man Figure (set 76206) is scaled to fit inside the mighty Hulkbuster.

2015 — The Hulk Buster Smash (set 76031) — A minifigure Iron Man can fit in the cockpit

2018 — The Hulkbuster Smash-Up (set 76104)

2020 — Iron Man Hulkbuster versus A.I.M. Agent (set 76164)

2023 — The Hulkbuster: The Battle of Wakanda (set 76247)

181

A CHRONICLE OF MIDDLE-EARTH

LEGO® *The Hobbit*™ and LEGO® *The Lord of the Rings*™ sets are released alongside blockbuster movie *The Hobbit: An Unexpected Journey* and its sequels, mapping a minifigure version of Middle-earth. Special pieces and unique figures make the two themes extra precious.

June 2012

Seven sets launch LEGO® *The Lord of the Rings*™. Four are based on first film *The Fellowship of the Ring*, two on follow-up *The Two Towers*, and one on epic finale *The Return of the King*.

New pieces made especially for the theme include Gollum's body and arms and the One Ring itself, all of which feature in Shelob Attacks (set 9470).

The largest set in the first wave is The Battle of Helm's Deep (set 9474). Its 1,368 pieces include a new style of LEGO horse with posable rear legs.

This huge Cave Troll figure is found only in The Mines of Moria (set 9473).

Lots of new hair and beard pieces are introduced in Middle-earth sets, including Bombur the Dwarf's braided beard with its built-in belly.

December 2012

"We put the "arg!" in Warg!"

LEGO® *The Hobbit*™ sets arrive in stores at the same time as *The Hobbit: An Unexpected Journey* ventures into cinemas. They come with many new parts, including scary Warg beasts.

An Unexpected Gathering (set 79003) depicts wizard Gandalf and his Dwarvish friends descending on Hobbit Bilbo Baggins' house for dinner!

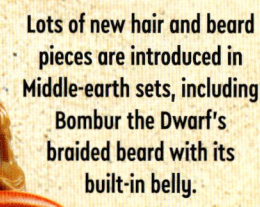

A CHRONICLE OF MIDDLE-EARTH

October 2014

Based on *The Hobbit: The Battle of the Five Armies*, The Lonely Mountain (set 79018) is the biggest LEGO *The Hobbit* set of all. Its mighty Smaug figure has a 17-in (42-cm) wingspan.

Smaug is made with 11 dark red dragon body parts, nine of which are found in no other set.

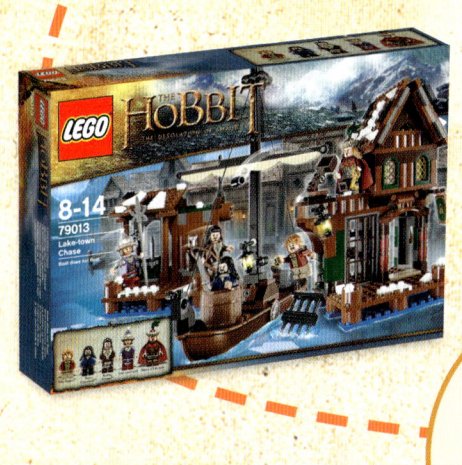

Tower of Orthanc includes a treelike Ent who can hold a minifigure in his mighty hands.

December 2013

Sets based on *The Hobbit: The Desolation of Smaug* include Lake-Town Chase (set 79013), with its breakaway prison wall and a unique barge made from two rowing boat pieces.

June 2013

Four new LEGO *The Lord of the Rings* sets include a Great Eagle swooping down on Battle at the Black Gate (set 79007) and the creepy King of the Dead sailing on the theme's only ship!

July 2013

Standing 28 in (73 cm) tall, the 2,359-piece Tower of Orthanc (set 10237) is the largest set in the LEGO *The Lord of the Rings* range, and one of the tallest LEGO sets ever made.

Pirate Ship Ambush (set 79008) comes with three ghoulish glow-in-the-dark minifigures.

183

2023
THE LORD OF THE RINGS: RIVENDELL

Ten years after LEGO® themes based on *The Lord of the Rings* and *The Hobbit* come to an end, the LEGO® Icons range takes a trip to Rivendell and returns with the mightiest Middle-earth set of all! This enormous display piece is packed with detail and peopled by hobbits, humans, elves, and dwarves!

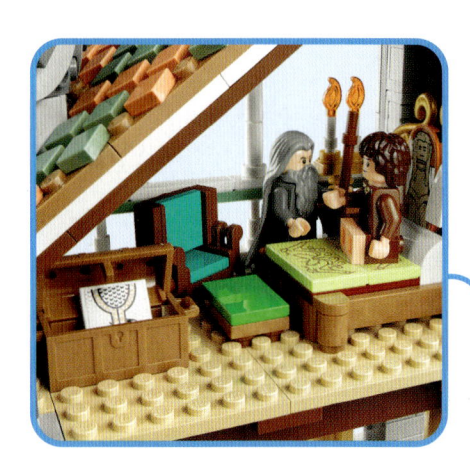

Frodo Baggins recovers from an injury in his uncle Bilbo's room. A chest here contains Bilbo's protective mithril coat and his trusty dagger, Sting.

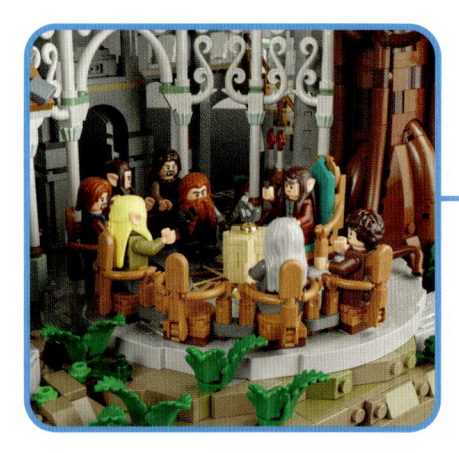

Humans, elves, dwarves, and hobbits come together at the Council of Elrond. Here, dwarf warrior Gimli tries to destroy the powerful Ruling Ring with his ax.

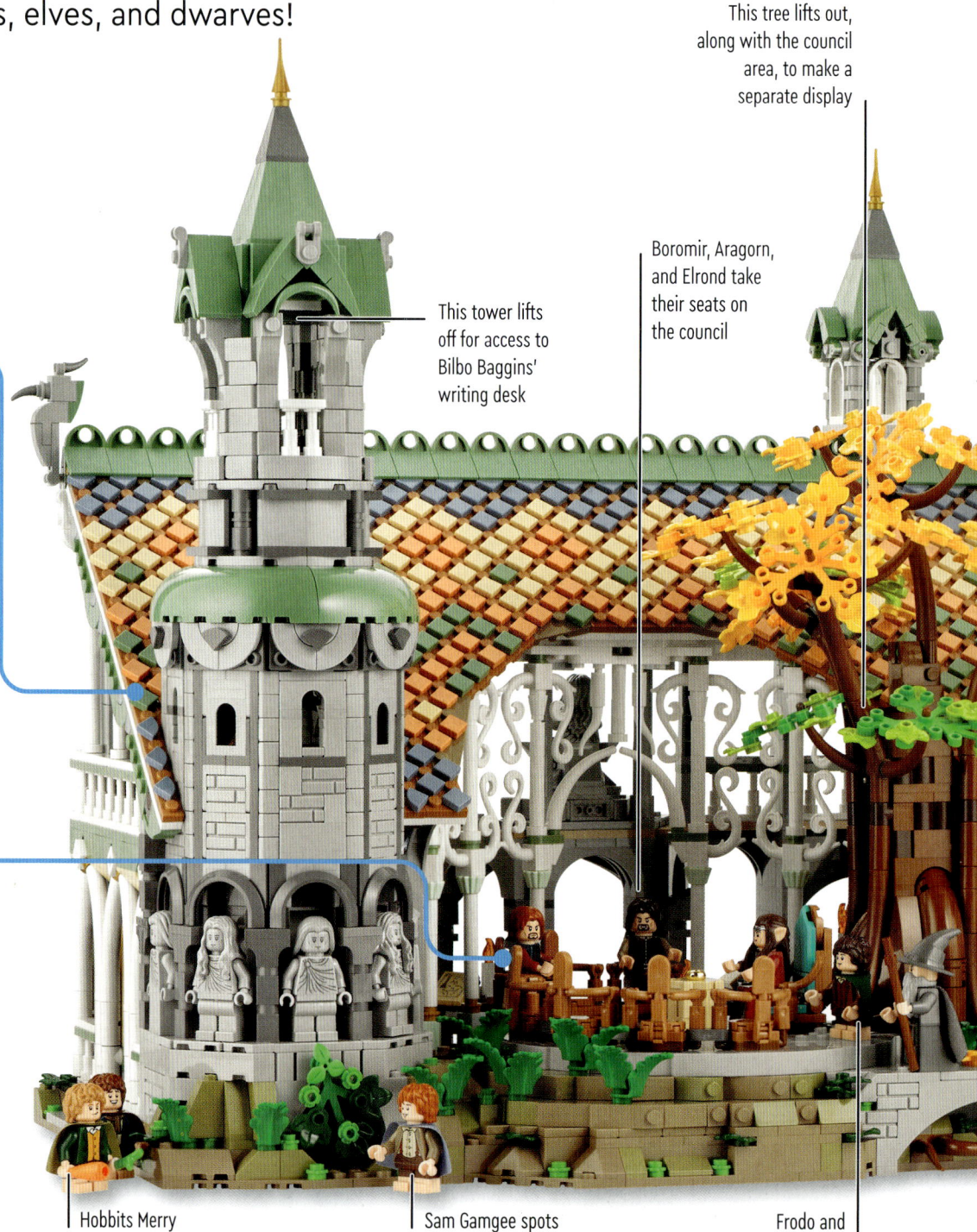

This tree lifts out, along with the council area, to make a separate display

This tower lifts off for access to Bilbo Baggins' writing desk

Boromir, Aragorn, and Elrond take their seats on the council

Hobbits Merry and Pippin

Sam Gamgee spots a good place to spy on the council!

Frodo and Gandalf arrive for the meeting

A CHRONICLE OF MIDDLE-EARTH

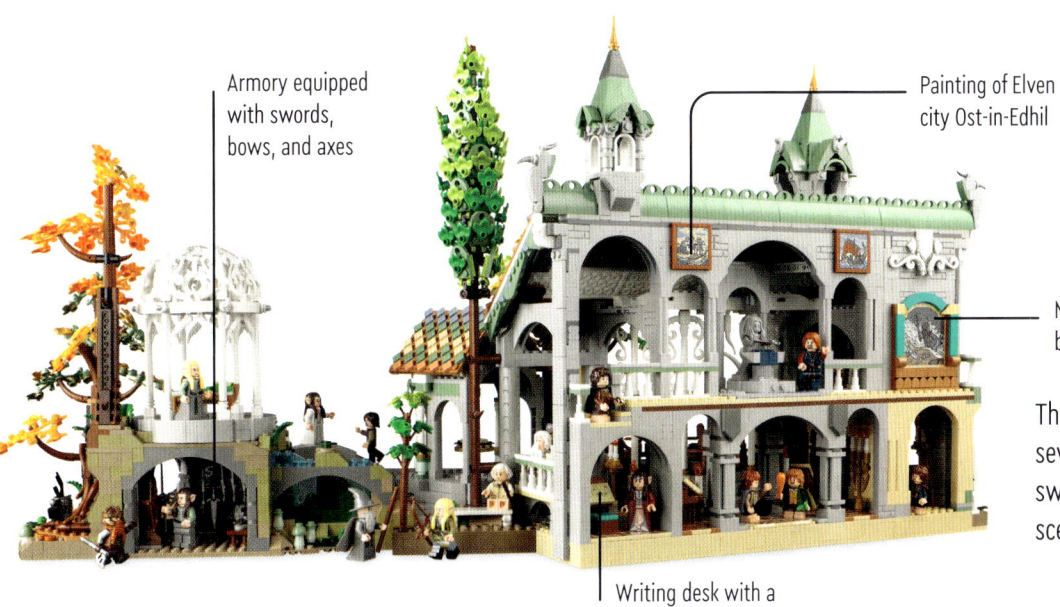

Armory equipped with swords, bows, and axes

Painting of Elven city Ost-in-Edhil

Mural showing Isildur battling Sauron

The back of the set reveals access to several rooms, a shrine to the broken sword Narsil, and artworks depicting scenes from Middle-earth history.

Writing desk with a map of Middle-earth

SET NUMBER	10316
PIECES	6,167
MINIFIGURES	21 (including statues)
SIZE	16 in (39 cm) tall, 29 in (72 cm) wide

Legolas brings bad news about the wretched Gollum!

Arwen convinces Elrond to remake the sword Narsil in this pavilion

Beyond the House of Elrond, Elven smiths forge the mighty sword Andúril. The Human Aragorn wields this blade on the quest to destroy the One Ring.

A lantern lights the way through the trees to the forge

Bilbo prepares to tell his tale to the council

Dwarves Gimli and Gloin don't want to be late!

These elves work in the forge beneath the pavilion

The mushrooms around the forge glow in the dark

185

CAN YOU DIG IT?

Based in a blocky world with a focus on building and exploration, video game *Minecraft* is ideally suited to life as a LEGO® theme. Just like its online inspiration, **LEGO® Minecraft®** spans diverse biomes (environments), is packed full of both friendly and ferocious mobs (creatures), and is, of course, endlessly rebuildable!

The first Minecraft set, simply named Micro World (set 21102), is released as part of the fan-designed LEGO® Ideas range. It comes with buildable microscale versions of player skin Steve and a creeper mob.

2012

The Snow Hideout includes a missile-launching Snow Golem mob!

You make me want to press paws!

This year's sets explore new Minecraft biomes, from desert in The Dungeon (set 21119) to icy tundra in The Snow Hideout (set 21120). Player skin Alex arrives in minifigure form, accompanied by a brick-built wolf.

2015

The Village (set 21128) is the first Minecraft set with more than 1,000 pieces. It splits into seven sections for rapid redesigns, and comes with new Villager mobs and a brick-built Iron Golem figure.

Colorful new Skin Packs re-create the in-game effect of customizing your player character.

2016

186

CAN YOU DIG IT?

Micro World has four modular sections that can be rearranged in many different ways.

LEGO Minecraft becomes a fully-fledged theme with two more microscale sets: Micro World—The Village (set 21105) and Micro World—The Nether (set 21106). Both come in satisfyingly cube-shaped boxes.

2013

2014

Micro World—The End (set 21107) completes the Micro World series with a scary Ender Dragon scene.

The first Crafting Box (set 21116) comes with building instructions for eight Minecraft models.

The first minifigure-scale Minecraft sets are packed full of new pieces, including cuboid minifigure and animal heads, pixelated minifigure tools and armor pieces, and four-legged Creeper bodies.

More new biomes burst into life in The Mushroom Island (set 21129) and The Ocean Monument (set 21136). The Mountain Cave (set 21137), meanwhile, becomes the biggest Minecraft set of all.

The Mushroom Island biome is home to colorful, cowlike creatures called mooshrooms.

2017

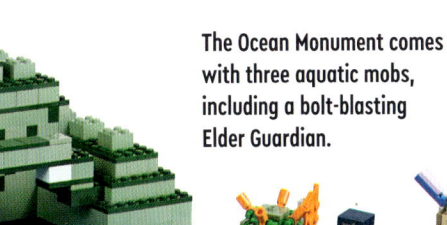

The Ocean Monument comes with three aquatic mobs, including a bolt-blasting Elder Guardian.

DELVE INTO MINECRAFT DUNGEONS AND MORE!

187

2018

New baby figures feature in sets such as The Zombie Cave (set 21141), while The Skull Arena (set 21145) comes with two ore minifigure skins. Elsewhere, the LEGO® BrickHeadz™ theme includes the biggest Steve figure yet.

LEGO BrickHeadz Steve & Creeper (set 41612) is the first of four Minecraft-themed BrickHeadz sets.

2019

Even bigger than BrickHeadz, this year's Minecraft sets include buildable characters such as Alex BigFig with Chicken (set 21149). More new minifigures include Pirate and Blacksmith skins and a Dragon Slayer skin.

2022

This year's largest set is 1,252-piece The Llama Village (set 21188), complete with Illager, Pillager, and Llama Herder minifigures. The Ice Castle (set 21186), meanwhile, boasts Royal Warrior and Yeti skins.

Call me Ocelot!

OK, but just call me Panda occasionally!

These player minifigures live the high life in The Modern Treehouse (set 21174).

2023

The Deep Dark Battle (set 21246) is the first set to venture into the Deep Dark biome, while The Iron Golem Fortress (set 21250) transforms into the biggest LEGO Minecraft mob yet, standing 8 in (20 cm) tall.

Following a fan vote to choose a new LEGO Minecraft minifigure, the winning Ninja skin is included in The Training Grounds (set 21183).

188

CAN YOU DIG IT?

The Dragon Slayer takes on an all-new Ender Dragon in The End Battle (set 21151).

The Redstone Battle (set 21163) celebrates new game *Minecraft Dungeons* with minifigure versions of heroes Hal, Hedwig, Hex, and Valorie, plus brick-built versions of their fearsome boss mob foes.

2020

New biome The Warped Forest (set 21168) introduces Piglin and Hoglin mobs, the latest *Minecraft Dungeons* boss is The Jungle Abomination (set 21176), and Panda and Ocelot looks provide the latest player skins.

This year's display sets include the oddly adorable BigFig Pig with Baby Zombie (set 21157).

2021

The Deep Dark Battle is dominated by a brick-built Warden mob.

2024

The first set to be based on spin-off game *Minecraft Legends* is The Devourer Showdown (set 21257). It stars a brick-built boss that can launch missiles from its mouth and bright green mucus blocks from its backpack!

189

THE MOUNTAIN CAVE

2017

The largest LEGO® Minecraft® set is so big it was revealed on social media in six stages! It was an appropriate launch for a set with modular sections that can be broken off and rearranged to make lots of different layouts. The set is packed full of surprises, including new mobs, hidden functions, secret shelters, and precious ores just waiting to be mined.

The creeper-head house is built with an open back and a lift-off roof for access to a cozy bedroom with a torch, a map, a furnace, and a creeper-head trophy.

Movable section of snow-capped mountainside

Detachable house roof

"Explodable" TNT platform

Train track corner section

Don't look directly at the Enderman mob's face!

Jumper plates show where railroad sections have been lifted out for use elsewhere

Eight stretches of railroad, the creeper-head house, and four other sections break away easily for rapid rearrangement of the Mountain Cave environment.

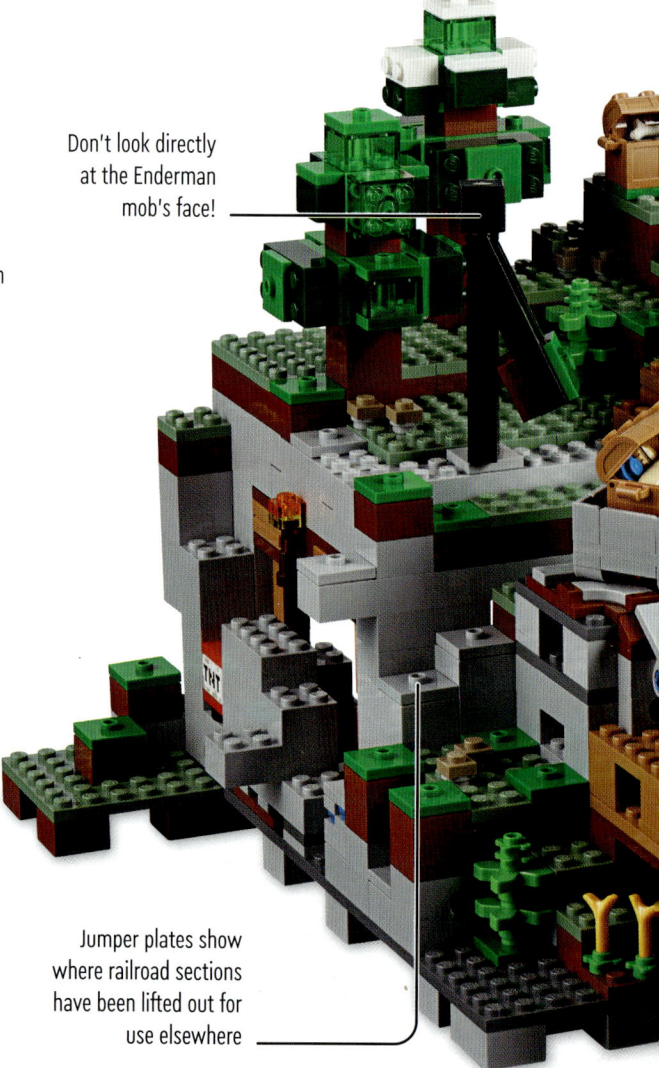

CAN YOU DIG IT?

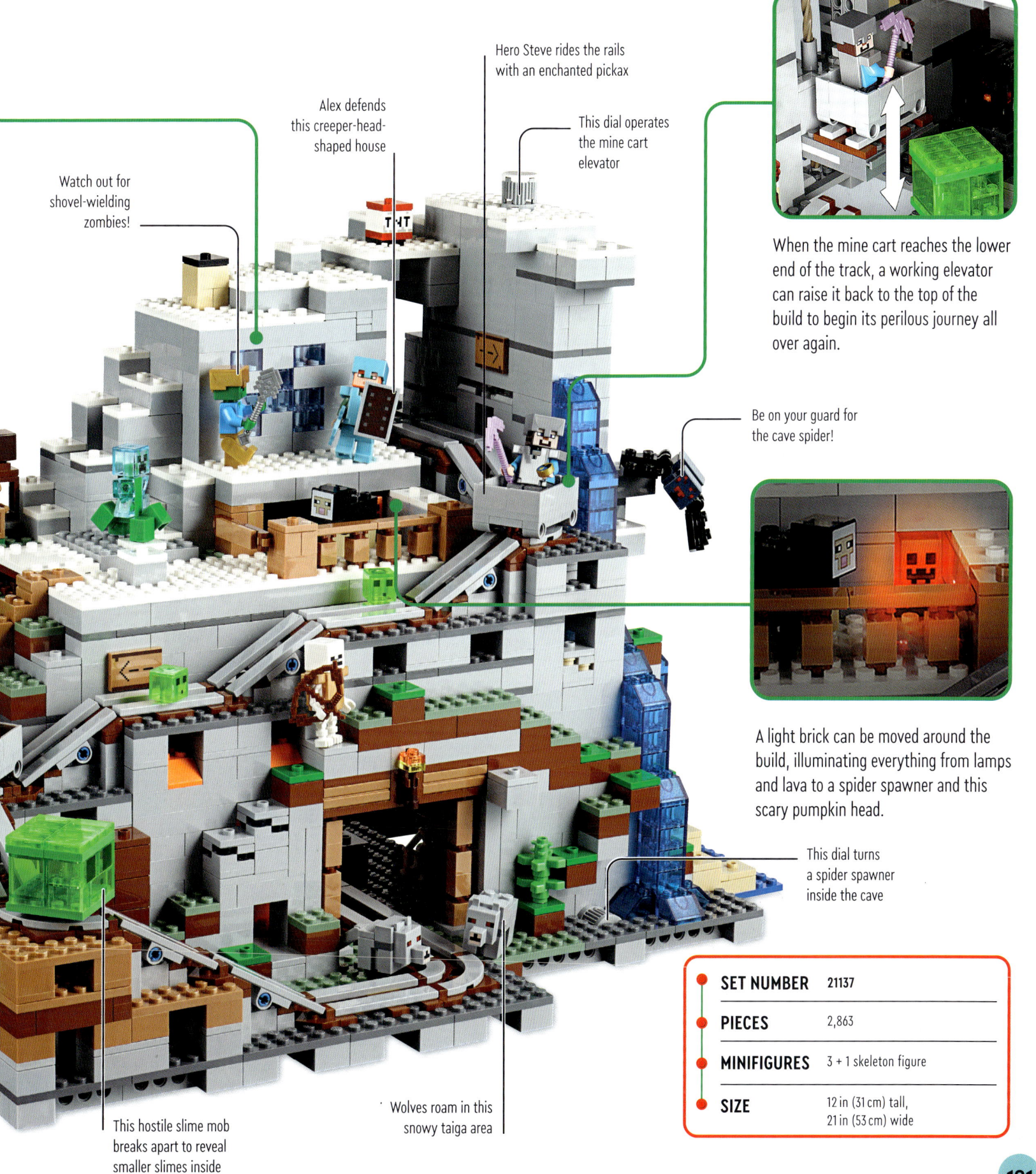

Watch out for shovel-wielding zombies!

Alex defends this creeper-head-shaped house

Hero Steve rides the rails with an enchanted pickax

This dial operates the mine cart elevator

When the mine cart reaches the lower end of the track, a working elevator can raise it back to the top of the build to begin its perilous journey all over again.

Be on your guard for the cave spider!

A light brick can be moved around the build, illuminating everything from lamps and lava to a spider spawner and this scary pumpkin head.

This dial turns a spider spawner inside the cave

This hostile slime mob breaks apart to reveal smaller slimes inside

Wolves roam in this snowy taiga area

SET NUMBER	21137
PIECES	2,863
MINIFIGURES	3 + 1 skeleton figure
SIZE	12 in (31 cm) tall, 21 in (53 cm) wide

191

MASSIVE MACHINES

Most LEGO® sets are meant for play, but ever since the 1970s there have also been larger, more realistic models intended for **display**. Many are based on real-life modes of transportation, and can whisk builders away on imaginative journeys, even when they never leave the shelf.

1975 — Known as LEGO® Expert in some countries, the LEGO® Hobby Set range launches with two vintage cars and a Formula 1 racer, each measuring about 11 in (28 cm) long.

1990 — With a detailed helicopter on an equally detailed trailer, the Model Team Whirl and Wheel Super Truck (set 5590) is the first standard LEGO set to have more than 1,000 pieces.

Whirl and Wheel Super Truck can be rebuilt as an airport fire engine.

2001 — The first vehicle in a new range of LEGO® Advanced Models is based on a 1916 biplane. The Sopwith Camel (set 3451) has an 18-in (46-cm) wingspan and a realistic rotating engine.

2006 — Following several vintage planes, Boeing 787 Dreamliner (set 10177) brings the Advanced Models range right up to date. Its 27-in (69-cm) wingspan is the largest of any LEGO plane.

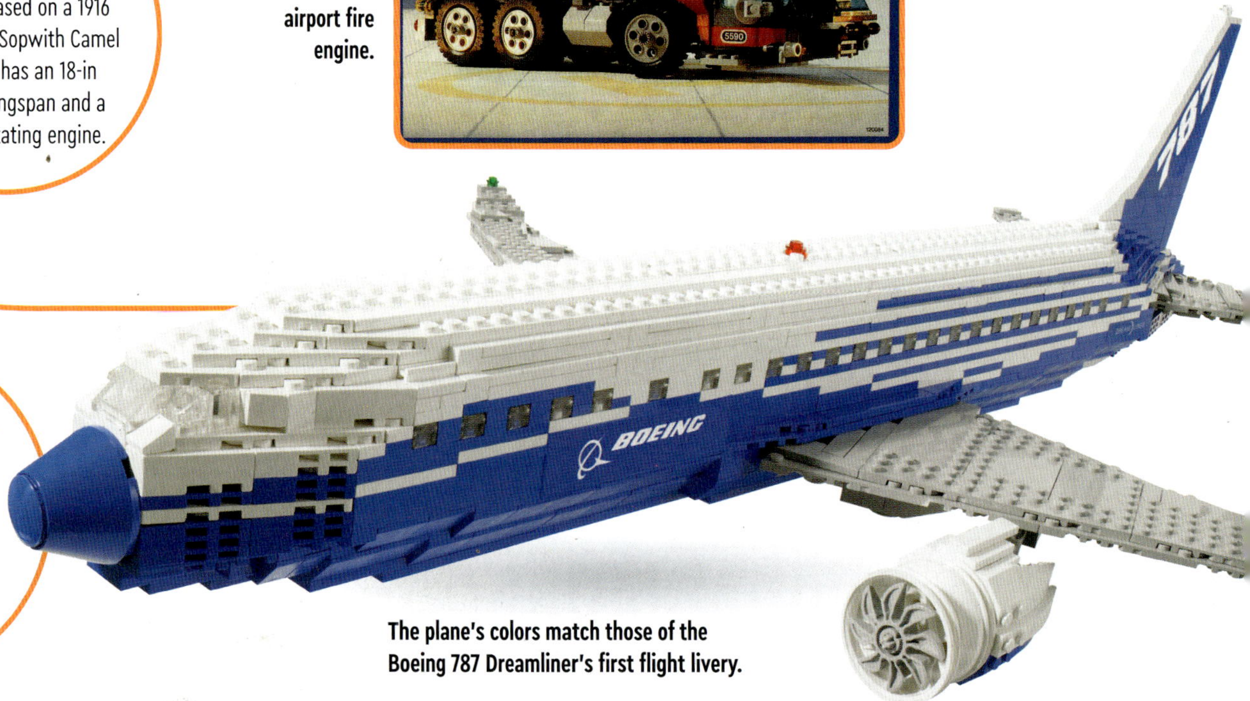

The plane's colors match those of the Boeing 787 Dreamliner's first flight livery.

MASSIVE MACHINES

With 237 pieces, 1926 Renault (set 391) is the largest of the first three Hobby Sets.

The Hobby Set range expands to include two motorbikes and one train—the 434-piece Thatcher Perkins Locomotive (set 396), based on a real engine from the 1860s.

1976

Like all Model Team sets, Formula 1 Racer (set 5540) has instructions for making two very different vehicles.

Like the Hobby Set range before it, LEGO® Model Team debuts with three large vehicle models, including an F1 racer. Only this time, the racing car can become an airplane!

The U.S.S. *Constellation* is later reissued as a LEGO® Legends set (set 10021).

The 973-piece U.S.S. *Constellation* is the last and largest Hobby Set. Based on an 18th-century frigate, it is the first LEGO set to have a brick-built display stand.

1986

1978

Advanced Models reach new heights of realism with the Volkswagen T1 Camper Van (set 10220). The 1960s icon boasts a fully furnished interior, complete with fabric curtains.

2011

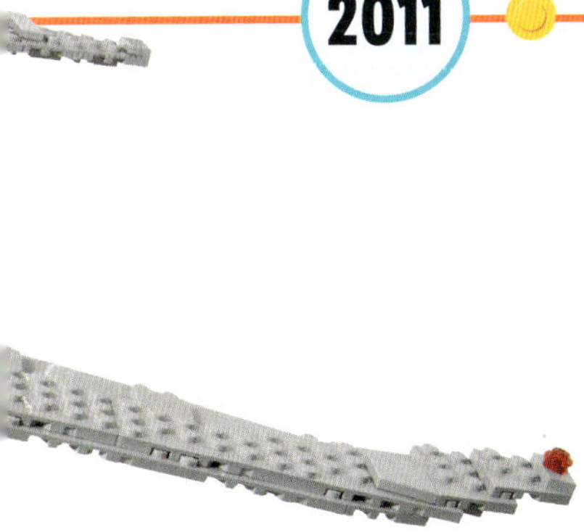

DON'T MISS THE CREATOR EXPERT BUS!

This model is based on the 1962 VW "splittie," so-called because of its split windshield.

193

The first large-scale LEGO® System motorcycle since 1976 is the Harley-Davidson Fat Boy (set 10269). The classic cruiser has 880 more pieces than its closest Hobby Set equivalent.

James Bond Aston Martin DB5 (set 10262) is the first large-scale LEGO vehicle to be based on a film series. Its functions include revolving license plates and an ejector seat.

2019

2018

London Bus (set 10258) becomes the biggest Creator Expert vehicle of all, with 1,686 pieces. The roof and upper deck both lift off to reveal details such as scuffed seats and litter.

2017

2014

A year after the Advanced Models range gets a rebrand as LEGO® Creator Expert, it launches the epic Maersk Line Triple-E (set 10241), a modern cargo ship measuring 25 in (65 cm) long.

The 1,518-part Maersk Line Triple-E comes with 128 Maersk-branded stickers.

MASSIVE MACHINES

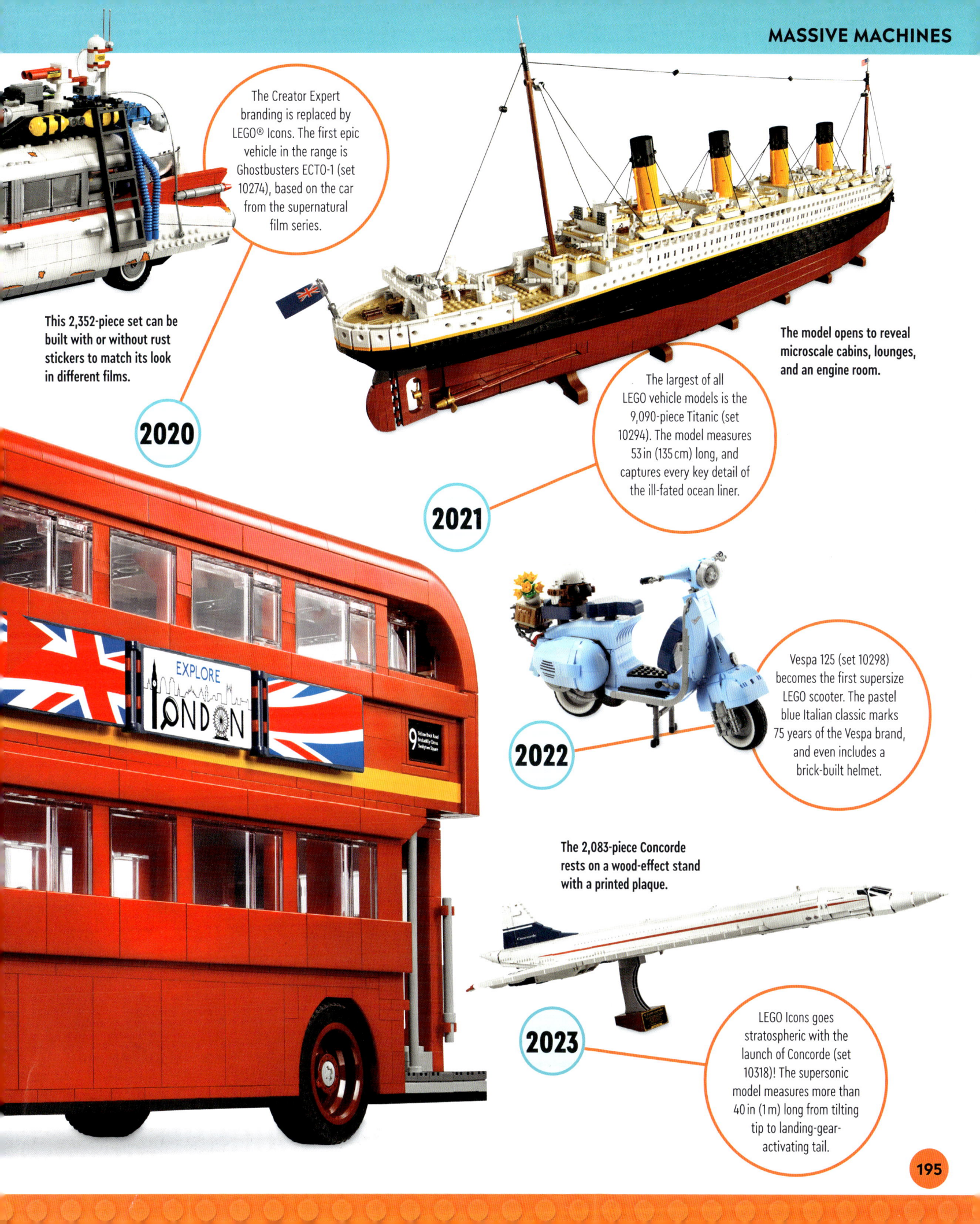

The Creator Expert branding is replaced by LEGO® Icons. The first epic vehicle in the range is Ghostbusters ECTO-1 (set 10274), based on the car from the supernatural film series.

This 2,352-piece set can be built with or without rust stickers to match its look in different films.

2020

The model opens to reveal microscale cabins, lounges, and an engine room.

The largest of all LEGO vehicle models is the 9,090-piece Titanic (set 10294). The model measures 53 in (135 cm) long, and captures every key detail of the ill-fated ocean liner.

2021

Vespa 125 (set 10298) becomes the first supersize LEGO scooter. The pastel blue Italian classic marks 75 years of the Vespa brand, and even includes a brick-built helmet.

2022

The 2,083-piece Concorde rests on a wood-effect stand with a printed plaque.

2023

LEGO Icons goes stratospheric with the launch of Concorde (set 10318)! The supersonic model measures more than 40 in (1 m) long from tilting tip to landing-gear-activating tail.

195

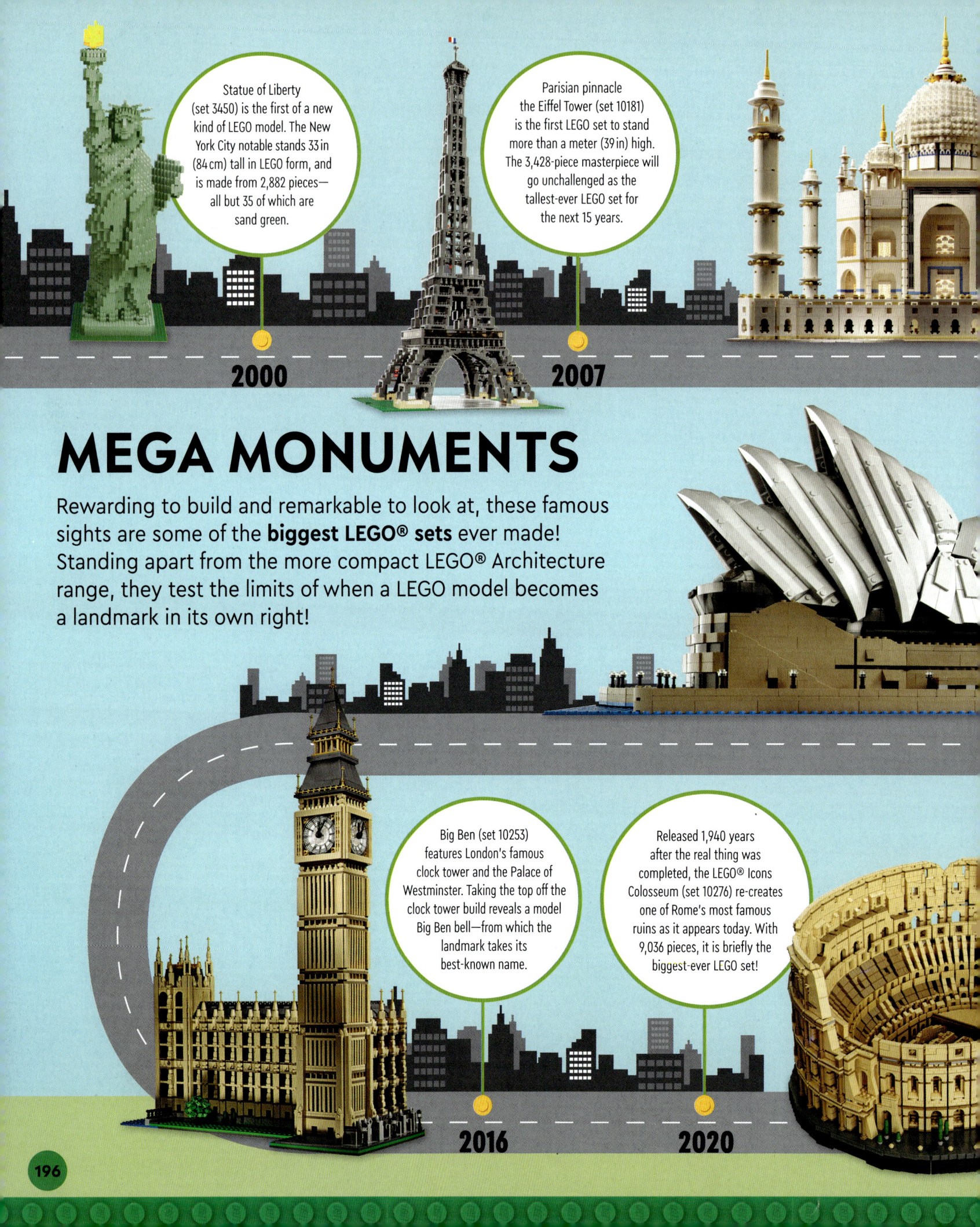

MEGA MONUMENTS

Rewarding to build and remarkable to look at, these famous sights are some of the **biggest LEGO® sets** ever made! Standing apart from the more compact LEGO® Architecture range, they test the limits of when a LEGO model becomes a landmark in its own right!

2000 — Statue of Liberty (set 3450) is the first of a new kind of LEGO model. The New York City notable stands 33 in (84 cm) tall in LEGO form, and is made from 2,882 pieces—all but 35 of which are sand green.

2007 — Parisian pinnacle the Eiffel Tower (set 10181) is the first LEGO set to stand more than a meter (39 in) high. The 3,428-piece masterpiece will go unchallenged as the tallest-ever LEGO set for the next 15 years.

2016 — Big Ben (set 10253) features London's famous clock tower and the Palace of Westminster. Taking the top off the clock tower build reveals a model Big Ben bell—from which the landmark takes its best-known name.

2020 — Released 1,940 years after the real thing was completed, the LEGO® Icons Colosseum (set 10276) re-creates one of Rome's most famous ruins as it appears today. With 9,036 pieces, it is briefly the biggest-ever LEGO set!

MEGA MONUMENTS

2008 — Launched as the largest-ever LEGO set, the Taj Mahal (set 10189) is made from 5,922 pieces. The imitation Jewel of India proves so popular that it is later reissued with one extra piece—a brick separator!

2010 — The first functional LEGO landmark, Tower Bridge (set 10214) opens in the middle, just like the real London river crossing. The 4,287-piece set is packed with realistic details, including a microscale red London bus.

2013 — The first real-world building in the LEGO® Creator Expert range, Australia's Sydney Opera House™ (set 10234) is also the first landmark set based on a 20th-century building, and the first from the Southern Hemisphere.

2021 — Camp Nou—FC Barcelona (set 10284) is one of three LEGO Icons soccer stadiums released between 2020 and 2022. The supersize Spanish arena has 5,509 pieces, and splits into five sections to show off its details.

2022 — What's taller than the 2007 Eiffel Tower model? In LEGO terms, only the 2022 Eiffel Tower (set 10307)! Topping out at 58 in (149 cm) high, it is also the first three-dimensional set to have more than 10,000 pieces.

FAIR PLAY

Starting with a single model for advanced builders in 2009, the **LEGO® Fairground Collection** has scaled new heights as part of the LEGO® Creator Expert range in the 2010s and LEGO® Icons in the 2020s. Big, bold, and packed full of brilliant engineering, each new set can be operated by hand or animated with the use of a LEGO motor.

The 2,464-piece Ferris Wheel (set 10247) stands 24 in (60 cm) tall. It comes with 10 minifigure passengers, and has room for three times as many in its brightly colored gondolas.

2015

Fairground Mixer (set 10244) is the Creator Expert set that turns the Fairground Collection into an ongoing series. It includes trucks to tow the attractions from place to place.

2014

2009

The 3,263-piece Grand Carousel (set 10196) has a sound brick that plays fairground music and a Power Functions motor to make the rides rise and fall as the carousel turns.

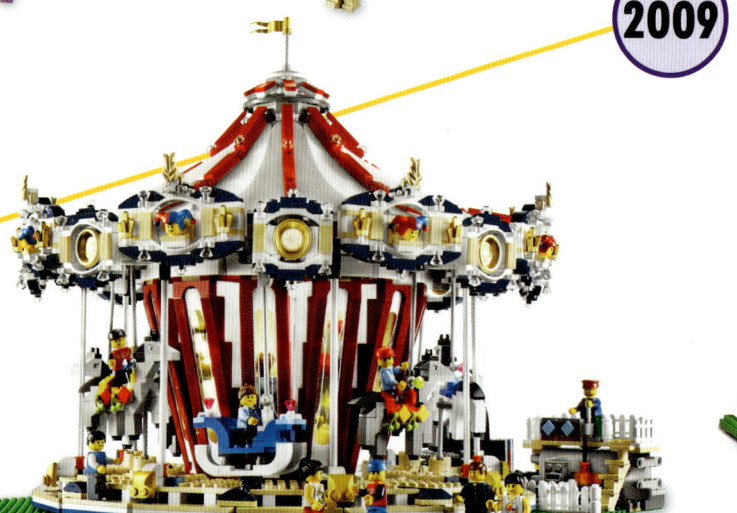

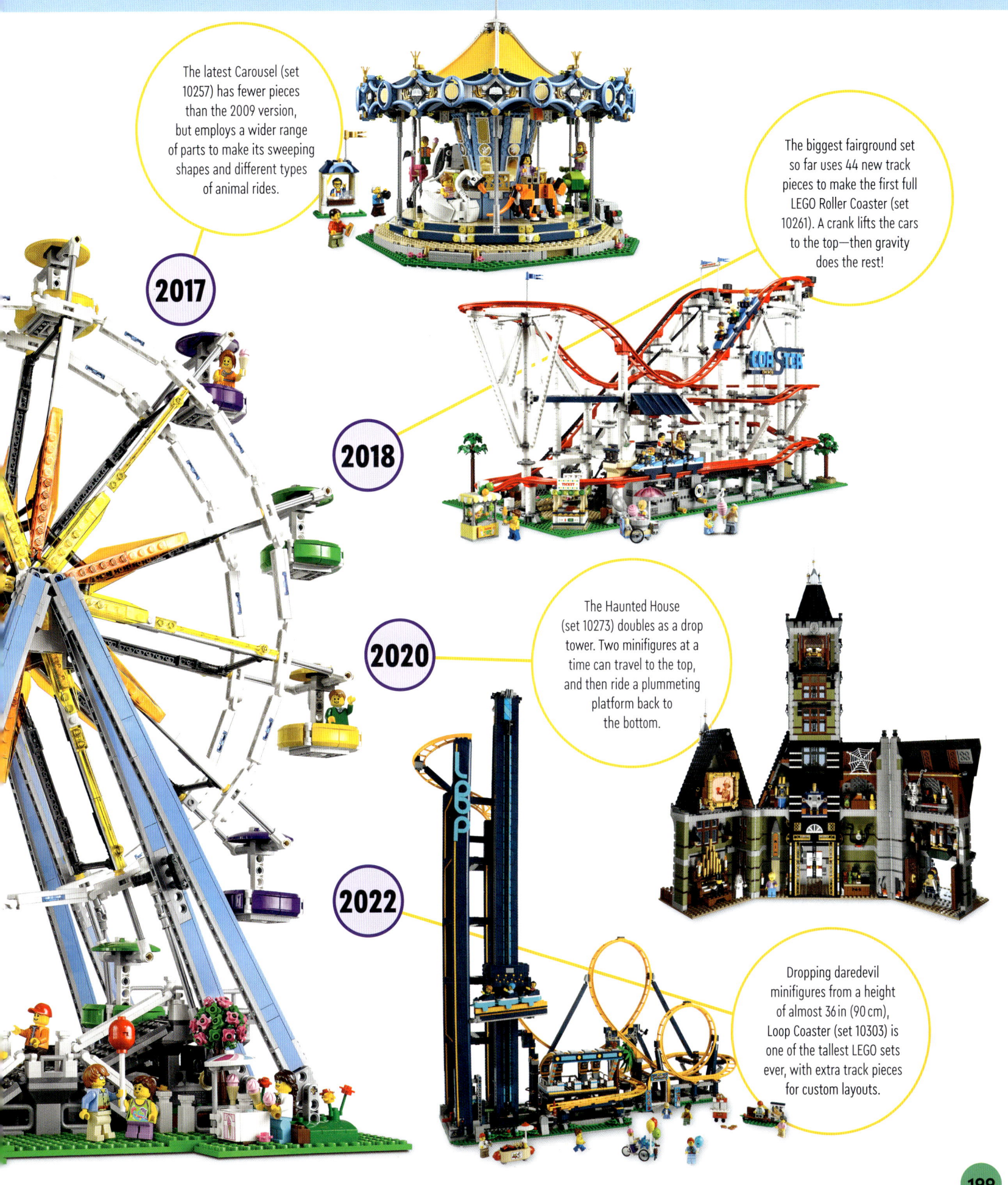

FAIR PLAY

2017 — The latest Carousel (set 10257) has fewer pieces than the 2009 version, but employs a wider range of parts to make its sweeping shapes and different types of animal rides.

2018 — The biggest fairground set so far uses 44 new track pieces to make the first full LEGO Roller Coaster (set 10261). A crank lifts the cars to the top—then gravity does the rest!

2020 — The Haunted House (set 10273) doubles as a drop tower. Two minifigures at a time can travel to the top, and then ride a plummeting platform back to the bottom.

2022 — Dropping daredevil minifigures from a height of almost 36 in (90 cm), Loop Coaster (set 10303) is one of the tallest LEGO sets ever, with extra track pieces for custom layouts.

BRICK FLICKS

LEGO® minifigures become supersize when they hit the big screen in 2014. The minifigure heroes of **THE LEGO® MOVIE™** wow audiences globally and start a trend for brick-based blockbusters. Three more **big-screen adventures** follow, and every one is awesome!

2014
THE LEGO® MOVIE™

Conceived in 2008 and made over the course of two years from 2012, THE LEGO MOVIE uses a unique form of digital animation that follows the rules of LEGO building. That means everything seen on screen could really be made from LEGO bricks, and the characters can only move like real minifigures! The film has its worldwide premiere in Los Angeles on February 1, 2014.

The film gets the whole world singing "Everything is Awesome"—a high-energy earworm that goes on to get an Oscar nomination for Best Original Song.

2017
THE LEGO® BATMAN MOVIE

When THE LEGO MOVIE left audiences wanting more, breakout costar LEGO® Batman™ was the obvious choice for a follow-up! Scriptwriting and storyboarding began in summer 2014, and the digital LEGO brick version of Gotham City was brought to life over the next two and a half years. Irish fans are the first to see THE LEGO BATMAN MOVIE when it premieres in Dublin on January 29, 2017.

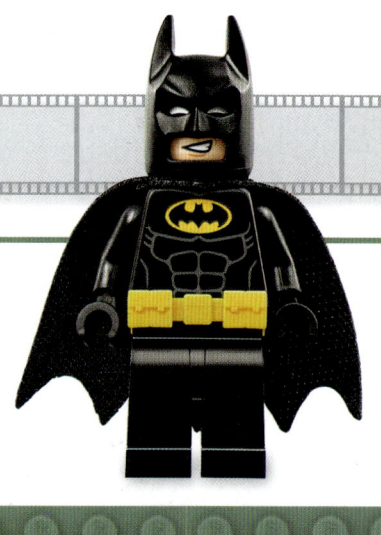

THE LEGO BATMAN MOVIE includes characters from throughout the Caped Crusader's 75-year history, including little-known villains such as Egghead and the Condiment King.

200

BRICK FLICKS

The star of THE LEGO MOVIE is Emmet Brickowski, but there wouldn't be a film without his Master Builder buddies Wyldstyle, Batman, Benny, Vitruvius, Unikitty, and MetalBeard.

The largest of 20 sets based on THE LEGO MOVIE is the 2,741-piece MetalBeard's Sea Cow (set 70810), complete with buildable MetalBeard and Queasy Kitty figures.

Found them!

Some characters from THE LEGO MOVIE are exclusively available as collectible Minifigures. They range from Abraham Lincoln and William Shakespeare to Velma Staplebot and "Where Are My Pants?" Guy.

Vehicles from the film made into LEGO sets include The Ultimate Batmobile (set 70917) and The Bat-Space Shuttle (set 70923), complete with Bat-Moon Buggy and Bat-Kayak.

Will Arnett isn't just the voice of LEGO Batman—he's also his face! Animators based the character's expressions on those of the actor as he recorded his lines.

There are 40 collectible Minifigures based on THE LEGO BATMAN MOVE, and eight of them are Batman! Variants include Glam Metal Batman and Mermaid Batman.

WATCH FOR MORE BRICK-BUILT BLOCKBUSTERS!

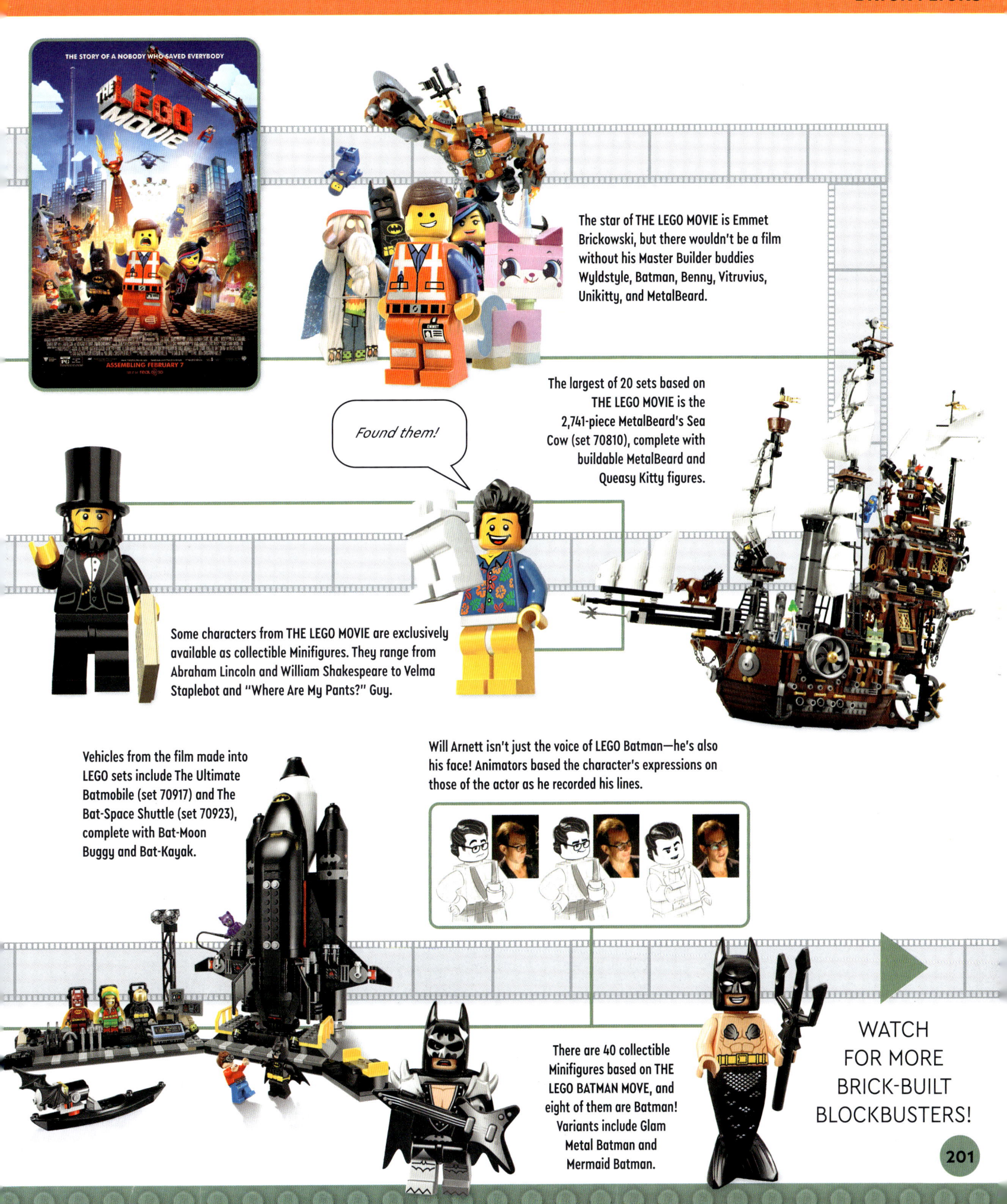

201

2017
THE LEGO® NINJAGO® MOVIE™

Plans for a movie based on the LEGO® NINJAGO® TV show were announced in 2013, but the smash-hit success of THE LEGO MOVIE changed ideas about what a LEGO film could be. A bigger, more ambitious adventure then began to take shape, reimagining the ninja team for a wider audience. The LEGO NINJAGO MOVIE has its red-carpet premiere in Los Angeles on September 16, 2017.

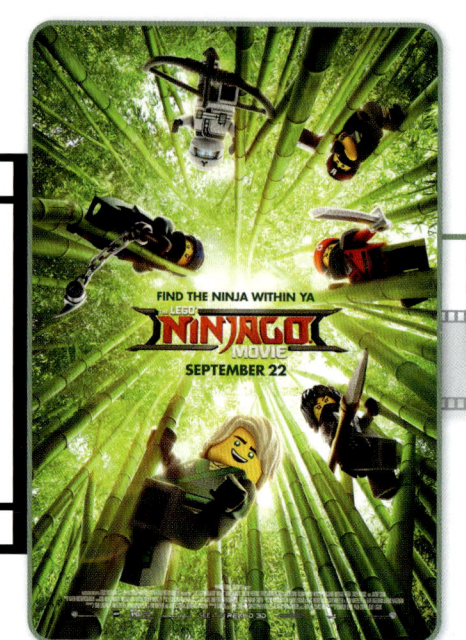

THE LEGO NINJAGO MOVIE is the first LEGO film where the landscape isn't entirely brick-built—but the lifelike jungles, beaches, and oceans are still all the work of highly skilled animators.

2019
THE LEGO® MOVIE 2™: THE SECOND PART

There was never any doubt that the stars of THE LEGO MOVIE would return in a sequel—they just had to wait their turn! A draft script was ready by the end of 2015, and production began in late 2017, using the latest animation tech to make the digital brick world look more realistic than ever. THE LEGO MOVIE 2: *The Second Part* debuts in Los Angeles on February 2, 2019.

Megastar Chris Pratt has a dual role in THE LEGO MOVIE 2, as Emmet and new character Rex Dangervest. He is also the inspiration for minifigures in LEGO® Marvel Super Heroes and LEGO® Jurassic World.

BRICK FLICKS

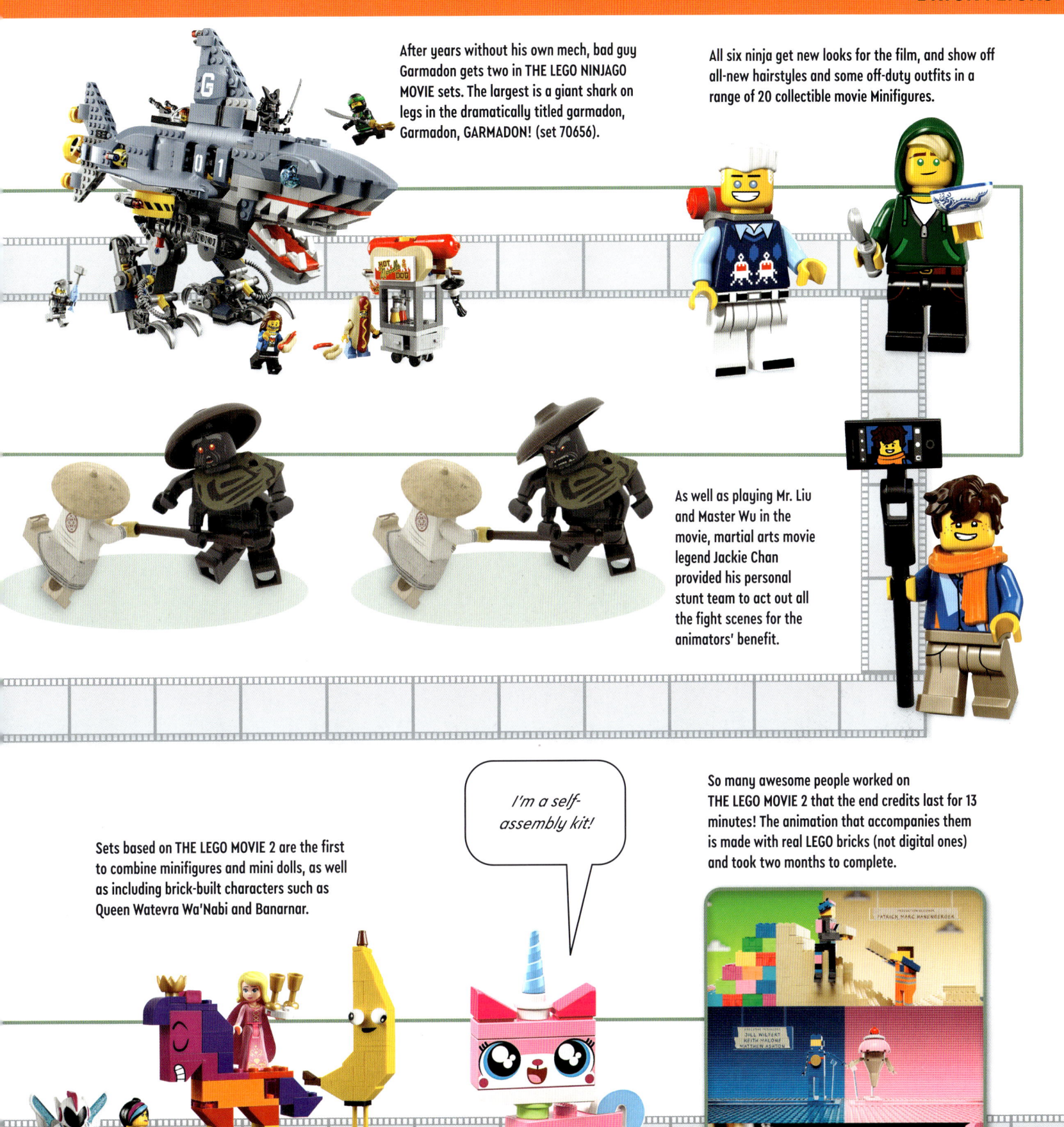

After years without his own mech, bad guy Garmadon gets two in THE LEGO NINJAGO MOVIE sets. The largest is a giant shark on legs in the dramatically titled garmadon, Garmadon, GARMADON! (set 70656).

All six ninja get new looks for the film, and show off all-new hairstyles and some off-duty outfits in a range of 20 collectible movie Minifigures.

As well as playing Mr. Liu and Master Wu in the movie, martial arts movie legend Jackie Chan provided his personal stunt team to act out all the fight scenes for the animators' benefit.

Sets based on THE LEGO MOVIE 2 are the first to combine minifigures and mini dolls, as well as including brick-built characters such as Queen Watevra Wa'Nabi and Banarnar.

I'm a self-assembly kit!

So many awesome people worked on THE LEGO MOVIE 2 that the end credits last for 13 minutes! The animation that accompanies them is made with real LEGO bricks (not digital ones) and took two months to complete.

203

2019

WELCOME TO APOCALYPSEBURG!

From the wreckage of Bricksburg comes the biggest set based on THE LEGO® MOVIE 2™. The city's own Statue of Liberty may have fallen, but it has found new purpose as a home for Emmet, Lucy, and their post-apocalyptic pals! The symbolic stronghold not only includes a coffee shop, a barber, and a police station, but also a gym, a spa, and a rooftop diner.

SET NUMBER	70840
PIECES	3,178
MINIFIGURES	12 + 1 skeleton figure
SIZE	20 in (52 cm) tall, 19 in (49 cm) wide

The inhabitants of Apocalypseburg live in old cargo containers. Lucy has one all to herself, where she keeps souvenirs from her pop-star past.

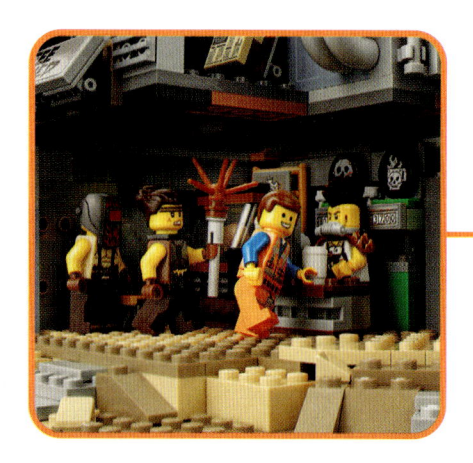

Society may have collapsed in THE LEGO MOVIE 2, but Larry the Barista is still selling overpriced coffee—and Emmet is still his best customer!

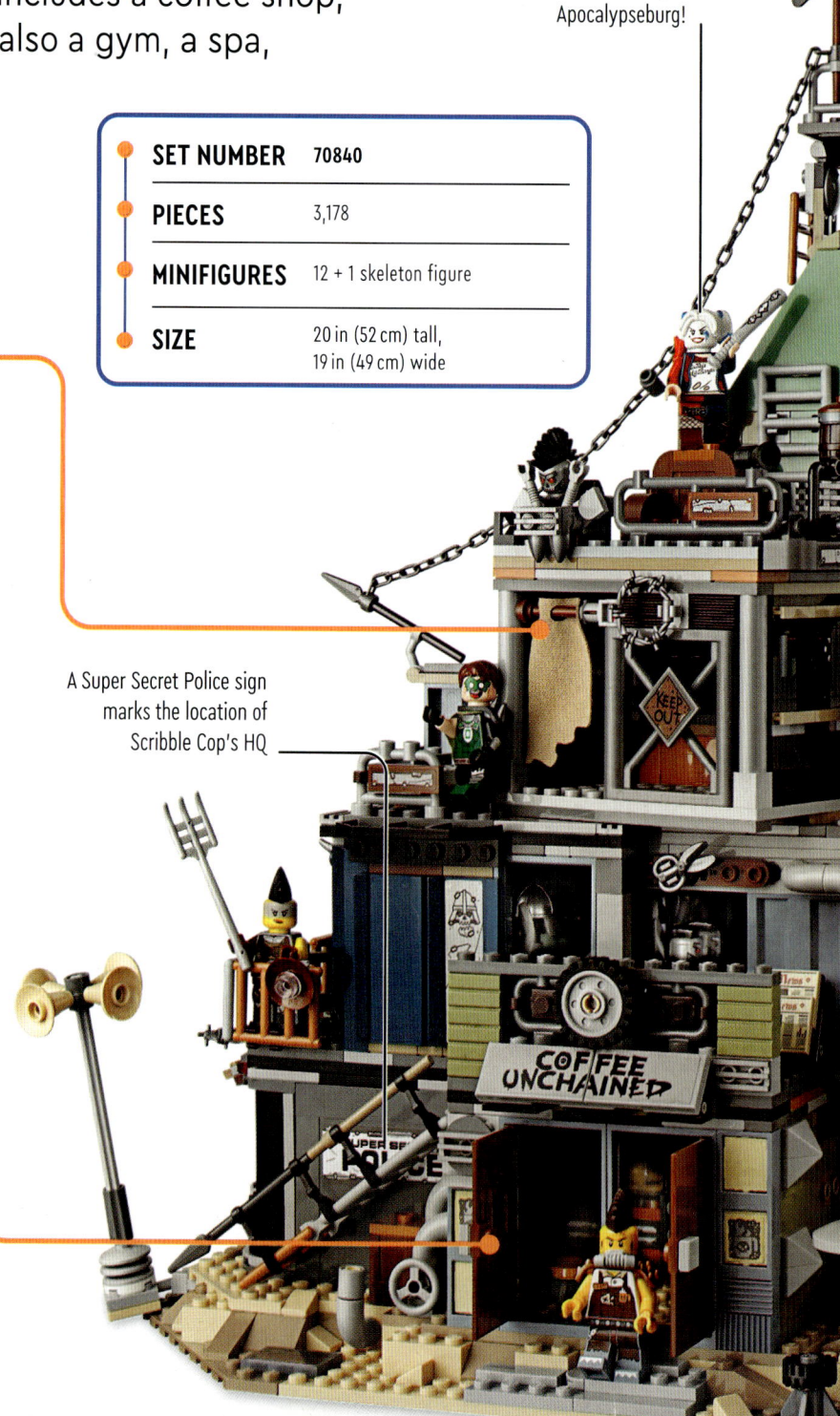

Harley Quinn is happier than most living in Apocalypseburg!

A Super Secret Police sign marks the location of Scribble Cop's HQ

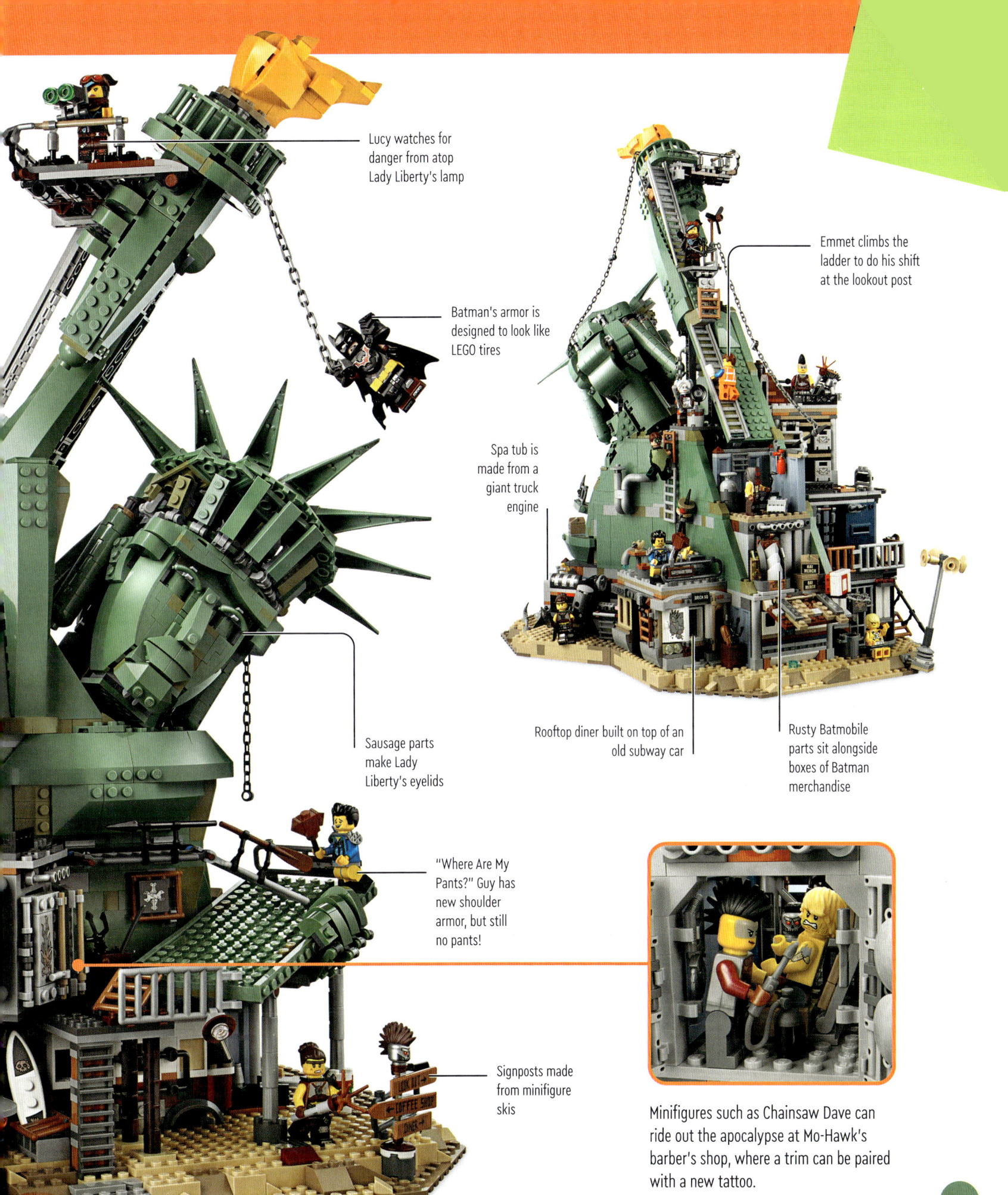

Lucy watches for danger from atop Lady Liberty's lamp

Batman's armor is designed to look like LEGO tires

Emmet climbs the ladder to do his shift at the lookout post

Spa tub is made from a giant truck engine

Sausage parts make Lady Liberty's eyelids

Rooftop diner built on top of an old subway car

Rusty Batmobile parts sit alongside boxes of Batman merchandise

"Where Are My Pants?" Guy has new shoulder armor, but still no pants!

Signposts made from minifigure skis

Minifigures such as Chainsaw Dave can ride out the apocalypse at Mo-Hawk's barber's shop, where a trim can be paired with a new tattoo.

205

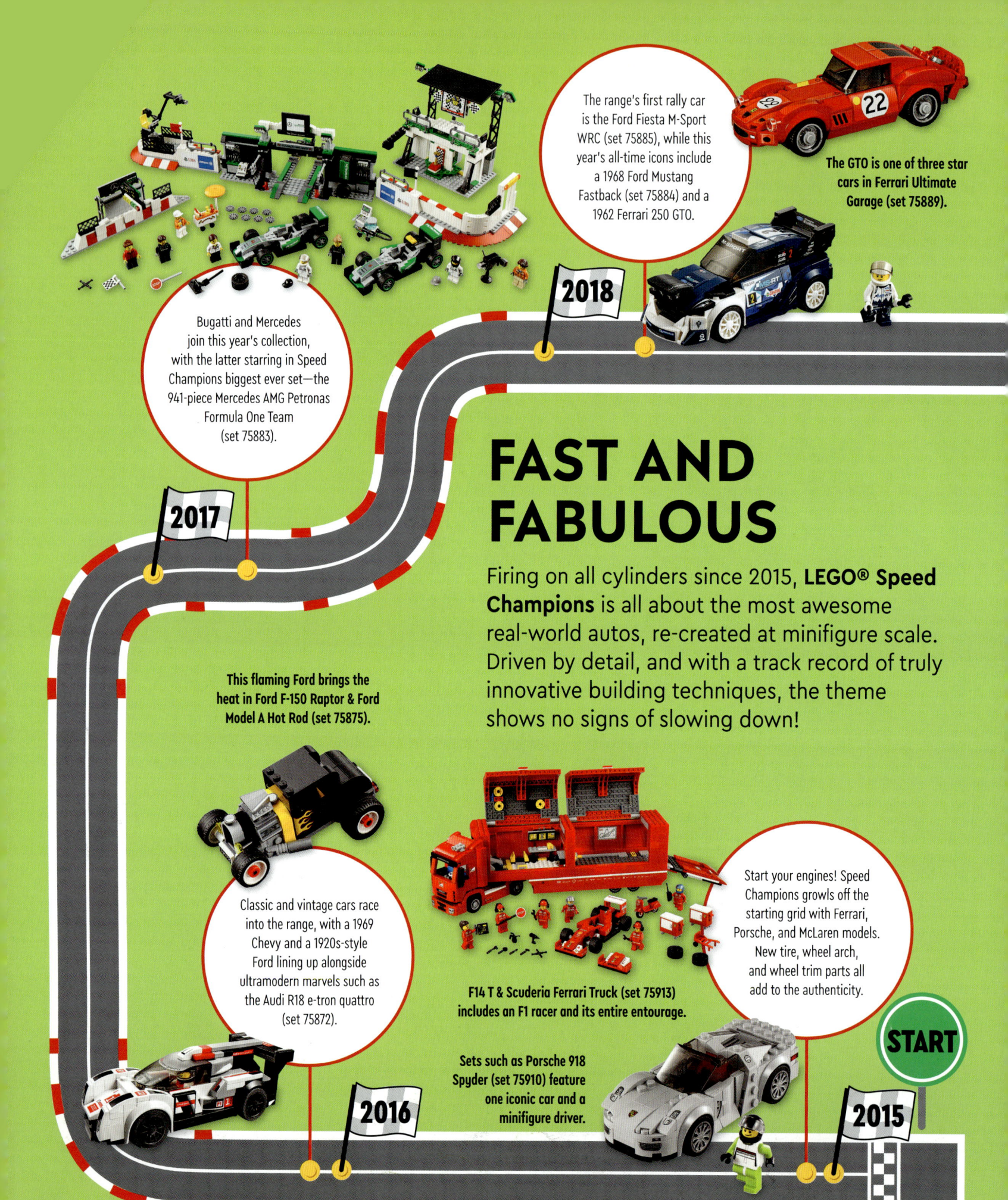

FAST AND FABULOUS

Firing on all cylinders since 2015, **LEGO® Speed Champions** is all about the most awesome real-world autos, re-created at minifigure scale. Driven by detail, and with a track record of truly innovative building techniques, the theme shows no signs of slowing down!

The range's first rally car is the Ford Fiesta M-Sport WRC (set 75885), while this year's all-time icons include a 1968 Ford Mustang Fastback (set 75884) and a 1962 Ferrari 250 GTO.

The GTO is one of three star cars in Ferrari Ultimate Garage (set 75889).

2018

Bugatti and Mercedes join this year's collection, with the latter starring in Speed Champions biggest ever set—the 941-piece Mercedes AMG Petronas Formula One Team (set 75883).

2017

This flaming Ford brings the heat in Ford F-150 Raptor & Ford Model A Hot Rod (set 75875).

Classic and vintage cars race into the range, with a 1969 Chevy and a 1920s-style Ford lining up alongside ultramodern marvels such as the Audi R18 e-tron quattro (set 75872).

2016

F14 T & Scuderia Ferrari Truck (set 75913) includes an F1 racer and its entire entourage.

Sets such as Porsche 918 Spyder (set 75910) feature one iconic car and a minifigure driver.

Start your engines! Speed Champions growls off the starting grid with Ferrari, Porsche, and McLaren models. New tire, wheel arch, and wheel trim parts all add to the authenticity.

START

2015

206

FAST AND FABULOUS

2019 — It's Dodge against Dodge and Mini versus Mini in this year's twin-packs, as 50-year-old classics feature alongside the latest machines from both car manufacturers.

The newer car from 1967 Mini Cooper S Rally and 2018 MINI John Cooper Works Buggy (set 75894) has working rubber-band suspension.

2020 — Things step up a gear as Speed Champions' cars go from being six studs wide to eight studs wide, bringing even more detail to the range's first Jaguar, Lamborghini, and Nissan sets.

Lamborghini Urus ST-X & Huracán Super Trofeo EVO (set 76899) is one of the most realistic Speed Champions sets so far.

The older car from 2018 Dodge Challenger SRT Demon and 1970 Dodge Charger R/T (set 75893) has a detachable supercharger.

2021 — The Koenigsegg Jesko (set 76900) and Toyota Supra (set 76901) put two more much-loved makers on the Speed Champions track, and the range gets its first ever dragster.

There are many more bricks in the Jesko set than there are real Jeskos in the world!

2023 — Updated chassis, wheel arch, and windshield pieces make sets such as Pagani Utopia (set 76915) some of the curviest and most true-to-life Speed Champions sets so far.

This 14-in (35-cm) dragster is part of Mopar Dodge//SRT Top Fuel Dragster and 1970 Dodge Challenger T/A (set 76904).

2022 — Aston Martin and Lotus join the lineup of LEGO supercars, and the range drives into the movies with cars belonging to James Bond, and Dom from the *Fast & Furious* franchise.

I'll try to bring it back in 298 pieces!

James Bond's 007 Aston Martin DB5 (set 76911) comes with swappable super-spy license plates.

The Lotus Evija (set 76907) has an upside-down minifigure snowboard as its spoiler.

2024 — You wait 10 years for a Speed Champions BMW, and then two zoom into view at once—in the 676-piece twin-pack BMW M4 GT3 & BMW M Hybrid V8 (set 76922).

207

JURASSIC WORLD

With DNA that can be traced back to 2001's LEGO® Studios sets, the **LEGO® Jurassic World™** theme burst into life in 2015, alongside the first *Jurassic World* movie. Since then, its minifigure heroes have faced prehistoric peril in sets inspired by the films and TV series.

Featuring movie-making minifigures on brick-built soundstages, the LEGO Studios theme includes two sets based on the filming of *Jurassic Park III*, complete with camera operators.

2001

Four sets based on animated series LEGO *Jurassic World: Legend of Isla Nublar* include the epic T. rex vs. Dino-Mech Battle (set 75938), complete with a brick-built robo-rex.

2019

Standing 16 in (42 cm) high with 3,120 pieces, Jurassic Park: T. Rex Rampage (set 75936) is the biggest build in the theme to date.

2020

This year's dinosaurs include a spiky Ankylosaurus, a long-necked Gallimimus and, in Dr. Wu's Lab: Baby Dinosaurs Breakout (set 75939), a baby Triceratops as big as a LEGO horse!

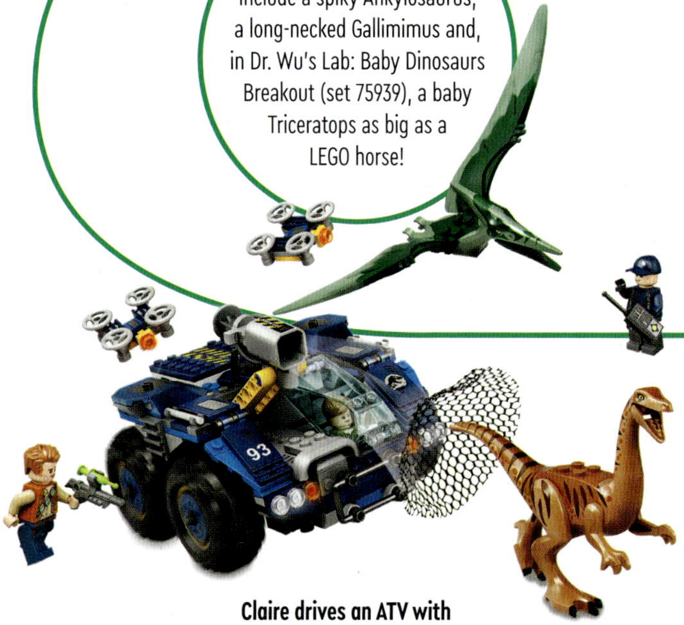

The teen heroes of animated series *Jurassic World Camp Cretaceous* star in this year's sets, along with a new Baryonyx figure and the theme's first brick-built dinosaur skeleton.

Kenji and Sammy have a close call in Carnotaurus Dinosaur Chase (set 76941).

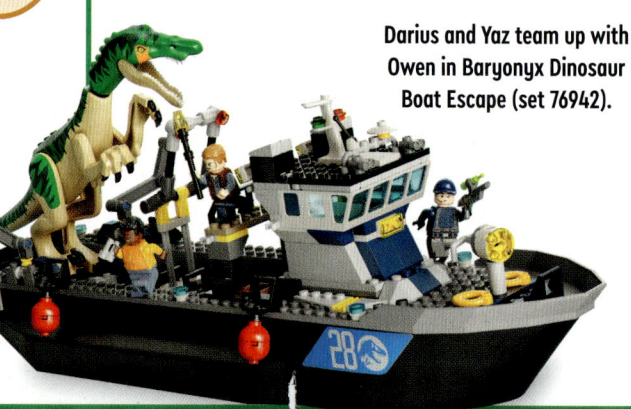

2021

Claire drives an ATV with detachable drones in Gallimimus and Pteranodon Breakout (set 75940).

Darius and Yaz team up with Owen in Baryonyx Dinosaur Boat Escape (set 76942).

208

JURASSIC WORLD

Help! I feel sick!

The first six LEGO Jurassic World sets introduce heroes Owen and Claire alongside a Pteranodon, a Dilophosaurus, a Tyrannosaurus rex, an Indominus rex, and four raptors.

Claire's nephew Zach and scientist Dr. Wu star in this year's biggest set, Indominus Rex Breakout (set 75919).

Every one of this year's dinosaur figures has posable limbs and snapping jaws.

2015

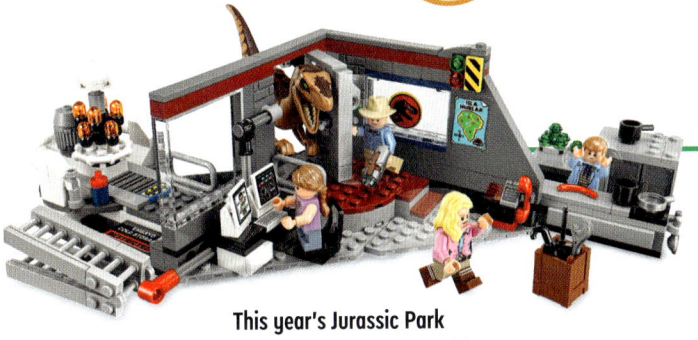

This year's Jurassic Park Velociraptor Chase (set 75932) is the first set to be based on the 1993 film that started it all.

Indoraptor Rampage at Lockwood Estate (set 75930) brings battling dinosaurs to new character Maisie's doorstep.

Sets inspired by blockbuster sequel *Jurassic World: Fallen Kingdom* include fearsome Carnotaurus, Indoraptor, and Stygimoloch figures, plus super-cute new baby dinosaur pieces.

2018

The prehistoric star of Quetzalcoatlus Plane Ambush (set 76947) has an 11.5-in (29-cm) wingspan!

Five sets celebrate the 30th anniversary of the original *Jurassic Park* film, including Brachiosaurus Discovery (set 76960), with its extra-tall dino figure and even taller tree build!

2022

From towering Giganotosaurus to plane-size Quetzalcoatlus, LEGO dinosaurs (and pterosaurs) are bigger than ever in sets based on thrilling threequel *Jurassic World Dominion*.

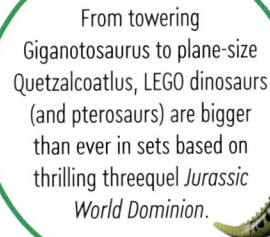

2023

The dinos in Giganotosaurus & Therizinosaurus Attack (set 76949) are so big that Owen and Claire need a tower to see them properly!

2024

Dinosaur Fossils: T. Rex Skull (set 76964) is a new kind of LEGO Jurassic World display set. It combines a snapping dino skull, a fossilized footprint, and a detailed display plaque.

209

BUILD ME UP!

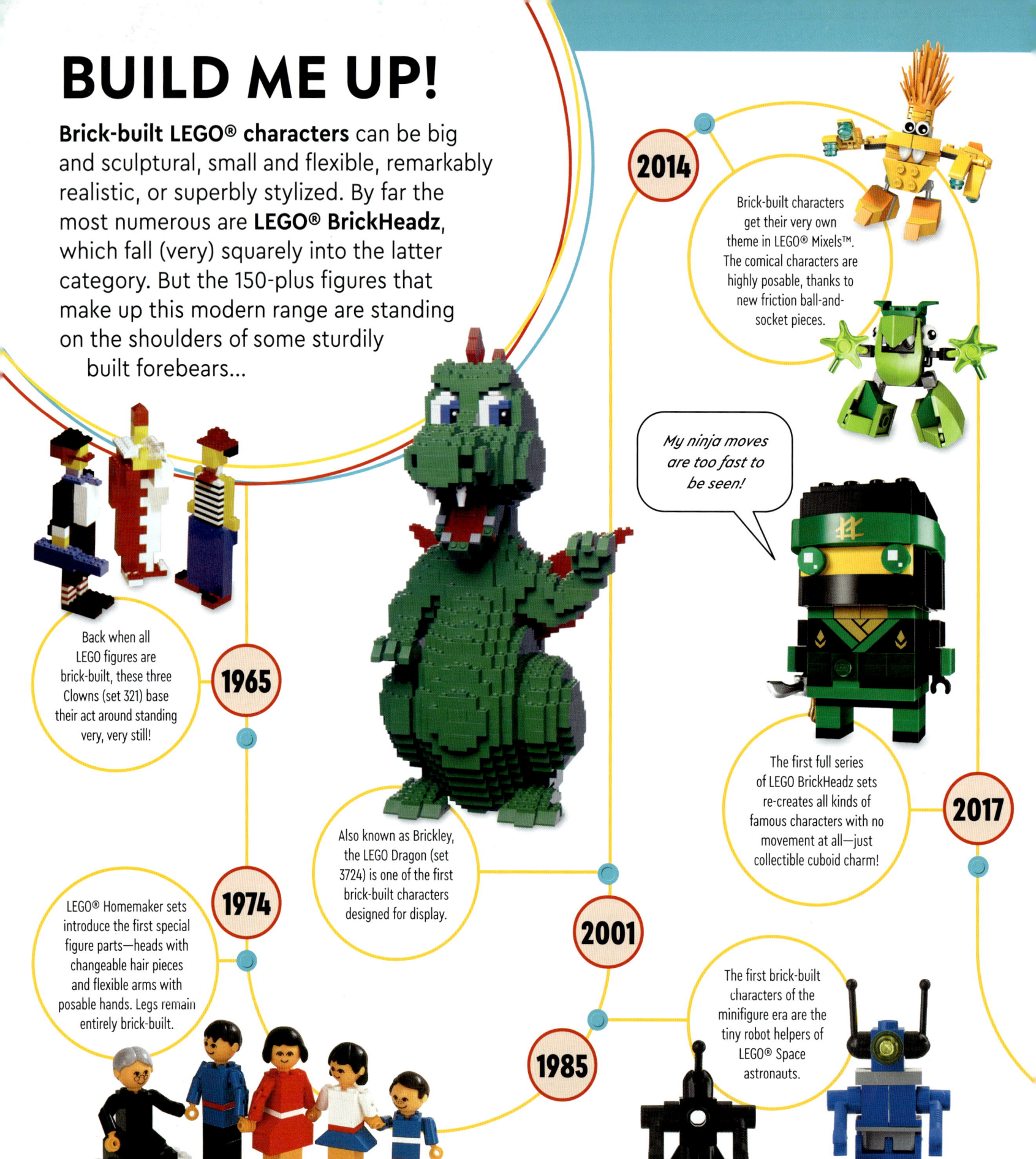

Brick-built LEGO® characters can be big and sculptural, small and flexible, remarkably realistic, or superbly stylized. By far the most numerous are **LEGO® BrickHeadz**, which fall (very) squarely into the latter category. But the 150-plus figures that make up this modern range are standing on the shoulders of some sturdily built forebears...

2014 — Brick-built characters get their very own theme in LEGO® Mixels™. The comical characters are highly posable, thanks to new friction ball-and-socket pieces.

My ninja moves are too fast to be seen!

2017 — The first full series of LEGO BrickHeadz sets re-creates all kinds of famous characters with no movement at all—just collectible cuboid charm!

1965 — Back when all LEGO figures are brick-built, these three Clowns (set 321) base their act around standing very, very still!

1974 — LEGO® Homemaker sets introduce the first special figure parts—heads with changeable hair pieces and flexible arms with posable hands. Legs remain entirely brick-built.

2001 — Also known as Brickley, the LEGO Dragon (set 3724) is one of the first brick-built characters designed for display.

1985 — The first brick-built characters of the minifigure era are the tiny robot helpers of LEGO® Space astronauts.

BUILD ME UP!

2019
A diverse year for LEGO BrickHeadz includes a Thanksgiving Scarecrow (set 40352), Lady Liberty (set 40367), and the stars of THE LEGO® MOVIE 2™.

2021
BrickHeadz sets branch out into buildable pets, including cats, hamsters, birds, and an adorable pair of Dalmatians (set 40479).

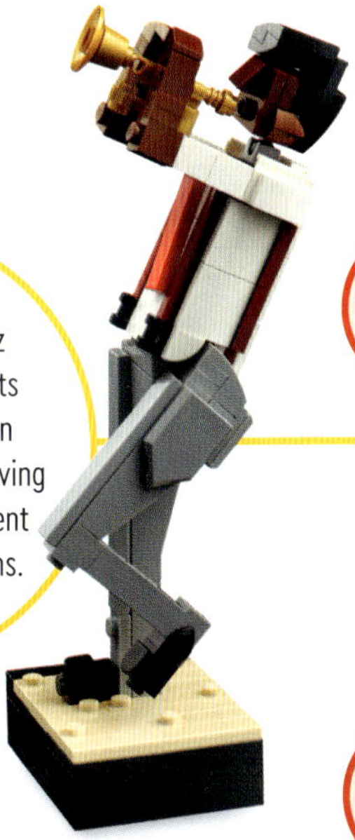

2022
The LEGO® Ideas Jazz Quartet (set 21334) puts a new, realistic spin on brick-built characters, giving a real sense of movement to its posable musicians.

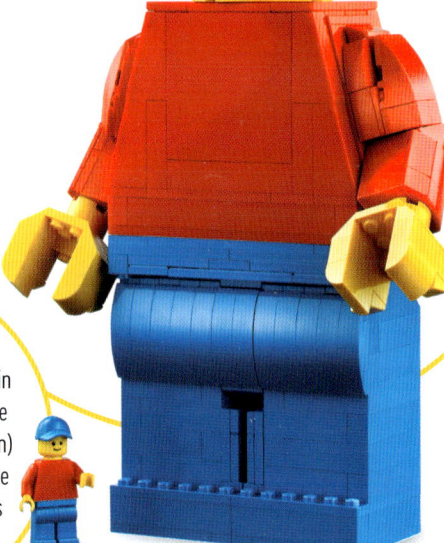

2023
Brick-built characters and minifigures join forces in Up-Scaled LEGO® Minifigure (set 40649). The 11-in (27-cm) figure doesn't just move like a minifigure, he also keeps one under his hat!

There's something very wrong with this mirror!

2018
This year's BrickHeadz sets include Go Brick Me (set 41597). The customizable brick-built figure can be made to look like anyone.

211

BRICKS THAT GO BUMP IN THE NIGHT

Some LEGO® themes are set in the real world and others in full-on fantasy lands. And in between? That's where the best **ghost stories** take place! With one foot in everyday life (or thereabouts), these themes also dip a toe into spine-tingling territories. Here, realistic castles have ghoulish guests and high schools turn into student-eating monsters at the flick of a switch or two!

1990

There's a strange, green glow coming from this year's LEGO® Castle sets. Peer into sets such as King's Mountain Fortress (set 6081), and you might just see the first glow-in-the-dark LEGO ghost figures!

You can blame me for a lot of sleepless knights!

1997

The first ever witch minifigure gave the Fright Knights their fearsome powers.

Two themes crank up the creepiness this year, as Bat Lord Basil and the Fright Knights take over LEGO Castle, and the Time Cruisers tackle ghosts and ghouls in sets such as Twisted Time Train (set 6497).

2002

It's frights, camera, action, as the LEGO® Studios theme corners the scary movie market. But don't worry—the vampire, werewolf, and monster minifigures in these sets are just actors in costumes... aren't they?

2003

Only the bravest builders dare to delve into this year's LEGO® Creator Halloween Bucket (set 7836)! It comes with more than 100 ideas for building black cats, pumpkins, dragons, and... penguins. Chilling!

2007

The LEGO Castle theme enters its Fantasy Era, starting with a plague of super-scary skeletons! There are skeleton ships, a skeleton tower, and even skeleton horses pulling the Skeletons' Prison Carriage (set 7092).

212

BRICKS THAT GO BUMP IN THE NIGHT

Monster Fighter heroes include awesome Ann Lee and hard-bitten Jack McHammer.

2015

The entire 14th series of collectible LEGO® Minifigures is themed around monsters of all shapes and sizes (OK, just minifigure-size). Creepy characters include a Gargoyle, a Banshee, and a Zombie Pirate.

2012

Bat monsters, a zombie bride and groom, and a glow-in-the-dark Ghost Train (set 9467) are among the menaces faced by scientist Dr. Rodney Rathbone and his team in the epic LEGO® Monster Fighters theme.

Woo-ooo-ooo... f!

Ten Hidden Side sets include this friendly ghost dog figure!

Eek! A ghost dog!

2019

There are more LEGO ghosts and monsters than ever before in the hugely haunted LEGO® Hidden Side theme. Some are minifigures, some are entire buildings, and some can only be seen using a special smartphone app.

It's all fun and games in Haunted House (set 10273), the latest attraction in the LEGO® Icons Fairground Collection. Meanwhile, Hidden Side reaches its epic conclusion with the coming of creepy Nehmaar Reem.

2020

Hidden Side heroes Jack and Parker tackle all manner of monstrous activity in Newbury Haunted High School (set 70425). An interactive app helps players scan for resident ghosts.

213

WORLDS OF WONDER

Most LEGO® themes involve a healthy dose of fantasy, but only a few take place in worlds entirely unlike our own. **Imaginary lands** explored in LEGO sets include the animal habitats of CHIMA, the enchanted realm of Elvendale, the ancient yet ultramodern kingdom of Knighton, and the boundless dimension of DREAMZzz™.

Laval and other main characters come in both minifigure and buildable figure form.

LEGO® Legends of Chima™ introduces a world where highly evolved animal tribes compete for power-giving CHI. The main tribes in the first year of sets are the Lions, led by Laval, and the Crocodiles, led by Cragger.

2013

The second year of LEGO Elves sets introduces villainous elf Ragana Shadowflame plus five big, buildable dragons. Four dragons are linked to the elements earth, wind, fire, and water, while the fifth one's element is love.

The NEXO KNIGHTS protect Knighton from Jestro and the Lava Army unleashed by his Book of Monsters.

Scanning the sets' many shields with a smartphone unlocks new powers in the NEXO KNIGHTS game app.

This year's newest fantasy land is Knighton, home of the LEGO® NEXO KNIGHTS™. Putting a futuristic spin on classic Castle sets, the theme's brave stars download digital power-ups to defeat the forces of evil.

2016

The NEXO KNIGHTS cross swords with Stone Monsters in this year's sets. The largest is Knighton Castle (set 70357), in which digital wizard Merlok 2.0 gets a mech suit to take on the rock-hard Stone Stompers.

The last LEGO Elves sets pit Emily and her elf friends against evil shape-shifting Noctura and her bat minions. Luckily, the Elves have Elemental Guardians on their side, including Rowan the Fire Lion and Liska the Earth Fox.

2017

Emily's sister, Sophie Jones, gets involved in the latest LEGO Elves adventures thanks to the crafty Cronan Darkroot, the Goblin King. Cute but cunning new goblin figures do Darkroot's bidding in all eight 2017 sets.

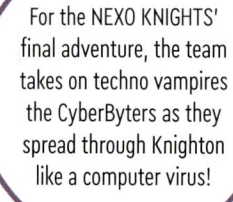

2018

For the NEXO KNIGHTS' final adventure, the team takes on techno vampires the CyberByters as they spread through Knighton like a computer virus!

214

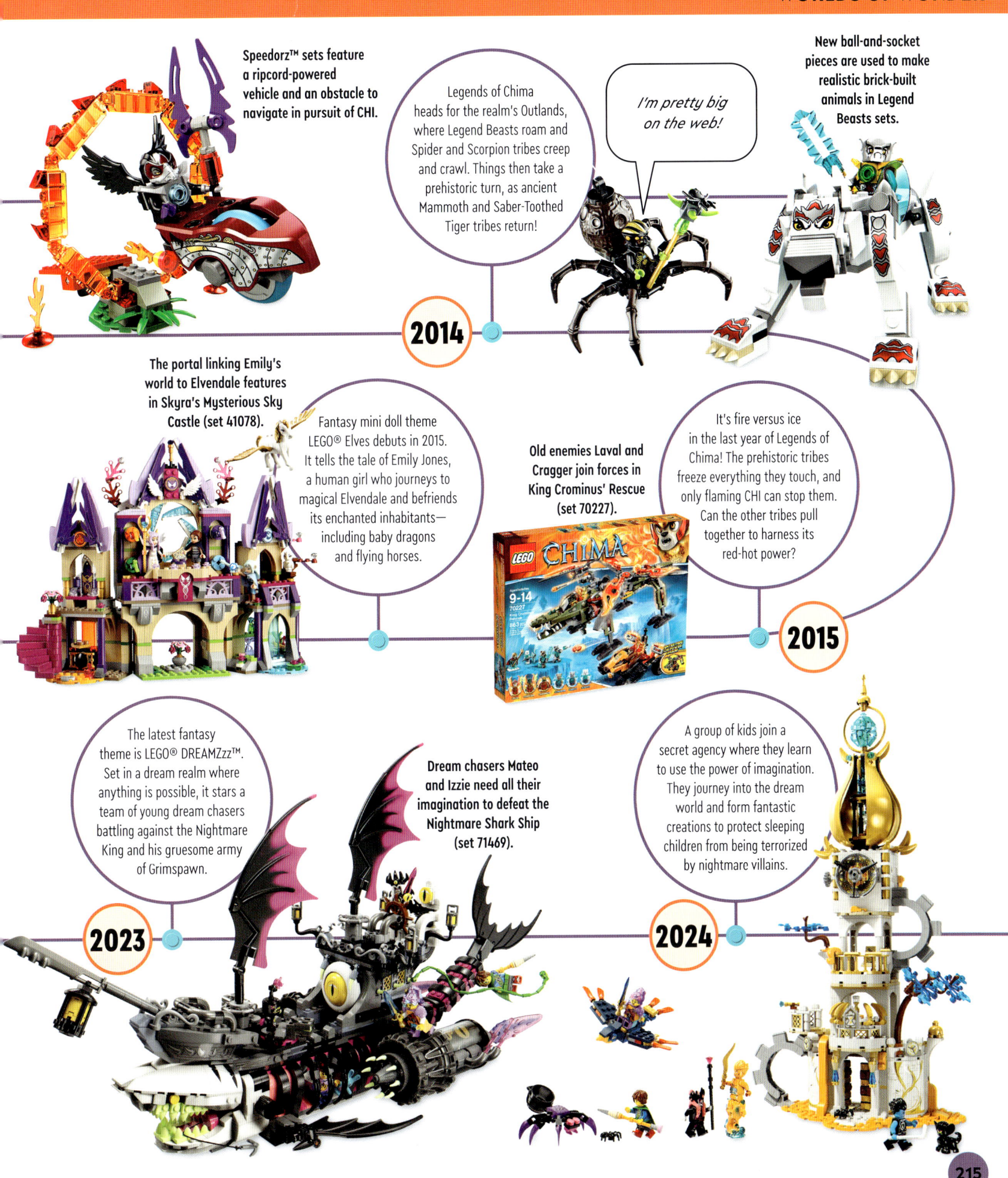

WORLDS OF WONDER

Speedorz™ sets feature a ripcord-powered vehicle and an obstacle to navigate in pursuit of CHI.

Legends of Chima heads for the realm's Outlands, where Legend Beasts roam and Spider and Scorpion tribes creep and crawl. Things then take a prehistoric turn, as ancient Mammoth and Saber-Toothed Tiger tribes return!

I'm pretty big on the web!

New ball-and-socket pieces are used to make realistic brick-built animals in Legend Beasts sets.

2014

The portal linking Emily's world to Elvendale features in Skyra's Mysterious Sky Castle (set 41078).

Fantasy mini doll theme LEGO® Elves debuts in 2015. It tells the tale of Emily Jones, a human girl who journeys to magical Elvendale and befriends its enchanted inhabitants—including baby dragons and flying horses.

Old enemies Laval and Cragger join forces in King Crominus' Rescue (set 70227).

It's fire versus ice in the last year of Legends of Chima! The prehistoric tribes freeze everything they touch, and only flaming CHI can stop them. Can the other tribes pull together to harness its red-hot power?

2015

The latest fantasy theme is LEGO® DREAMZzz™. Set in a dream realm where anything is possible, it stars a team of young dream chasers battling against the Nightmare King and his gruesome army of Grimspawn.

Dream chasers Mateo and Izzie need all their imagination to defeat the Nightmare Shark Ship (set 71469).

A group of kids join a secret agency where they learn to use the power of imagination. They journey into the dream world and form fantastic creations to protect sleeping children from being terrorized by nightmare villains.

2023

2024

215

TV TIMES

Lots of LEGO® themes have their own TV show, but only a few original **TV shows** get their own LEGO themes and sets! Builds are all based on small-screen favorites—from animated adventures and comedy classics to live-action dramas and bingeable box sets.

Two *Airbender* sets are released, both featuring the show's hero, Aang.

The first minifigure themes to be based on TV shows are LEGO® SpongeBob SquarePants™ and LEGO® Avatar: The Last Airbender, both based on Nickelodeon animated series.

2006

The Krusty Krab (set 3825) is the first of 14 SpongeBob sets.

The Flintstones (set 21316) is based on the 1960s Hanna-Barbera cartoon series.

The Upside Down (set 75810) turns Netflix series *Stranger Things* on its head with a design that works whichever way up you display it. Meanwhile, LEGO Ideas meets *The Flintstones*.

2019

You can count on 123 Sesame Street (set 21324) to capture the magic of TV's longest-running Muppet show! A range of collectible Muppet Minifigures will follow in 2022.

2020

Cookie Monster, Oscar, Big Bird, Elmo, and Bert and Ernie all appear in this LEGO Ideas set.

2021

Netflix's much-loved makeover show gets a LEGO glow-up in Queer Eye—The Fab 5 Loft (set 10291). The set includes a "transformation chamber" and a Bruley the dog figure.

TV TIMES

2013 — Cowabunga! The LEGO® Teenage Mutant Ninja Turtles™ launch into action in sets such as Shellraiser Street Chase (set 79104), inspired by their latest TV adventures.

2015 — Doctor Who (set 21304) includes an unfolding TARDIS time machine.

Zoinks! A minifigure Mystery Inc. investigates creepy crooks in five LEGO® Scooby-Doo™ sets, while LEGO® Ideas pays tribute to the world's longest-running TV sci-fi series.

The Mystery Machine (set 75902) re-creates the Scooby Gang's classic van.

2018 — After debuting in LEGO® DIMENSIONS, LEGO® The Powerpuff Girls™ get their very own theme. Mojo Jojo Strikes (set 41288) is the largest set based on the Cartoon Network super heroes.

2022 — The Office (set 21336) becomes the fourth LEGO Ideas set based on a smash-hit US sitcom, following sets based on *The Big Bang Theory*, *Friends*, and *Seinfeld*.

2023 — The LEGO® Gabby's Dollhouse theme re-creates the preschool show's star in mini doll form, with unique new LEGO figures as her various feline friends.

Kitty Fairy's Garden Party (set 10787) includes special Pandy Paws and Kitty Fairy figures.

BIG-SCREEN BUILDS

There's more to **LEGO® movies** than just THE LEGO® MOVIE™! Since 1999, some of the silver screen's most famous stories and best-loved characters have been turned into brickbusting sets, enabling fans to replay classic moments or direct their own new adventures.

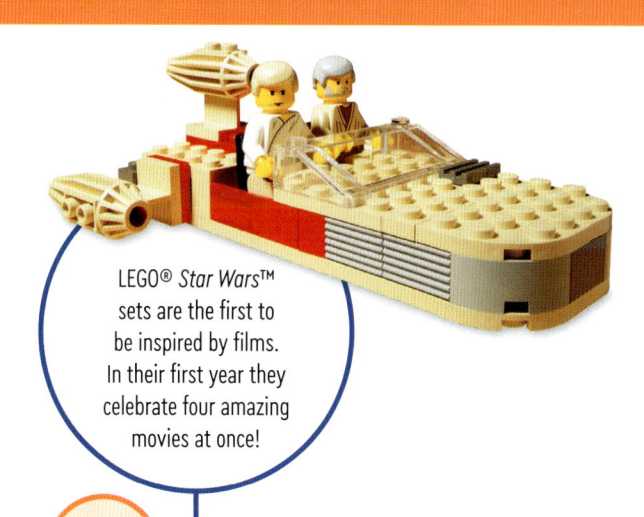

LEGO® *Star Wars*™ sets are the first to be inspired by films. In their first year they celebrate four amazing movies at once!

1999

As *The Hobbit: An Unexpected Journey* heads for cinemas, LEGO® *The Hobbit*™ and LEGO® *The Lord of the Rings*™ sets venture into stores!

2012

2013

Based on *Back to the Future*, The DeLorean Time Machine (set 21103) is the first of several LEGO® Ideas sets inspired by classic films.

2014

This year's film-themed sets are based on Teenage Mutant Ninja Turtles... and a surprise box-office smash called THE LEGO® MOVIE™.

2016

Sets based on two different *Ghostbusters* films include Firehouse Headquarters (set 75827), one of the biggest LEGO sets ever made.

218

BIG-SCREEN BUILDS

2001 — The first LEGO® Harry Potter™ sets debut in the same year as LEGO® Studios sets based on the making of *Jurassic Park III*.

2002 — LEGO Studios sets based on this year's *Spider-Man* movie are the first of many to feature big-screen Super Heroes.

2010 — LEGO® *Prince of Persia*™, LEGO® *Toy Story*™, and LEGO® DUPLO® *Cars*™ sets are the first of many to be based on Disney and Disney Pixar films.

2008 — LEGO® *Indiana Jones*™ and LEGO® Speed Racer sets tie in with two of this year's most hotly anticipated movies.

2020 — A blockbuster year sees sets based on *Minions: The Rise of Gru*, *Trolls World Tour*, and even Universal's 1931 version of *Frankenstein*!

2022 — Four spectacular sets based on the first *Avatar* film precede five more that will accompany *Avatar: The Way of Water* the following year.

219

NEXT-LEVEL SETS

The first LEGO® theme based on a **video game** was 2013's LEGO® Minecraft®. Since then, themes based on Super Mario™ and Sonic the Hedgehog™ have brought new kinds of gameplay to LEGO sets while others have celebrated the latest adventure games, classic consoles, and arcade icons.

2015
The first Sonic the Hedgehog minifigure features in a LEGO® DIMENSIONS set. The same theme also boasts sets based on puzzle game *Portal 2* and classic arcade compilation series *Midway Arcade*.

2022
The LEGO® Icons Horizon Forbidden West: Tallneck (set 76989) is a 1,222-piece display set celebrating the "big guys" of the smash-hit action RPG. It also includes a unique minifigure of the game's hero, Aloy.

2022
The second classic console to be replicated in LEGO bricks is the LEGO Icons Atari 2600 (set 10306). The set slides open to reveal a minifigure gamer blasting his way through 1970s space simulator *Asteroids*!

2023
Sonic's own theme puts a new spin on buildable video games, with high-speed minifigure launchers. LEGO® Sonic the Hedgehog™ sets also include brand-new Tails and Amy Rose minifigures and an epic Eggman figure.

2022
Princess Peach is the latest interactive figure in this year's Super Mario sets, while The Mighty Bowser (set 71411) becomes the theme's biggest set as a 2,807-piece, fireball-spitting sculpture.

NEXT-LEVEL SETS

2019
The LEGO® Overwatch® theme comprises seven play sets based on the much-loved multiplayer action game, and one display set, Junkrat & Roadhog (set 75977), capturing all the chaos of Junkertown!

2020
The LEGO® Super Mario™ theme introduces a new kind of figure with sensors, speakers, and screens! These allow Mario to collect coins, react to perils, and use power-ups in buildable, playable game levels.

2022
The Blue Blur returns in Sonic the Hedgehog—Green Hill Zone (set 21331). Multiple versions of the LEGO® Ideas set can be built in different ways and joined together to create a longer, custom course.

2021
The Mario Bros. team up as Luigi leaps into LEGO Super Mario sets. Meanwhile, Master Your Adventure (set 71380) is the theme's first Maker Set for creating custom challenges with unique rewards.

2020
Mario also stars in this year's Nintendo Entertainment System (set 71374), a 2,646-piece re-creation of the classic 1980s console complete with controller, cartridge, and side-scrolling TV screen.

2023
The fourth year of Super Mario sets is all about the apes, with Donkey Kong's Tree House (set 71424), Diddy Kong's Mine Cart Ride (set 71425), and Dixie Kong's Jungle Jam (set 71421).

2023
LEGO Icons goes back to the dawn of gaming with the 2,651-piece PAC-MAN Arcade (set 10323). Turn the handle on the side to see the classic characters move around the brick-built maze.

2024
Six sets based on creative game series Animal Crossing feature minifigure versions of much-loved characters and celebrate all-star settings such as Nook's Cranny & Rosie's House (set 77050).

THE 2020s

2020

LEGO® Monkie Kid™ puts a new spin on an ancient Chinese adventure story.

LEGO® Art, LEGO® DOTS, and LEGO® Brick Sketches™ celebrate the stylish side of building.

The star of LEGO® Super Mario™ is a new kind of figure that reacts to movement and special Action Bricks.

2022

LEGOLAND® Water Park Gardaland and LEGOLAND® New York open their gates in Italy and the US, respectively.

The LEGO Group celebrates its 90th birthday with the 90 Years of Play campaign.

LEGO® Avatar sets re-create the epic *Avatar* films, complete with unique Na'vi figures.

LEGO® Sonic the Hedgehog™ spins into action with help from a buildable speed sphere!

LEGO® Gabby's Dollhouse sets re-create the miniature world of the much-loved TV show.

Online LEGO gaming gets bigger than ever with the launch of LEGO® Fortnite®.

2021

Lovable little movie icons get smaller still in LEGO® Trolls World Tour and LEGO® Minions: *The Rise of Gru* sets.

The LEGO® Icons Botanical Collection comes into bloom with lifelike, life-size plant builds.

Six golden ninja minifigures (and a golden Master Wu) mark 10 years of LEGO® NINJAGO®.

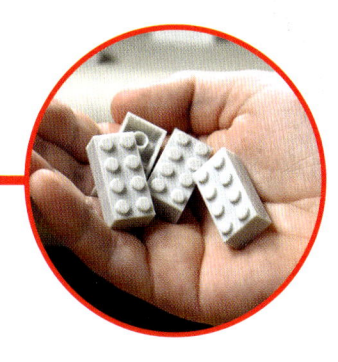

The LEGO Group produces a prototype LEGO brick made from recycled plastic bottles.

2023

The LEGO® Friends clock up 10 Years of Friendship!

Recyclable paper-based bags start to replace plastic ones in LEGO sets.

LEGOLAND® Korea opens as Asia's largest LEGO attraction.

Kids with big imaginations take on the Nightmare King in fantasy theme LEGO® DREAMZzz™.

2024

Thomas Kirk Kristiansen becomes chairman of the LEGO Group.

Fab new minifigures star in LEGO® Animal Crossing™, based on the smash-hit video game.

Special sets and never-before-seen minifigures mark the 25th anniversary of LEGO® *Star Wars*™.

The LEGO Group opens its most sustainable factory so far in Binh Duong province, Vietnam.

223

YEARS OF THE MONKIE

In 2020, an ancient Chinese classic got a 21st-century LEGO® reboot. Inspired by tales of the mythical Monkey King, **LEGO® Monkie Kid™** follows the adventures of a noodle delivery boy who fights the forces of evil with help from his friends, his magical golden staff, and the occasional celestial being!

1592

The novel *Journey to the West* is published in China. It blends a seventh-century travelogue with folk tales of the mythical Monkey King. In time, it comes to be seen as a defining classic of Chinese literature.

2018–2019

LEGO designers are inspired by *Journey to the West* and work with families in China to turn it into a LEGO play theme. In 2019, a collectible LEGO® Minifigure Monkey King is released.

This year's new minifigures include moon-dwelling, live-streaming celestial being Chang'e and her Lunar Rabbit Robot.

Monkie Kid's home town of Megapolis comes to life in The City of Lanterns (set 80036). The 2,187-piece set includes a bubble tea shop, a karaoke booth, a LEGO Store, and a Pigsy-themed railroad.

2022

Spider Queen's Arachnoid Base (set 80022) is one of many sets in which Monkie Kid turns his magic staff into a flying machine.

2023

A cursed scroll puts Monkie Kid in conflict with all-new demons in this year's epic storyline. The scroll itself is found in just one set—hidden under a four-poster bed in Dragon of the East Palace (set 80049).

The Mighty Azure Lion (set 80048) leads this year's baddies—the Demon Kings of Lion Camel Ridge.

224

YEARS OF THE MONKIE

Monkey King Warrior Mech (set 80012) has more metallic gold parts than any other set.

More than 400 years in the making, the first LEGO Monkie Kid sets launch alongside an animated TV special. Monkey King himself appears just once in the first wave—in Monkey King Warrior Mech.

The first eight sets introduce Monkie Kid and his friends, including Mei, Sandy, Pigsy, and Sandy's pet cat, Mo.

2020

The Legendary Flower Fruit Mountain includes four minifigures of Monkey King at different stages in his life.

The Flaming Foundry (set 80016) is the largest of three sets to accompany the new, animated LEGO *Monkie Kid* TV series.

2021

While most of this year's sets focus on Monkie Kid's latest TV adventures, The Legendary Flower Fruit Mountain (set 80024) is a 1,949-piece retelling of the original Monkey King's action-packed early life.

2024

Lifting the giant staff out of the East Palace set reveals Monkie Kid's minifigure-scale version underneath.

Sets celebrating five years of the LEGO Monkie Kid theme include a limited edition Monkie Kid 5th Anniversary Cake (set 6476261), topped off with a Monkey King minifigure wearing a party hat!

STATEMENT PIECES

All LEGO® sets are miniature **works of art**, but some are made especially for lovers of craft, culture, and classic design. These are the centerpieces to give your home a gallery glow-up and the accessories to turn your wardrobe into a talking point. You can call it the LEGO look!

The first LEGO range with a focus on craft and style is LEGO® SCALA™. Sets include buildable bracelets, pendants, and other wearable works of art.

1979–1980

Connoisseurs of classic design can tap away on the LEGO Ideas Typewriter (set 21327), which has moving keys, a working carriage mechanism, and plenty of mid-century charm.

2021

LEGO® DOTS is all about making personalized patterns with the smallest LEGO elements. Bracelets, bag tags, message boards, and more can all be made into detailed designs.

2020–2023

The LEGO® Icons Botanical Collection begins with Flower Bouquet (set 10280) and Bonsai Tree (set 10281), both designed to make your home beautiful with no need for watering!

LEGO Icons set Everyone is Awesome (set 40516) is a different kind of statement piece—designed not only to look great but also to celebrate social diversity and inclusion.

226

STATEMENT PIECES

2003–2006 — Bracelets are just the beginning in LEGO® CLIKITS™ craft sets. Click-on parts make statement pillows, picture frames, memo holders, and more.

2009–2011 — Sets made for Japanese design store MUJI combine LEGO bricks and hole-punched paper to make unique ornaments with a minimalist look.

2020 — The dedicated LEGO® Art range debuts with four large mosaic builds, including Andy Warhol's Marilyn Monroe (set 31197), which can be built in four different pop art colorways.

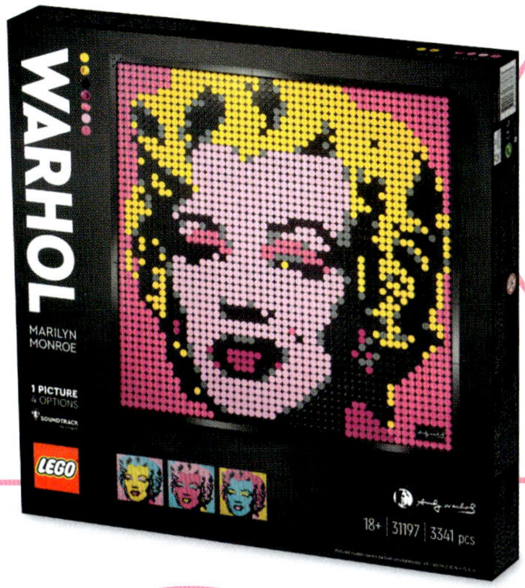

2018 — The LEGO® Ideas Ship in a Bottle (set 21313) re-creates a kind of folk art popular since the 1800s. There's no mystery about how the ship got inside the bottle, but it still looks cool!

2022 — LEGO Ideas pays tribute to Vincent Van Gogh with The Starry Night (set 21333), a 2,316-piece brick "painting," complete with a Van Gogh minifigure to add a final flourish!

2023 — The Botanical Collection celebrates the timeless craft of flower arranging with Wildflower Bouquet (set 10313) and Dried Flower Centerpiece (set 10314).

LEGO Art set Hokusai—The Great Wave (set 31208) uses 1,810 pieces to re-create one of the great works of Japanese printmaking.

227

TIME, PIECES

In the 20th century it was rare for LEGO® sets to have more than 1,000 pieces. But since the year 2000, the **biggest LEGO sets** have been getting even bigger! Here are the 21st-century sets that have passed the baton of "biggest set ever" from one generation to the next.

The LEGO® Star Wars™ Imperial Star Destroyer (set 10030) also includes a tiny *Tantive IV*.

I'm just happy that a minifigure was the biggest anything!

The first LEGO Statue of Liberty (set 3450) is also the first set with more than 2,000 pieces.

The LEGO *Star Wars* Death Star II (set 10143) has a circumference of 60 in (152 cm).

This buildable LEGO® Minifigure (set 3723) is the biggest set for just two weeks!

1,850 pieces	2,882 pieces	3,096 pieces	3,441 pieces
Nov 1, 2000	Nov 15, 2000	2002	2005

228

TIME, PIECES

The Ultimate Collector's *Millennium Falcon* (set 10179) keeps LEGO *Star Wars* on top.

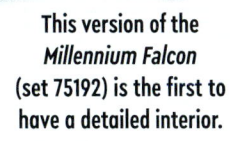

This version of the *Millennium Falcon* (set 75192) is the first to have a detailed interior.

The majestic Taj Mahal (set 10189) is the undisputed biggest set ever for a decade.

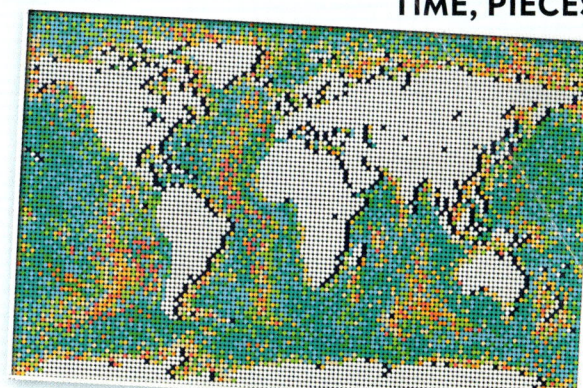

World Map (set 31203) is more than 40 in (100 cm) wide and includes 11,170 1×1 round pieces!

Rome's iconic Colosseum (set 10276) has more pieces than four Statue of Liberty sets!

5,197 pieces	5,922 pieces	7,541 pieces	9,036 pieces	11,695 pieces
2007	2008	2017	2020	2021

LEARNING CURVE

LEGO® bricks and learning have always gone together, and today's **LEGO® Education** sets are the latest in a long line of resources made for schools. Here are just a few ideas that have clicked in classrooms over the years—exploring everything from engineering and coding to physics and feelings!

1949 — The first LEGO products made for schools are "Byggeklodser" (building bricks) for early learners.

1962 — The first European school sets boast a bumper selection of bricks in neat wooden boxes.

2004 — The World Robot Olympiad™ is the latest LEGO MINDSTORMS challenge for students.

2005 — The LEGO Education name is introduced on sets such as Community Workers (set 9247).

2009 — The first generation of LEGO® WeDo sets bring school robotics to younger audiences.

2013 — First launched in 1998, LEGO® Soft Bricks return for squishy, supersize building fun.

2016 — Build Me "Emotions" (set 45018) helps younger children explore each other's feelings.

2017  — STEAM sets for preschoolers combine Science, Technology, Engineering, Art, and Math.

STEAM Park (set 45024) explores gears, motion, measurement, and more.

2020 — LEGO Education launches SPIKE™ Prime as the colorful successor to LEGO MINDSTORMS.

LEARNING CURVE

1962–1969 — School sets in the US range from plain cardboard boxes to suitcases full of bricks!

1972 — Bricks are used to solve logic puzzles in one-off math set Thinking with LEGO (set 1512).

1980 — The LEGO Group sets up a department to promote the importance of learning through play.

This year's school sets are the first to include minifigures for creative role play.

1986 — LEGO® Technic Control sets for schools are the first to blend building and computer coding!

1988 — The LEGO education division becomes LEGO® Dacta™, from the Greek for a skilled teacher.

1998 — LEGO® MINDSTORMS® for schools brings smart bricks and real robots into the classroom. FIRST and the LEGO Group join forces to create FIRST LEGO® League, a new robotics contest.

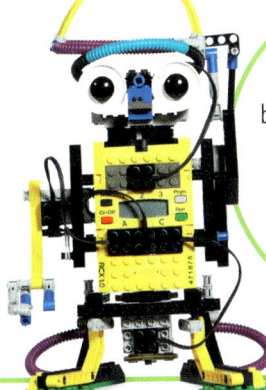

FIRST LEGO® League is a STEM (Science, Technology, Engineering, and Math) program where teams of children around the world enter their LEGO robots into fun contests, gaining valuable life skills.

2021 — The BricQ Motion range uses pistons, sails, weights, and more to explore physical forces.

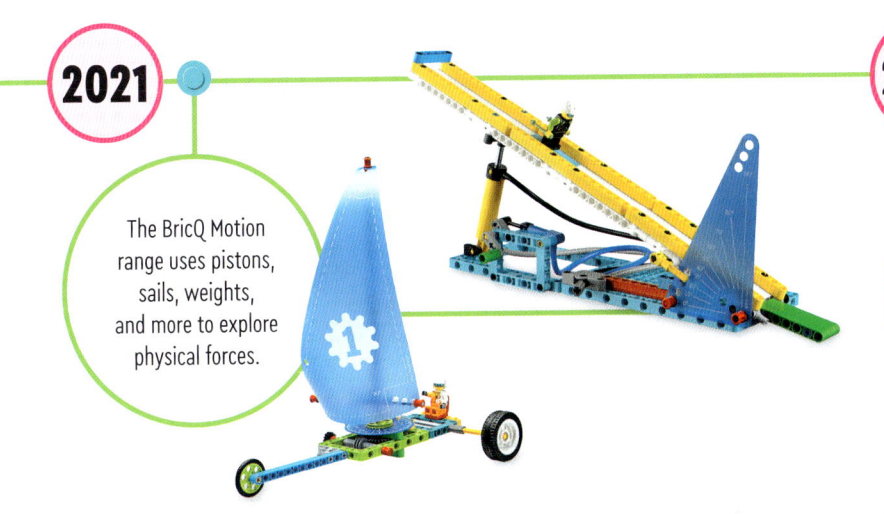

2023 — Classroom kit Hannah's STEAM Heroes gets kids thinking about cool 21st century careers.

Rebuild The World with Bee Rescue
Featuring Hannah's STEAM Heroes: Julie & Jeff Russell

BRICKISH BROADCASTING

Just like LEGO® sets, **small-screen LEGO shows** come in all shapes and sizes. There are short animations for younger children, action adventure series for older kids, and nail-biting reality contests that the whole family can enjoy. Some air on traditional TV, others on streaming services, and some are YouTube exclusives.

1987 — The first LEGO TV show is Claymation series *Edward and Friends*, starring Edward Elephant and other LEGO® FABULAND™ characters. It airs in Canada, New Zealand, and the UK.

2015 — There's something for everyone in a year that launches the LEGO® *Elves* series, the LEGO *Star Wars: Droid Tales* miniseries, and TV special LEGO® *Scooby-Doo™: Knight Time Terror!*

2016 — As LEGO® NEXO KNIGHTS™ and LEGO *Star Wars: The Freemaker Adventures* air on TV, new series based on LEGO® BIONICLE® and LEGO Friends are the first to debut on Netflix.

2017 — British fan builders become TV stars in the first ever series of reality show LEGO® *Masters*, and Unikitty from THE LEGO® MOVIE™ sparkles in her own animated series.

2018 — There's more from Heartlake City in LEGO *Friends: Girls on a Mission*, and Australian and German versions of LEGO *Masters* showcase more of the world's best builders.

2019 — LEGO® *City Adventures* and LEGO® *Jurassic World: Legend of Isla Nublar* are new on Nickelodeon, while LEGO® *Hidden Side* is the first LEGO series to debut on YouTube.

232

BRICKISH BROADCASTING

2002 — The first live-action LEGO TV series is *Galidor: Defenders of the Outer Dimension*. Fans can re-create the ambitious sci-fi adventure with a range of buildable action figures.

2005 — Minifigures make their TV debut in LEGO® *Star Wars™: Revenge of the Brick*, a five-minute comedy version of *Star Wars: Revenge of the Sith* made for Cartoon Network.

2011 — LEGO *NINJAGO: Masters of Spinjitzu* launches alongside the first LEGO® NINJAGO® sets. It becomes the longest-running LEGO series of all, clocking up 215 episodes by 2022.

2014 — Buildable monsters the LEGO® Mixels™ star in a self-titled series, and a special episode of animated sitcom *The Simpsons* sees TV's most famous family turn into minifigures.

2013 — LEGO® *Legends of Chima™* explores a whole new world of animal characters, while miniseries *The Yoda Chronicles* adds some new names to the LEGO *Star Wars* universe.

2012 — Animated special LEGO *Friends: New Girl in Town* shows the stars of LEGO® Friends as real girls rather than LEGO mini dolls, and sets up a series of half-hour adventures.

2020 — LEGO® Monkie Kid™ sets launch alongside TV special *Monkie Kid: A Hero Is Born*. A LEGO *Monkie Kid* series follows, becoming one of the most popular children's animated shows in China.

2020–2022 — All-new versions of LEGO *Masters* air in China, Denmark, France, the Netherlands, New Zealand, Norway, Poland, Spain, Sweden, and the US, securing its smash-hit status!

2023 — LEGO® DREAMZzz™: *Trials of the Dream Chasers* keeps everyone wide awake, LEGO *Friends: The Next Chapter* turns the page, and LEGO *NINJAGO: Dragons Rising* spins all-new ninja tales!

233

DESIGNING A LEGO® SET

It can take as long as two years for a **LEGO® set** concept to get all the way from a designer's head and into eager builders' hands. The stages in between involve lots of experimentation, imagination, and collaboration between different kinds of experts, including the biggest LEGO experts of all—kids!

Stage 1

Most new LEGO sets are part of a wider play theme. These themes grow out of story ideas that are made into pictures and shown to children, who choose their favorites. A successful theme may combine the best bits of several different story ideas.

Stage 6

Many sets feature unique stickers or printed designs to add detail to a build and its minifigures. As soon as a set designer has a rough idea of what these should look like, they brief a graphic designer who specializes in 2D designs.

Stage 7

Team members share ideas and advice throughout the set design process. They also work with dedicated model coaches, who build and play with work-in-progress sets to offer a second opinion on things like building complexity and sturdiness.

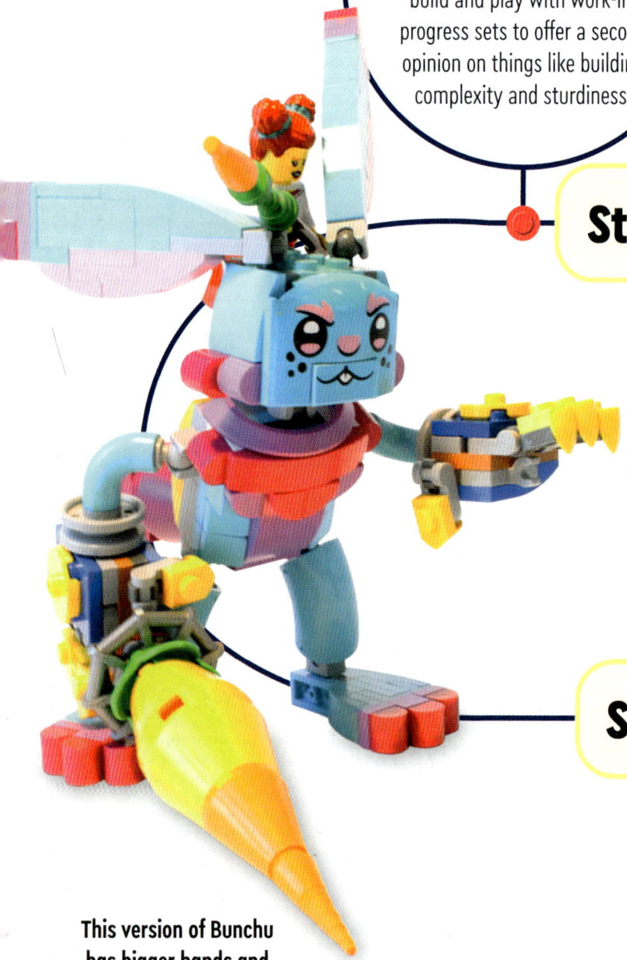

Stage 8

Children get involved again when a model is advanced enough to look and feel like a "real" LEGO set. Designers gain valuable insights as kids from all kinds of backgrounds are invited to build and play with a set in whatever way feels right to them.

Stage 9

When a model designer is happy with their model, they call a Model Quality Meeting. Here designers, model coaches, and building instruction designers carefully construct the model, to make sure the build experience is the best it can possibly be.

This version of Bunchu has bigger hands and shorter legs than the final design.

Bunchu's hands are more familiar here, but his feet are not!

DESIGNING A

Stage 2
When a theme is selected, it gets its own team of LEGO designers. They get together and start to turn story points into set ideas. They plan how many sets there should be, how big each one will be, and what will make each one special.

LEGO® DREAMZzz™ designers at an ideas meeting.

Stage 3
The design stage for individual sets begins when team members each take away one idea and start to develop it in detail. Some designers reach for bricks right away, while others sketch out their ideas on paper or use digital design tools.

These three concept sketches explore possibilities for Bunchu the Bunny from LEGO DREAMZzz.

Stage 5
To refine new parts for production, mechanical engineers, mold engineers, and quality engineers work together to produce factory prototypes. Some are sent to the designers for approval, and the rest are put through rigorous safety testing.

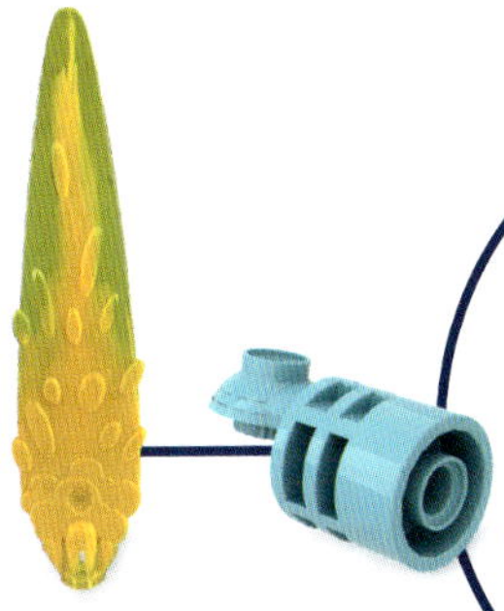

New elements in LEGO DREAMZzz sets include tubular limb joints and dream flame pieces.

Stage 4
If a set designer decides that their model needs an entirely new part, they work with an element designer to create something that will be useful in other sets too. A rough, 3D-printed version of the new part can be ready to use within days.

Stage 10
Once the building process is approved, a building instruction designer uses special LEGO software to create clear step-by-step instructions based on potentially hundreds of photos that they took at the Model Quality Meeting.

Finishing touches
When the set design is approved for production, the packaging can be finalized with eye-catching model photography and important information such as the precise number of pieces. The set is now ready for the factory and the world!

235

INSIDE THE FACTORY

A single **LEGO® factory** can make a vast variety of bricks and perfectly formed elements every hour, but nothing about the process is rushed. Every step of element production is a finely tuned marvel of modern engineering, built on decades of technical expertise and an unshakable belief that only the best is good enough.

Stage 1
LEGO bricks start out in the factory as colorless granulates. These are each smaller than a grain of rice!

Stage 7
The bricks fall onto conveyor belts and into large crates. Some from each batch are taken away to make sure they meet the LEGO Group quality standards.

Stage 8
Crates full of finished bricks are collected by robot vehicles, labeled, and stored in high-bay warehouses. In some factories, stacks of bricks can reach 121 ft (37 m) high!

Stage 9 
When a particular crate is needed, a robot crane knows exactly where it is! It can slide a crate out from anywhere in the stacks and then send it on its way.

Stage 10
Elements that need a graphic design on them are sent to a decoration department, where giant printers apply different colors in turn.

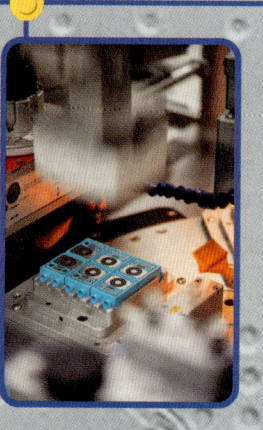

Stage 11 
Elements made up of several pieces (such as torsos with arms and hands) are sent to their own special assembly machines before heading for the packing department.

236

Stage 2: Pumps move the granulate around the factory, delivering it from huge storage silos to hundreds of molding machines making different LEGO elements.

Stage 3: En route, the granulate is heated just enough to remove any moisture and then mixed with the pigment that will give the finished LEGO bricks their color.

Stage 4: The ... pigmen... temper... 590°F (310°C), creating a thick, gooey liquid up to three times hotter than boiling water.

Stage 5: The molding machines inject the liquid into every corner of their metal molds and subject them to pressures of up to 7.1 tons per square in (1 metric ton per cm^2).

Stage 6: Inside the molds, the liquid cools and hardens to exactly the right shape in around 10 to 15 seconds. When the molds open, finished LEGO bricks drop out.

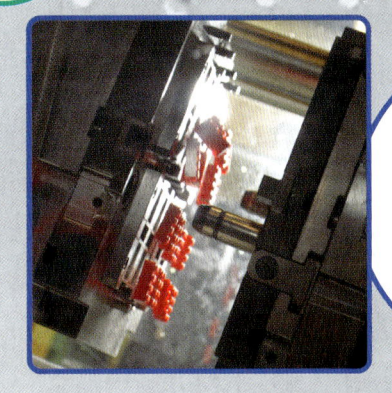

Stage 12: Bricks of different kinds meet for the first time in the packing department, where machines count out and group the precise parts needed for a specific set.

Stage 13: As sets begin to take shape, high-precision scales weigh the element selections to ensure no part is missing. The parts are then sealed inside numbered bags.

Stage 14: Another machine groups the bags for each set and packs them into boxes. These are weighed again, sealed, and then packed into larger boxes for distribution.

Stage 15: Robot cranes load the packaged sets onto pallets for delivery to retailers. They may be on store shelves within days—and in builders' collections for decades!

237

THE CHANGING LEGO® LOGO

The **LEGO® logo** has taken many forms on its way to becoming a worldwide symbol of quality! Red has been its key color since the 1940s, with friendly balloon lettering making its debut in the 1950s. The classic square logo was devised in the 1970s, then subtly refined for the 21st century.

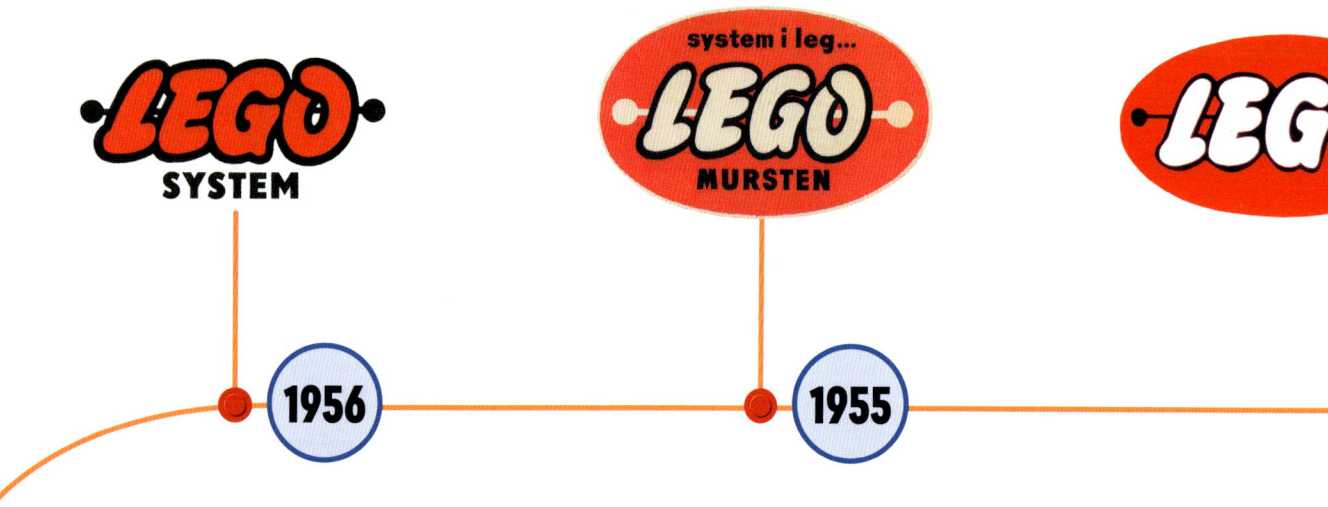

1936

1956 — LEGO SYSTEM

1955 — system i leg… LEGO MURSTEN

1958 — LEGO System / LEGO System / LEGO SYSTEM

THE CHANGING LEGO LOGO

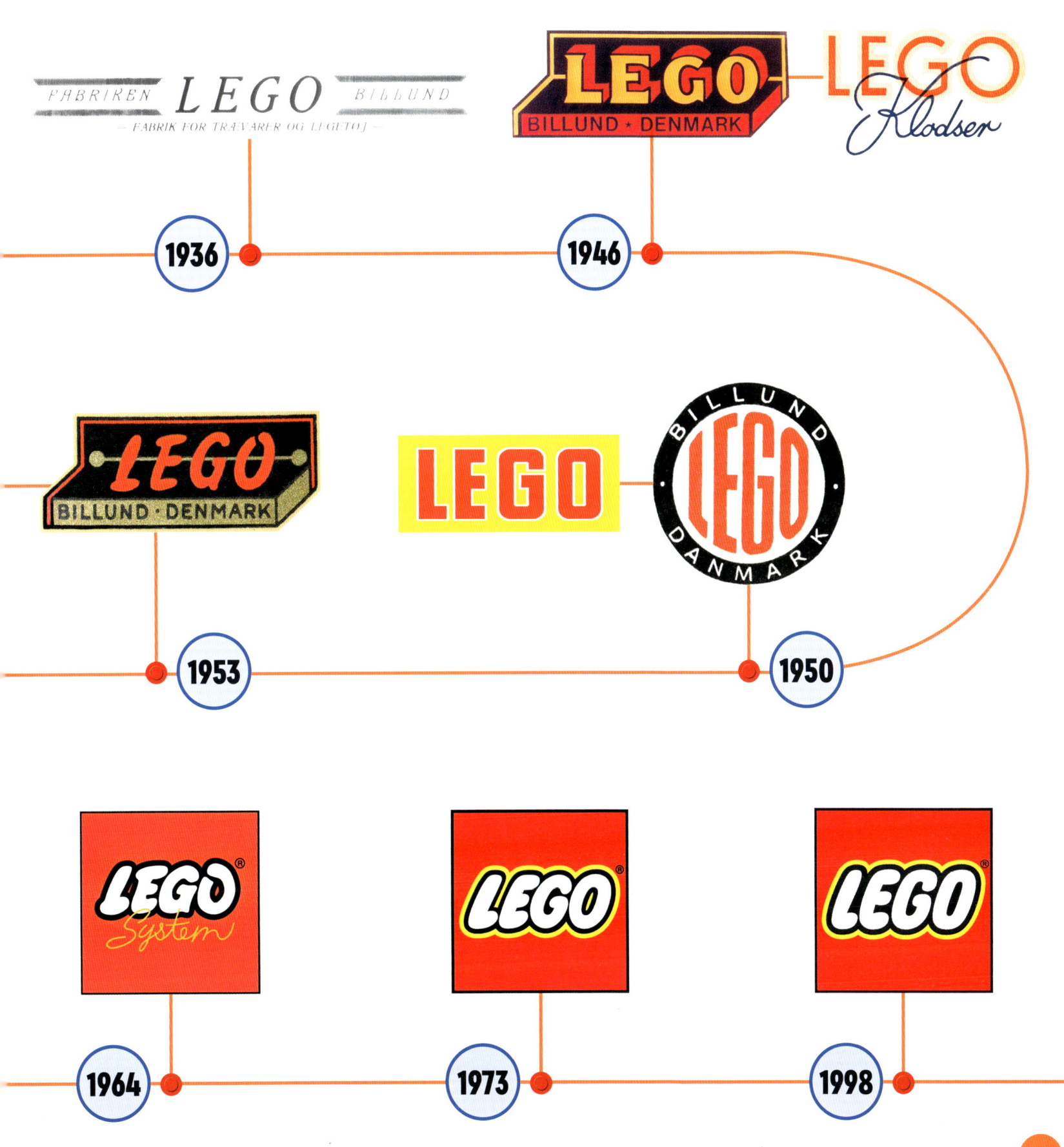

- 1936
- 1946
- 1953
- 1950
- 1964
- 1973
- 1998

FROM POST TO POSTS

The LEGO Group has always found ways to stay in touch with **LEGO® fans** around the world—first through fan club magazines alone, and now with websites and apps as well. Today, the latest LEGO updates are shared in LEGO® *Life* magazine, on the LEGO® Insiders Club website, and on various social media.

1950s — In the days before LEGO® Clubs, the LEGO Group in Germany prints the first publication just for LEGO fans. Titled the LEGO® *Post*, it includes a map of Denmark and tips for taking care of your LEGO bricks.

New Club magazines in the 1990s include LEGO® *Innovations* in Canada, LEGO® *Mania* in the US, and LEGO® *World Club Magazine* for fans in Europe, Asia, and the Pacific.

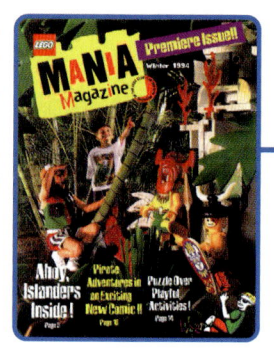

2002  — LEGO Clubs around the globe come together, with a single LEGO *Magazine* to unite them all. Meanwhile, LEGO.com hosts the first official LEGO message boards and LEGO Club pages.

The LEGO Club gets a new mascot—minifigure member Max. He goes on to star in two new publications: LEGO® *Club Magazine* and LEGO® *Club Jr.*, for kids ages six and under.

2004 — US Club members who sign up to become LEGO® BrickMasters get a bigger magazine, exclusive sets, LEGO design software, and a LEGOLAND® ticket sent direct to their door.

2005 — The LEGO Group launches its own YouTube channel and sets up the LEGO® Ambassador Program as a way to communicate with adult fan groups around the world.

2007

2008  — My LEGO® Network is the first LEGO social site for kids, hosted on LEGO.com. Users can create profile pages, chat with friends, show off their LEGO creations, and even make music!

240

FROM POST TO POSTS

1960s
The Samsonite Corporation publishes *Snap: The Fun Book for LEGO Club Members* in the US in 1963, and the first official LEGO Clubs launch in Canada in 1966 and Sweden in 1967.

1970s
The LEGO Group sends its first newsletter to British builders in 1974. A regular bulletin for Dutch fans follows in 1976, with the lyrics for a LEGO radio jingle inside its first issue.

1980s
The UK gets a fully-fledged LEGO Club in 1981, with *Bricks 'n Pieces* as its regular magazine. The LEGO Builders Club launches in the US six years later, along with *Brick Kicks* magazine.

1990s
The first LEGO® Technic Club launches in the UK in 1996 – the same year that LEGO.com goes live. The LEGO Group now has a whole new way to communicate with fans around the world.

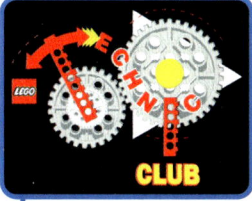

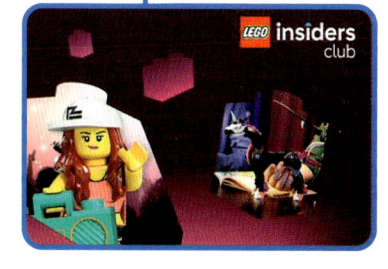

2011
LEGO BrickMasters becomes LEGO® Master Builder Academy, rewarding members with six exclusive sets per year. Meanwhile, the LEGO Group joins Facebook and Twitter.

2012
The LEGO Club launches a new magazine for fans of LEGO® Friends, and the first Instagram post from the LEGO Group shows a minifigure out for a stroll! #brickstagram #instagood #blessed

2017
The LEGO Club becomes LEGO® Life—combining a magazine with an app for sharing photos of builds, watching LEGO videos, and communicating in the universal language of LEGO emoji!

2023
The LEGO Group joins TikTok, and the new LEGO® Insiders Club launches as a website and app packed full of building tips, challenges, games, and videos, alongside LEGO Life.

You must be 13 or older to use most third-party social media sites.

WONDER LANDS

Visit any **LEGOLAND® Park** around the world and you'll see amazing LEGO® models, travel on thrilling LEGO rides, and maybe even stay in a LEGO themed room. But no two LEGOLAND resorts are the same, and each new opening puts a fresh spin on a concept that first wowed crowds more than 50 years ago.

The LEGO factory in Denmark attracts so many visitors every year that the owner of the LEGO Group, Godtfred Kirk Christiansen, decides to build a theme park next door!

A display for visitors at the Billund factory in 1961

c. 1965

LEGOLAND® Florida launches as the largest LEGO attraction in the US. It includes a water park and a celebrated botanical garden that first opened to the public in 1936.

2011

The first LEGO resort in Asia, LEGOLAND® Malaysia celebrates nothing but amazing Eastern architecture in a sprawling Miniland area that took three years to build.

2012

The first indoor Miniland nestles under a huge dome at LEGOLAND® Dubai in the UAE. Its centerpiece is a 55-ft (17-m) model of the world's tallest building, the Burj Khalifa.

2016

LEGOLAND® Japan's Miniland re-creations include Nagoya Castle and Kyoto's Golden Pavilion. The park is also home to a LEGO cherry blossom tree made from more than 800,000 bricks!

2017

242

WONDER LANDS

1968 — LEGOLAND® Billund opens to huge crowds on June 7. Attractions include a driving school, puppet shows, and a train ride around the brick-built Miniland model village.

1996 — Eighty million bricks are used to build LEGOLAND® Windsor in the UK! It hosts 1.4 million visitors in its first year and remains the world's largest LEGOLAND Park until 2021.

2002 — LEGOLAND® Deutschland in southern Germany opens in 2002. It unveils the world's biggest Miniland model in 2005, and welcomes guests to the first LEGO campsite in 2008.

The Allianz Arena soccer stadium at LEGOLAND Deutschland is made from more than one million bricks.

1999 — The first LEGOLAND Park in the US is LEGOLAND® California. Designed around a lake and close to the seaside, it soon expands to encompass a huge aquarium and a water park.

Concept art for LEGOLAND California from the mid 1990s

2021 — When LEGOLAND® New York opens in the US, it becomes the world's largest LEGO resort. Its rides include a virtual-reality adventure that turns visitors into minifigures.

The first LEGO themed water park in Europe is Italy's LEGOLAND® Water Park Gardaland. It combines 370,000 gallons of water with more than five million LEGO bricks.

2022 — Spanning 70 acres on a river island, LEGOLAND® Korea opens as Asia's largest LEGO resort. Its on-site hotel has rooms themed around pirates, knights, and ninja!

LEGOLAND Korea opens on May 5, celebrated as Children's Day in East Asia.

2025 — A new LEGOLAND resort is set to open in Shanghai—the first to open in China.

243

WHAT'S IN STORE?

With more than 1,000 outposts on six continents, you're never very far away from a **LEGO® Store**! No two are exactly the same, but all let you make your own minifigures, fill boxes with your own selection of bricks, and see the latest sets come to life in digital 3D.

1992 — Looking like a giant LEGO brick construction site, the LEGO® Imagination Center in Minnesota is a Mono Store—the forerunner of modern LEGO Stores.

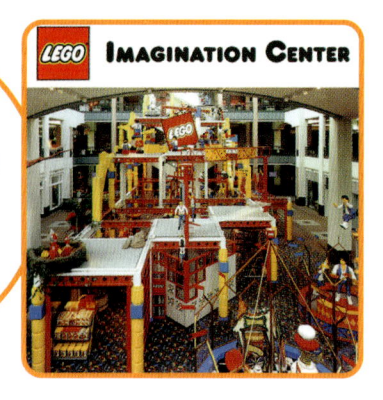

2014 — Abu Dhabi in the United Arab Emirates is home to the first LEGO Store in the Middle East—complete with a life-size, brick-built camel!

2016 — China's first LEGO Store is the world's largest—for six months! An even bigger store opens in London, UK, just in time for Christmas.

2018 — The vast London Store is the first to feature a LEGO® Mosaic Maker photo booth.

2019 — LEGO Stores around the world start selling exclusive minifigure parts in time for Halloween 2019.

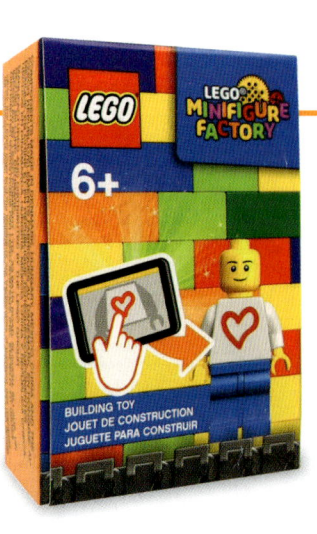

The first African LEGO Store opens in South Africa. Its attractions include a 15,041-piece mosaic of the continent's amazing wildlife.

Albany, New York, is home to the 100th LEGO Store in the US and Canada, while the Berlin Store in Germany is the first to offer custom-printed minifigures.

WHAT'S IN STORE?

2002 — The first LEGO Stores open in Germany, Russia, and the UK, complete with supersize builds, Pick-a-Brick walls, and all the latest LEGO sets.

2009 — LEGO Stores around the world start offering free monthly mini model-building sessions.

2013 — In New York, the 100th LEGO Store to open globally gives away special celebratory bricks.

2012 — The first LEGO set of a LEGO Store is LEGO® Brand Retail Store (set 3300003), given away at LEGO Store grand openings throughout the year!

2021 — The LEGO Store on New York's Fifth Avenue is the only store to feature a Brick Lab area, where wraparound screens and 3D scanners put your builds into an immersive adventure.

The first floating LEGO Store is found on board German cruise ship the *AIDAprima*!

2023 — One of the world's largest LEGO Stores opens in Sydney, Australia. Inside, LEGO fans can find a two-story rainbow gum tree and a 549,378-piece model of the Sydney Harbour Bridge.

Each minifigure and animal has a story to tell about the history of the Sydney Harbor Bridge.

245

WELCOME TO OUR HOUSE

In 2017, a long-held dream became a reality when the **LEGO® House** in Billund, Denmark, opened to the public for the first time. The "Home of the Brick™" took three years to build, and this one-of-a-kind visitor attraction now welcomes hundreds of thousands of LEGO fans through its doors each year.

1990 — The LEGO Group opens a staff museum at its headquarters in Billund. The LEGO® Idea House is packed full of classic sets and tells the company's story for LEGO employees and their guests.

2015 — The LEGO House reaches its full height in October, as the last of many huge steel beams are welded and bolted into place. The next step is to clad the bare building in shiny, LEGO brick-shaped tiles.

2016 — The interior of the LEGO House begins to take shape, starting with the central staircase. In spring of this year, work begins to build the life-size LEGO style furniture and the many themed play experiences.

2017 — On September 27, 2017, the LEGO House is finally ready for its grand opening! The event is attended by members of the Danish royal family, and by LEGO fans of all ages from around the world.

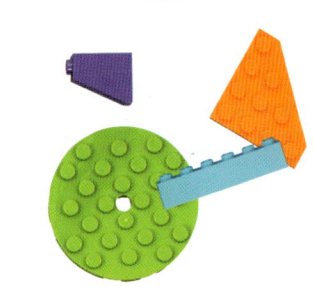

246

WELCOME TO OUR HOUSE

2010 — The popularity of the Idea House convinces the LEGO Group owner Kjeld Kirk Kristiansen of the need for something bigger—a purpose-built celebration of the LEGO brick that is open to the public.

2012 — Danish architect Bjarke Ingels comes up with an idea to bring Kjeld Kirk's vision to life: a building shaped like a stack of giant LEGO bricks that people can choose to pass through or climb over!

2014 — Three generations of the Kirk Kristiansen family lay the foundation stones for the LEGO House as building work begins in August. By Christmas, the huge basement floor is just about complete!

2013 — LEGO designers start to plan the enormous builds that will go on display in the new LEGO House. Their ideas include the most complex LEGO creation of all time: the epic Tree of Creativity.

2022 — The LEGO House celebrates its fifth birthday and welcomes its one millionth guest! The lucky-numbered visitor is a seven-year-old from Germany, who leaves with a lifetime LEGO House pass!

LEGO House covers an area of 3 acres (12,000 m^2) and resembles a stack of 21 giant LEGO bricks.

247

LEGO® HOUSE

2017

Ever since it opened, the LEGO® House has stocked a special LEGO® Architecture model in its shop. This miniature version of the Home of the Brick™ makes the perfect souvenir, reminding visitors of the different themed zones and experiences they enjoyed inside. The only thing it's missing is a built-in basement vault!

The Green Zone is an amazing minifigure world, where you can create your own characters and make your own stop-motion movies.

In the Yellow Zone, visitors build unique flowers and creatures before bringing them to life in a thriving digital ecosystem!

In the real LEGO House, the basement is home to the History Collection—an enormous display of sets spanning almost 100 years.

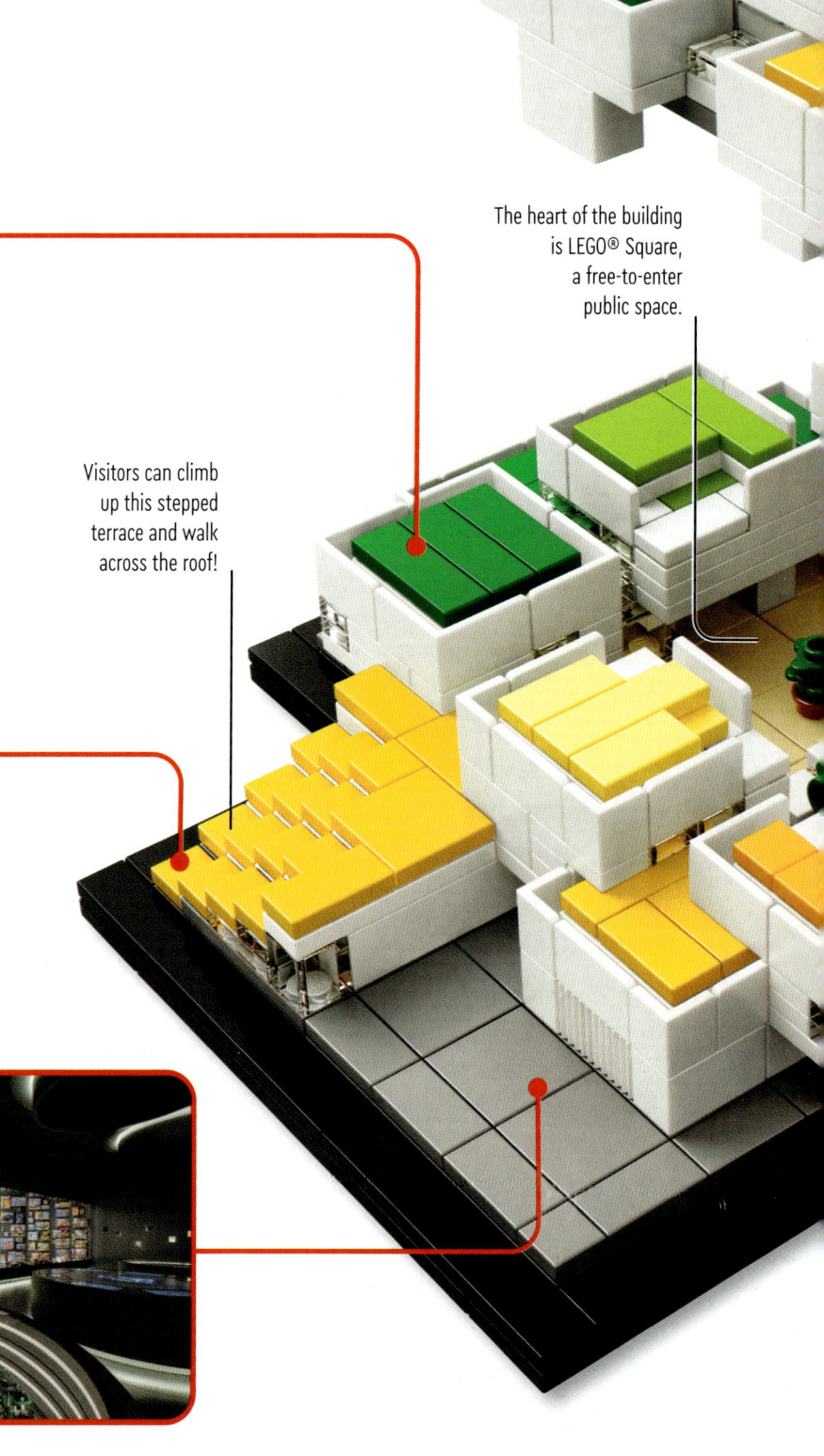

The heart of the building is LEGO® Square, a free-to-enter public space.

Visitors can climb up this stepped terrace and walk across the roof!

WELCOME TO OUR HOUSE

SET NUMBER	21037
PIECES	774
SIZE	2 in (6 cm) high, 8 in (22 cm) wide

At the top of the LEGO House, the Masterpiece Gallery showcases amazing fan builds and three half-ton (450-kg) giant brick dinosaurs!

The Blue Zone is all about testing and learning—from minifigure racing cars to builds to change the world and LEGO® MINDSTORMS® robots.

Creativity knows no bounds in the Red Zone, where millions of bricks are waiting to be put together in brand-new ways.

In the restaurant, diners build their food order from LEGO bricks, then collect their meal in a brick box served by LEGO robots!

249

TOMORROW'S WORLD

The LEGO Group has always taken its social responsibilities seriously, and in the 21st century it has stepped up its focus on **sustainability and the environment** in a big way. Here are just some of the milestones that are helping to keep the company clean and green into the 2050s and beyond...

2003 — The LEGO Group is the first toy company to sign up to the United Nations Global Compact—a list of fundamental responsibilities toward the planet and its people.

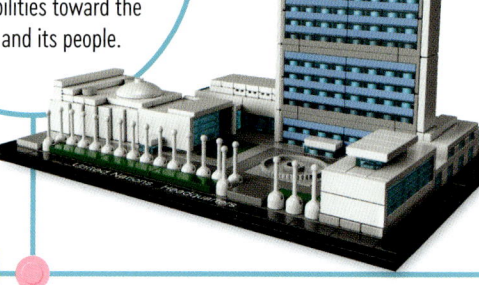

2018  — The first bio-polyethylene (bio-PE) LEGO elements are launched, made from sustainably sourced Brazilian sugarcane. More than 200 LEGO elements are now made from bio-PE.

2020 — The LEGO Group joins the Ellen MacArthur Foundation, committing to an economy based around reuse and recycling. Paper bags replace single-use plastic bags in LEGO Stores.

2021 — The LEGO Group helps give young people a voice at the COP26 climate-change conference and installs more than 20,000 solar panels at its factories around the world.

This 10-step booklet for COP26 leaders is created with input from more than 6,000 children.

2023 — Paper-based bags start to replace plastic ones in LEGO sets. The LEGO Group invests in e-methanol, made with renewable energy and biogenic CO2, for some of its plastic production.

2024 — The LEGO Group opens its most sustainable factory so far in Binh Duong Province, Vietnam, which will feature rooftop solar panels. A solar farm is to be built on a neighboring plot of land.

PLANS FOR THE FUTURE ▶

TOMORROW'S WORLD

2008 — The LEGO Group announces its Planet Promise: to strive to play its part in helping to build a sustainable future and make a positive impact on society and the planet, which our children will inherit.

2013 — LEGO set boxes start to get smaller relative to their contents, saving thousands of tons of cardboard and allowing sets to be distributed with fewer truck journeys.

2014 — The LEGO Group launches its Engage-to-Reduce program, working with suppliers to cut greenhouse gas emissions across the entire company.

Cleaning up emissions is my life's mission!

This employee gift set from 2015 celebrates the involvement of the LEGO Group with offshore wind power.

2017 — For the first time, wind farms funded by the parent company of the LEGO Group generate more annual energy than is used by LEGO factories and offices around the world.

2015 — Starting this year, all paper and cardboard used in LEGO products and packaging is made from 100% Forest Stewardship Council–certified sources.

2025 — The LEGO Group aims to reach its target of sending zero waste to landfills and to eliminate single-use plastics from LEGO packaging.

2026 — The LEGO Group plans to open a landscaped solar park in Billund, Denmark, designed to generate as much energy as is used by its factories and offices in the country every year.

2032 — By this date, the LEGO Group aims to reduce its worldwide carbon emissions by at least 37 percent compared to 2019, in line with the United Nations' Paris Climate Accords.

2050 — The LEGO Group has pledged to cut carbon emissions across its entire supply chain to net zero by the middle of the century.

251

INDEX

Main entries are **bold**

A
Advanced Models 74, **192-93**, 194
advent calendars 36, 46, 74, 91, 108, 137
Adventurers 26, 38, 70, **82-85**
Agents 38, 96, 116
Alpha Team 94, 117
Andrea's Modern Mansion (set) **168-69**
Angry Birds Movie, The 142
animal figures **66-67**
Apocalypseburg, **204-05**
apps 21, 25, 59, 60, 80, 162, 173, 213, 214, 241
Aquaraiders 83
Aqua Raiders 85, 97
Aquazone 70, 82-83
Architecture 96, **134-35**, 196, 248-49
Art 173, 178, 222, 227
Atlantis 84-85, 140
Automatic Binding Bricks 10-11, 12
Avatar 152, 219, 222
Avatar: the Last Airbender 96, 216
Avengers 176-77, 179
   Advent Calendar 178

B
Bach, Eric 57
Back to the Future 218
Batcave—Shadow Box (set) **174-75**
BATMAN MOVIE, THE LEGO 143, 200-01
BELVILLE 27, 64, 71
Berard, Jamie 128-31
bicycles 19, 40
BIONICLE 47, 90, 95, **100-03**, 141, 161
   Netflix series 232
Black Panther 177, 178-79

board games 10, 65, 90, 107, 158
BOOST 80, 143
Braille Bricks 143
brick-built characters **210-11**
BrickHeadz 99, 108, 136, 142, 152, 172, 177, 188, **210-11**
Brickley 210
BrickMasters 240-41
bricks, development **12-13**
BricQ Motion range 231
Brok, Eric 129
BTS 163
Buildable Figures 90, 141, 177
Bunchu the Bunny 234-35

C
Cars, DUPLO 31, 140, 150-51, 219
Castle 32, 35, 36, **44-49**, 66-67
   Advent Calendar 36
CD-ROMs 95, 101
Chan, Jackie 203
Christiansen, Godtfred Kirk 8, 11, 242
Christiansen, Niels B. 142
Christmas sets **136-37**
City 19, 24-25, 43, 46, 67, 97, 120, **122-27**
   Advent Calendar 137
   City Jungle 67, 124
CLIKITS 65, 96, 227
Clumsy Hans 8
"clutch power" 10
craft and culture **226-27**
Creator 20-21, 75, **112-15**
   Creator 3in1 47, 97, 112-13, 115, 121
   Creator Expert 129, 141, 194-95, 197, 198-99
CUUSOO 119, 141, 163

D
Dacta 231
DC Batman 96, 170-71
DC Comics Super Heroes **170-75**
Deep Sea Explorers 67, 125
designing sets **234-35**
DIMENSIONS 143, 217, 220
Dino 85, 141
Dino Attack 85, 97
Dino 2010 85, 97
Dinosaurs 95
Discovery Channel 96, 118
Disney Castle (set) **154-55**
Disney *Frozen* 150
Disney Pixar 31, 150
Disney Princess 141, 150, 152, 154-55
DOTS 222, 226
Downtown (set) **126-27**
Dragon Knights 44, 46-47
DREAMZzz 215, 223, 233, 235
DUPLO 17, **28-31**, 32, 64, 71, 74, 150-51, 171, 219
   DUPLO *Cars*, 31, 141, 150-51, 219
   DUPLO *Disney Princess* 30, 150
   DUPLO Dolls 30, 65
   PRIMO 70

E
Education, 31, **230-31**
   SPIKE range 81, 230
Edward and Friends TV show 62, 232
Eldorado Fortress (set) **76-77**
Elves 142, 214-15
   TV show 232
Europa 72
EXO-FORCE 96, 116-17

252

INDEX

"Expert Builder" sets 57
Explore 30
Exploriens 52-53
Extreme Team subtheme 42

F
Faber, Christian 100-01
FABULAND 33, **62-63**, 151, 232
    figures 64
Factory (theme) 24, 96, 129, 163
factory, LEGO production **236-37**
Fairground **198-99**
fan clubs **240-41**
Fantastic Beasts 108
figures (other than minifigures) **64-67**
FIRST LEGO League 79, 231
Flex System 57
FRIENDS 39, 65, 121, 140,
    164-69, 223
    TV and Netflix shows 164, 232-33
Fright Knights 45, 212
Furukawa, Satoshi 119
Futuron 51, 54

G
Gabby's Dollhouse 217, 222
Galaxy Squad 52, 117
Galidor sets 65, 94
    TV show 233
Galilei, Galileo 120
Games 90, 97, 107
    figures 65
Ghostbusters 195, 218
ghosts and ghouls **212-13**
Graabæk, Astrid 128-29
Gravity Games 95, 98
Gringotts Wizarding Bank Collectors'
    Edition (set) **110-11**
Grubb, Anderson Ward 131

H
Hamilton, Margaret 120
Harry Potter 36-37, 38, 66-67, 94, **106-11**, 219
    Advent Calendar 108
Hero Factory 102, 141
Hidden Side 143, 213
    YouTube series 232
Hobbit, The 141, **182-83**, 218
Hobby sets 33, 192-95
Holm, Dagny 8
Homemaker 32, 34-35, 210
hospitals 34, 41, 123, 166
Hubble Space Telescope 121
Hulkbuster (set) **180-81**
Hydronauts 82-83

I
Icons 25, 53, 76-77, 130, 184-85
    195-97, 213, 220-21
    Botanical Collection 223, 226
Ideas 26-27, 47, 120, 153, **162-63**,
    211, 216-17, 226-27
imaginary lands **214-15**
Indiana Jones 96, **138-39**, 219
International Space Station 119, 121
Inventor 113
Iron Man 177-81
Island Xtreme Stunts 95

J
Jemison, Mae 120
Jurassic World 30, 142, 202,
    208-09
    TV show 232

K
Klodser 9
Knights' Kingdom 46-47
Knudsen, Jens Nygaard 34
Knudstorp, Jørgen Vig 97
Krentz, Daniel August 44
Kristiansen, Kjeld Kirk 11, 14-15, 28, 33,
    97, 247
Kristensen, Knud Møller 18
Kristiansen, Ole Kirk 8-11, 17, 69, 128, 142
Kristiansen, Thomas Kirk 142, 223
Kubus 10

L
largest sets **228-29**
Legends 42-43, 45, 73, 193
Legends of Chima 140, 214-15, 233
"leg godt" 8
LEGO Clubs 68-69, **240-41**
LEGO Foundation 69
LEGO House 135, 143, **246-47**
LEGO House (set) **248-49**
LEGOLAND Parks **242-43**
    Billund, Denmark 17, 32, 242-43
    California 71, 73, 243
    Dubai 142, 242
    Florida 140, 242
    Günzburg, Germany 94, 243
    Korea 223, 243
    Malaysia 141, 242
    Nagoya, Japan 143, 242
    New York 222, 243
    Windsor, UK 243
LEGOLAND Water Park Gardaland, Italy
    222, 243
LEGO logo 71, **238-39**
    DUPLO 28, 31
LEGO MOVIE, THE 53, 142, 200-01
LEGO MOVIE 2, THE 30, 202-04
LEGO Prize 68
LEGO stores **244-45**
LEGO World Cup 69
Liebherr Crawler Crane LR 13000 (set)
    60-61
Life on Mars 53
light bricks 20-21
Lion Knights 45, 46-47
Lion Knights' Castle (set) **48-49**
Lord of the Rings, The 141,
    182-85, 218
Lord of the Rings: Rivendell (set)
    184-85

253

M

Marvel Super Heroes 36, 152, **176-77**, 202
Massachusetts Institute of Technology (MIT) 78-79
Master Builder Academy 241
Mata Nui **100-03**
McVeigh, Chris 130
mechs 84, 90-91, 96, 116-17, 157, 158-59, 161, 179, 180-81, 203, 208, 225
Microfighters 90
microfigures 90, 153, 161, 176
Mickey and Friends subtheme 152-53
Mickey Mouse 94
Middle-earth **182-85**
Mighty Dinosaurs 114-15
Mighty Micros 172, 177
Millennium Falcon 86, 91, 229
Millennium Falcon (set) **92-93**,
MINDSTORMS 70, **78-81**, 90, 249
MINDSTORMS for Schools 230-31
Mindstorms: Children, Computers, and Powerful Ideas (book) 78
Minecraft 140, **186-91**
mini dolls 65, 140, 142, 152, 165, 168-69, 203
minifigure accessories **38-39**
Minifigures (collectible) 36, 99, 108, 140, **144-49**, 151, 153, 172, 179, 201, 203, 213, 216, 224
minifigures, development of **34-37**
minifigure teams **116-17**
Miniland 242-43
Minions: *The Rise of Gru* 27, 223
Minitalia 32
Mixels 141, 210, 233
Model Quality Meeting 234
Model Team sets 69, 192-93
Modular Buildings Collection **128-31**
Modulex 16
Mogensen, Andreas 119
Monypoli board game 10

Monkie Kid 39, 222, **224-25**
    TV shows 233
Monorail Transport System (set) **54-55**
Monster Fighters 141, 213
Mosaic Maker photo booth 244
motors **20-21**
Mountain Cave, The (set) **190-91**
movies **218-19**
    LEGO movies **200-05**
Mr. Gold 146
Müller, Florian 130
Muppets 216
museums 9, **132-33**, 134, 246
My LEGO Network 240

N

NASA 118-21, 162
Natural History Museum (set) **132-33**
NEXO KNIGHTS 143, 214
    TV show 232
Nickelodeon TV shows 96, 216, 232
Ninja 46
NINJAGO 39, 141, **156-61**, 223
    TV show 157, 233
Ninjago City Markets (set) **160-61**
NINJAGO MOVIE, THE LEGO 143, 202-03

O

Octan Energy 43, 122-23, 130
Ole Kirk Foundation 17
OLO 32
Orient Express train, The (set) **26-27**
Overwatch 143, 221

P

Pakbaz, Stephen 119
Papert, Professor Seymour 78-79
Paradisa 43, 71
Pharaoh's Quest 85, 141
Pirates 35, 67, 69, **72-77**
    Advent Calendar 74
Pirates of the Caribbean 140, 151

plastic types 17, 142
Pneumatic sets 56
police 40-41, 50, 52, 62, 105, 122-25, 130, 147, 204
Powered UP 21, 25, 59
Power Functions 21, 24, 59, 97, 112, 198
Power Miners 84, 97
Powerpuff Girls, The 217
Pratt, Chris 202
preschool sets 29, 230
PRIMO 29, 70
Prince of Persia 66, 140, 151, 219
Psiaki, Mike 131
Pull-along toys 8-9, 19, 150

Q

QUATRO 31, 96

R

Racers 19, 20, 94, **104-05**
RES-Q subtheme 42
Ride, Sally 120
Roboforce 53
robots 52, 65, 70, **78-81**, 95, 102, 231, 249
Rock Raiders 71, 82, 84
Roman, Nancy Grace 120
Royal Knights 44
Ryaa, Jan 57

S

Samsonite luggage company 11, 16-17, 241
SCALA 33, 64, 70, 226
Schwartz, Jordan 129
Scooby-Doo 143, 217
    TV special 232
Serious Play 95
set design **234-35**
"Slammer" cars 104
Slizers, Technic 59, 101

INDEX

smart brick 78-79, 80-81
Soccer 98
Soft Bricks 230
sound bricks 20-21
Space 32, 36, **50-56**, **118-21**
Speed Champions 19, 142, **206-07**
Speed Racer 96, 219
Spider-Man 95, 177-79
SPIKE 81, 230
SpongeBob SquarePants 96, 216
sports **98-99**
Sports 37, 95
Spybotics 81, 95
Star Wars 19, 21, 36-37, 71, **86-93**, 95, 97, 218, 223, 228-29
    Advent Calendar 91
    TV shows 232-33
STEAM sets 230
storybooks (FABULAND) 62-63
stud-and-tube principle 10
Studios 208, 212, 219
Super Heroes 30, 36, 141, **170-81**
Superman 30, 170-73
Super Mario 220-21, 222
sustainability **250-51**
"System in Play" 10, 14

T
Talbott, Wes 130
Technic 20-21, **56-61**, 69
    Control Center 20, 70, 78
    figures 64, 68
Teenage Mutant Ninja Turtles 140, 217, 218
Terapi range 17
Thomas & Friends 31
Throwbots 59
Time Cruisers 71, 116, 212
Tiny Turbos 105
Toa 101-03
Town 32, **40-43**, 55, 95
Town Plan **14-15**

Toy Industry Hall of Fame 69, 97
Toy Story 31, 140, 151, 152, 219
train sets **22-27**
transportation, large models **192-95**
Tree of Creativity 247
TV shows **216-17**, **232-33**

U
UFO sets 53
Ultra Agents 117, 142
Unikitty 142, 201
    TV show 232
Unitron 52, 55

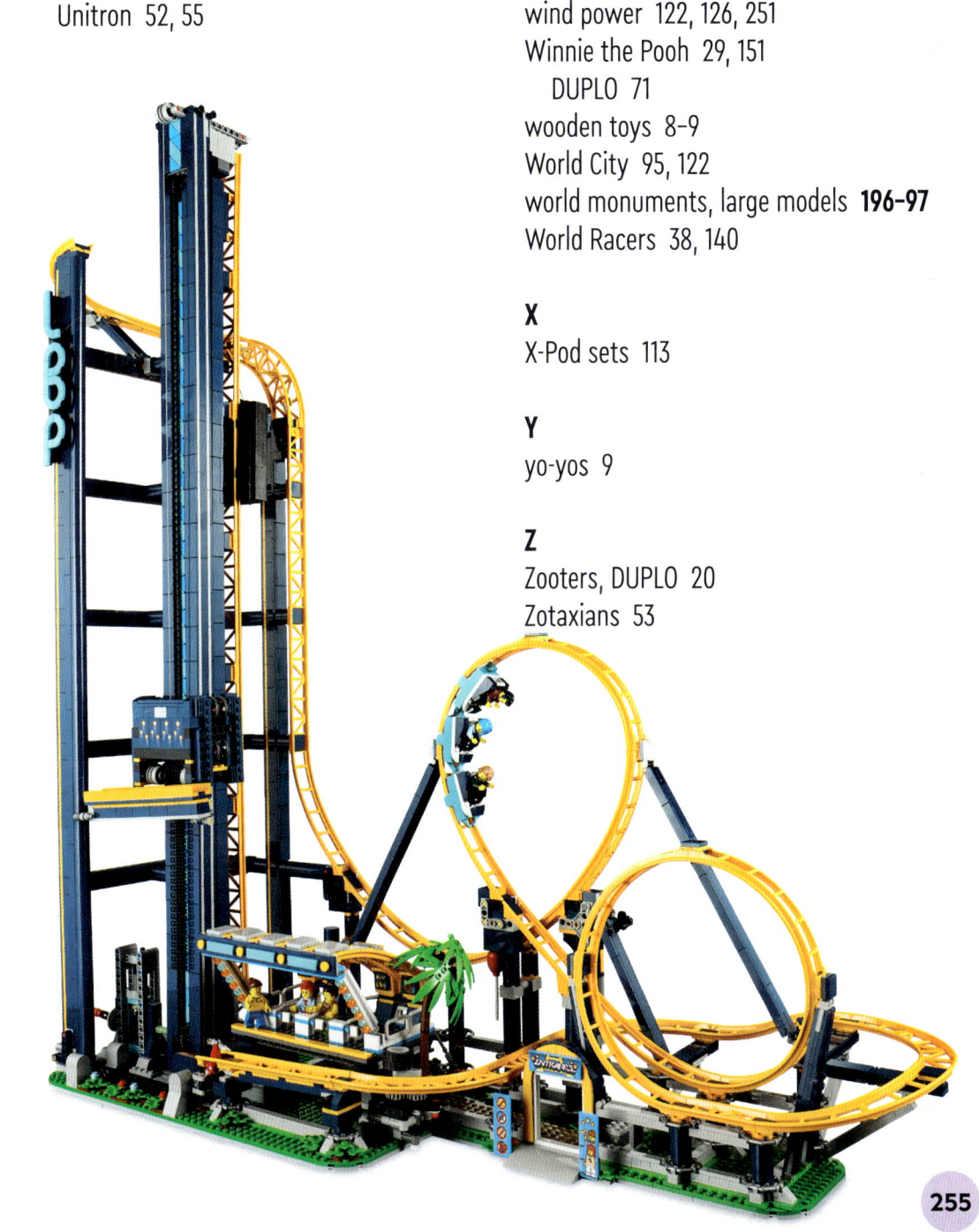

V
Vas, Nick 131
video games 71, 86-87, 95, 100, 104, 106, 124, 143, 170-71, 176-79, 186, **220-21**

W
Walt Disney Company 29, **150-51**
Welcome to Apocalypseburg! (set) **204-05**
Western 39, 67, 71, 72, 83
wheels 13, 17, **18-19**
wheelchair 19, 125, 148
wind power 122, 126, 251
Winnie the Pooh 29, 151
    DUPLO 71
wooden toys 8-9
World City 95, 122
world monuments, large models **196-97**
World Racers 38, 140

X
X-Pod sets 113

Y
yo-yos 9

Z
Zooters, DUPLO 20
Zotaxians 53

255

Senior Editor Helen Murray
Project Editor Lisa Stock
Editor Kathryn Hill
Senior US Editor Megan Douglass
Senior Designer Lauren Adams
Designers James McKeag and LS Design: Sadie Thomas, Rhys Thomas, Samantha Richiardi, and Tory Gordon-Harris
Senior Production Editor Jennifer Murray
Senior Production Controller Lloyd Robertson
Managing Editor Paula Regan
Managing Art Editor Jo Connor
Managing Director Mark Searle

First American Edition, 2024
Published in the United States by DK Publishing,
a division of Penguin Random House LLC
1745 Broadway, 20th Floor, New York, NY 10019

Page design copyright © 2024 Dorling Kindersley Limited
24 25 26 27 28 10 9 8 7 6 5 4 3 2 1
001–340362–Oct/2024

LEGO, the LEGO logo, the Minifigure, the Brick and Knob configurations, DUPLO, BELVILLE, DREAMZzz, EXO-FORCE, the FRIENDS, HIDDEN SIDE and MINIFIGURES logos, BIONICLE, MINDSTORMS, LEGENDS OF CHIMA, NINJAGO, NEXO KNIGHTS, LEGOLAND, and SERIOUS PLAY are trademarks and/or copyrights of the LEGO Group. © 2024 The LEGO Group. All rights reserved.

Manufactured by Dorling Kindersley, One Embassy Gardens, 8 Viaduct Gardens, London SW11 7BW, under license from the LEGO Group.
All rights reserved.

Without limiting the rights under the copyright reserved above, no part of this publication may be reproduced, stored in or introduced into a retrieval system, or transmitted, in any form, or by any means (electronic, mechanical, photocopying, recording, or otherwise), without the prior written permission of the copyright owner.

A catalog record for this book
is available from the Library of Congress.
ISBN: 978-0-5938-4416-8

Printed and bound in China

www.dk.com
www.LEGO.com

MIX
Paper | Supporting responsible forestry
FSC® C018179

This book was made with Forest Stewardship Council™ certified paper—one small step in DK's commitment to a sustainable future. Learn more at www.dk.com/uk/information/sustainability

Acknowledgments

DK would like to thank Randi Sørensen, Heidi K. Jensen, Martin Leighton Lindhart, Lydia Barram, Kristian Reimer Hauge, and the LEGO® DREAMZzz™ design team at the LEGO Group.
DK also thanks Aanchal Singal for picture research, Selina Wood for editorial assistance, Thelma-Jane Robb and Lisa Sodeau for design assistance, and Julia March for proofreading and indexing.

THE LEGO MOVIE, THE LEGO BATMAN MOVIE, and THE LEGO NINJAGO MOVIE © The LEGO Group & Warner Bros Entertainment Inc. (s24)

Copyright © 2024 DC. All related characters and elements are trademarks of and © DC. Products used courtesy of Warner Bros. Entertainment Inc. and DC. (s24)

Copyright © 2024 Warner Bros. Entertainment Inc. WIZARDING WORLD characters, names and related indicia are © & ™ Warner Bros. Entertainment Inc. WB SHIELD: © & ™ WBEI.
Publishing Rights © JKR. (s24)

© Warner Bros. Entertainment Inc. All rights reserved.

Content on p140, pp186–191 © 2024 Mojang AB. TM Microsoft Corporation.

THE HOBBIT: AN UNEXPECTED JOURNEY, THE HOBBIT: THE DESOLATION OF SMAUG and THE HOBBIT: BATTLE OF FIVE ARMIES and the names of the characters, items, events and places therein are TM of The Saul Zaentz Company d/b/a Middle-Earth Enterprises under license to New Line Productions, Inc. (s24)

© New Line Productions, Inc. All rights reserved.
THE LORD OF THE RINGS: THE FELLOWSHIP OF THE RING, THE LORD OF THE RINGS: THE TWO TOWERS and THE LORD OF THE RINGS: THE RETURN OF THE KING and the names of the characters, items, events and places therein are ™ of The Saul Zaentz Company d/b/a Middle-Earth Enterprises under license to New Line Productions, Inc. (s24)

© 2024 Disney Enterprises, Inc. All rights reserved.
Pixar properties © Disney/Pixar
Based on the "Winnie the Pooh" works,
by A. A. Milne and E. H. Shepard.

Porsche is a trademark of Porsche.

Star Wars and Indiana Jones and all characters, names, and all related indicia are trademarks of & © Lucasfilm Ltd. 2024.
All Rights Reserved. Used under Authorization.

© 2024 20th Century Studios

Marvel and all characters, names, and all related indicia are trademarks of & © 2024 MARVEL.

© Universal City Studios LLC and Amblin Entertainment, Inc.
All Rights Reserved.

DreamWorks Trolls © DreamWorks Animation LLC.
All Rights Reserved.

DreamWorks Gabby's Dollhouse © DreamWorks Animation LLC.
All rights reserved.

Minions Franchise © Universal City Studios LLC. All Rights Reserved.

© AIDA Cruises

Additional picture credits:
First British Toy Fair photo courtesy of the British Toy and Hobby Association (p10);
Modulex photo courtesy of Tim Johnson and Francesco Spreafico for New Elementary (p16);
LEGO Homemaker photo courtesy of Daniel Konstanski (p35);
LEGO Foundation photo courtesy of the LEGO Foundation (p69);
BIONICLE concept art courtesy of Christian Faber (p101).